244 HOUSE PLANS FOR BETTER LIVING

Contents

Index to Designs

HOME PLANNERS, INC.
23761 RESEARCH DRIVE, FARMINGTON HILLS, MICHIGAN 48024

Volume 130. Home Planners' titles are published four times per year by Home Planners, Inc., 23761 Research Drive, Farmington Hills, Michigan 48024. All designs and illustrative material Copyright © MCMLXXXVI by Home Planners, Inc. All rights reserved. Reproduction in any manner or form not permitted. Printed in the United States of America. International Standard Book Number (ISBN): 0-918894-56-5.

How To Read Floor Plans and Blueprints

Selecting the most suitable house plan for your family is a matter of matching your needs, tastes, and life-style against the many designs we offer. When you study the floor plans in this issue, and the blueprints that you may subsequently order, remember that they are simply a two-dimensional representation of what will eventually be a three-dimensional reality.

Floor plans are easy to read. Rooms are clearly labeled, with dimensions given in feet and inches. Most symbols are logical and self-explanatory: The location of bathroom fixtures, planters, fireplaces, tile floors, cabinets and counters, sinks, appliances, closets, sloped or beamed ceilings will be obvious.

A blueprint, although much more detailed, is also easy to read; all it demands is concentration. The blueprints that we offer come in many large sheets, each one of which contains a different kind of information. One sheet contains foundation and excavation drawings, another has a precise plot plan. An elevations sheet deals with the exterior walls of the house; section drawings show precise dimensions, fittings, doors, windows, and roof structures. Our detailed floor plans give the construction information needed by your contractor. And each set of blueprints contains a lengthy materials list with size and quantities of all necessary components. Using this list, a contractor and suppliers can make a start at calculating costs for you.

When you first study a floor plan or blueprint, imagine that you are walking through the house. By mentally visualizing each room in three dimensions, you can transform the technical data and symbols into something more real.

Start at the front door. It's preferable to have a foyer or entrance hall in which to receive guests. A closet here is desirable; a powder room is a plus.

Look for good traffic circulation as you study the floor plan. You should not have to pass all the way through one main room to reach another. From the entrance area you should have direct access to the three principal areas of a house—the living, work, and sleeping zones. For example, a foyer might provide separate entrances to the living room, kitchen, patio, and a hallway or staircase leading to the bedrooms.

Study the layout of each zone. Most people expect the living room to be protected from cross traffic. The kitchen, on the other hand, should connect with the dining room—and perhaps also the utility room, basement, garage, patio or deck, or a secondary entrance. A homemaker whose workday centers in the kitchen may have special requirements: a window that faces the backyard; a clear view of the family room where children play; a garage or driveway entrance that allows for a short trip with groceries; laundry facilities close at hand. Check for efficient placement of kitchen cabinets, counters, and appliances. Is there enough room in the kitchen for additional appliances, for eating in? Is there a dining nook?

Perhaps this part of the house contains a family room or a den/bedroom/office. It's advantageous to have a bathroom or powder room in this section.

As you study the plan, you may encounter a staircase, indicated by a group of parallel lines, the number of lines equaling the number of steps. Arrows labeled "up" mean that the staircase leads to a higher level, and those pointing down mean it leads to a lower one. Staircases in a split-level will have both up and down arrows on one staircase because two levels are depicted in one drawing and an extra level in another.

Notice the location of the stairways. Is too much floor space lost to them? Will you find yourself making too many trips?

Study the sleeping quarters. Are the bedrooms situated as you like? You may want the master bedroom near the kids, or you may want it as far away as possible. Is there at least one closet per person in each bedroom or a double one for a couple? Bathrooms should be convenient to each bedroom—if not adjoining, then with hallway access and on the same floor.

Once you are familiar with the relative positions of the rooms, look for such structural details as:

• Sufficient uninterrupted wall space for furniture arrangement.

• Adequate room dimensions.

• Potential heating or cooling problems—i.e., a room over a garage or next to the laundry.

• Window and door placement for good ventilation and natural light.

• Location of doorways—avoid having a basement staircase or a bathroom in view of the dining room.

• Adequate auxiliary space—closets, storage, bathrooms, countertops.

• Separation of activity areas. (Will noise from the recreation room disturb sleeping children or a parent at work?)

As you complete your mental walk through the house, bear in mind your family's long-range needs. A good house plan will allow for some adjustments now and additions in the future.

Each member of your family may find the listing of his, or her, favorite features a most helpful exercise. Why not try it?

THE DESIGN CATEGORY SERIES . . .

presents Home Planners' complete selection of designs in six different books. The designs have been categorized as follows: Two-Story Homes, 1½-Story Homes, One-Story Homes *over* 2000 Sq. Ft., One-Story Homes *under* 2000 Sq. Ft., Multi-Level Homes, Vacation Homes. Editing the designs in this fashion allows for the selection of a single book featuring only designs which satisfy one's specific house type preference. This immensely facilitates the selection of a family's favorite design. For those who are undecided about their house type preferences a selection, or the Complete Collection, may be obtained so the entire Home Planners' design selection can be reviewed.

Design 302774

1,370 Sq. Ft. - First Floor
969 Sq. Ft. - Second Floor; 38,305 Cu. Ft.

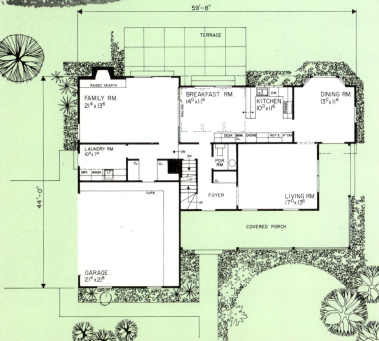

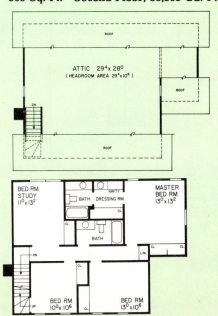

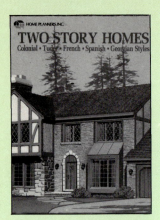
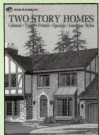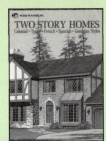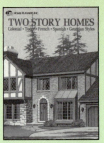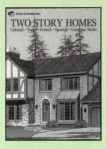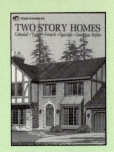

THE TWO STORY HOME . . .

has long been recognized as the most cost-effective type of home to build. When one considers that two levels of livability are sandwiched between a minimum amount of foundation and roof, this construction dollar economy becomes evident. The designs on the following pages are but a sampling of the variety that awaits the reader of this 288 page book. Sections include Heritage Houses, Tudor, French, Southern Colonial, Farmhouses and Contemporaries. There are homes to satisfy a wide variety of building budgets. Of particular interest are designs whose floor plans accommodate optional exterior styles.

Design 302800

999 Sq. Ft. - First Floor
997 Sq. Ft. - Second Floor; 31,390 Cu. Ft.

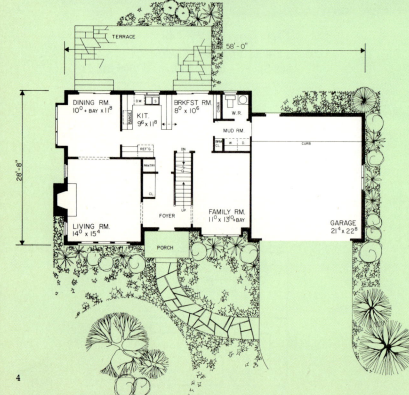

● This Tudor design has many fine features. The exterior is enhanced by front and side bay windows in the family and dining rooms. Along with an outstanding exterior, it also contains a modern and efficient floor plan within its modest proportions. Flanking the entrance foyer is a comfortable living room. The U-shaped kitchen is conveniently located between the dining and breakfast rooms.

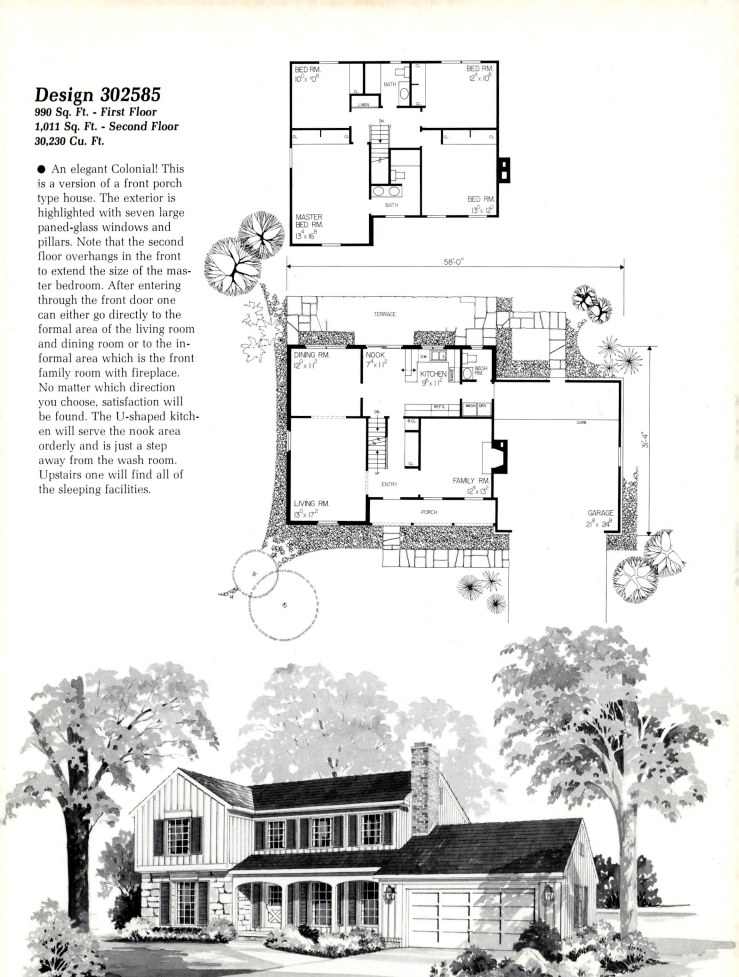

Design 302585

990 Sq. Ft. - First Floor
1,011 Sq. Ft. - Second Floor
30,230 Cu. Ft.

● An elegant Colonial! This is a version of a front porch type house. The exterior is highlighted with seven large paned-glass windows and pillars. Note that the second floor overhangs in the front to extend the size of the master bedroom. After entering through the front door one can either go directly to the formal area of the living room and dining room or to the informal area which is the front family room with fireplace. No matter which direction you choose, satisfaction will be found. The U-shaped kitchen will serve the nook area orderly and is just a step away from the wash room. Upstairs one will find all of the sleeping facilities.

BED RM. 10⁰ x 10⁸

BED RM. 12⁴ x 10⁸

BATH

LINEN

CL

DN.

BED RM. 13⁰ x 12⁰

BATH

MASTER BED RM. 13⁴ x 16⁸

58'-0"

TERRACE

DINING RM. 12⁰ x 11²

NOOK 7⁴ x 11²

KITCHEN 9⁶ x 11²

WASH RM.

REF'G.

WASH DRY.

B.CL.

DN.

UP

CL.

ENTRY

FAMILY RM. 12⁴ x 13²

CURB

LIVING RM. 13⁰ x 17²

PORCH

GARAGE 21⁸ x 24⁸

31'-4"

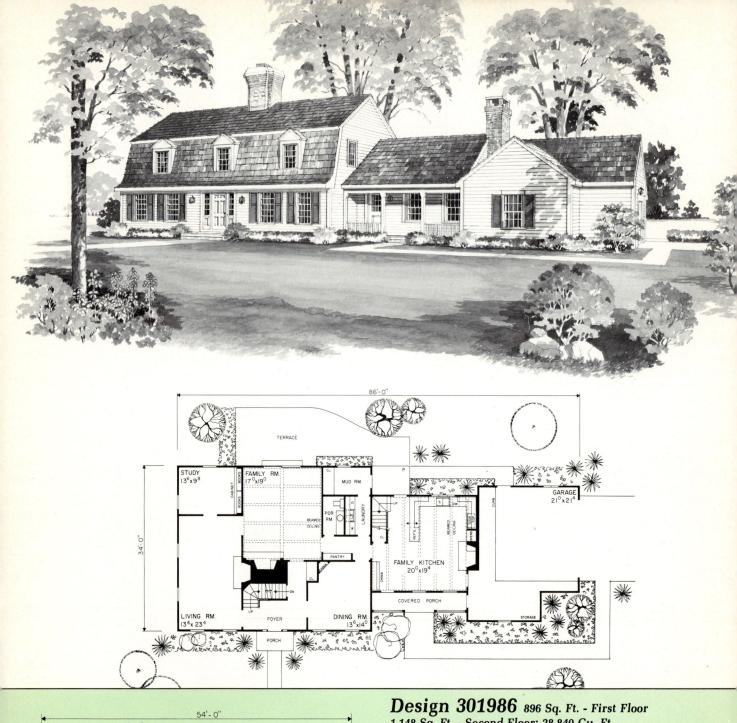

Design 301986 896 Sq. Ft. - First Floor
1,148 Sq. Ft. - Second Floor; 28,840 Cu. Ft.

● This design with its distinctive Gambrel roof will spell charm wherever it may be situated - far out in the country, or on a busy thoroughfare. Compact and economical to build, it will be easy on the budget. Note the location of the family room. It is over the garage on the second floor.

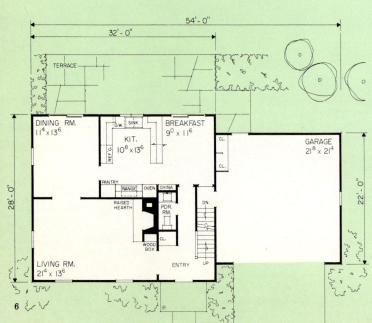

Design 302320 *1,856 Sq. Ft. - First Floor; 1,171 Sq. Ft. - Second Floor; 46,699 Cu. Ft.*

● A charming Colonial adaptation with a Gambrel roof front exterior and a Salt Box rear. The focal point of family activities will be the spacious family kitchen with its beamed ceiling and fireplace. Blueprints include details for both three and four bedroom options. In addition to the family kitchen, note beamed ceiling family room with fireplace. Don't miss the study with built-in book shelves and cabinets. Gracious living will be enjoyed throughout this design.

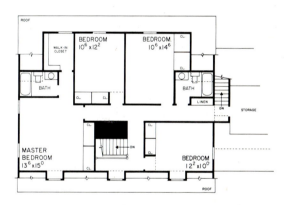

OPTIONAL SECOND FLOOR PLAN

Design 302586

984 Sq. Ft. - First Floor
1,003 Sq. Ft. - Second Floor; 30,080 Cu. Ft.

● A stately Tudor! With four large bedrooms. And lots of living space . . . formal living and dining rooms, a family room with a traditional fireplace, a spacious kitchen with nook.

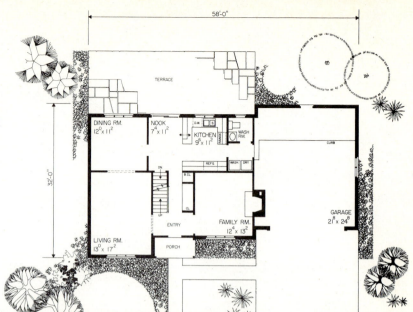

Design 302732

1,071 Sq. Ft. - First Floor
1,022 Sq. Ft. - Second Floor; 34,210 Cu. Ft.

● The two-story front entry hall will be dramatic indeed. Note the efficient kitchen adjacent to informal family room, formal dining room. Upstairs, three big bedrooms, two baths.

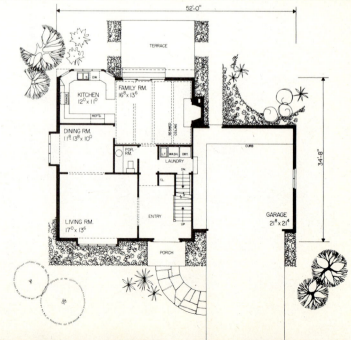

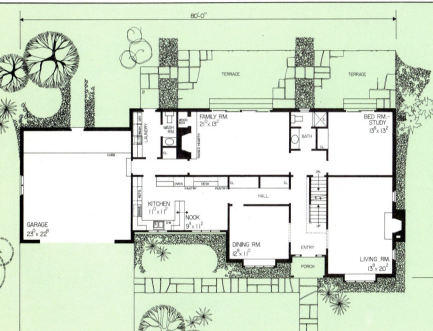

Design 302577

1,718 Sq. Ft. - First Floor
1,147 Sq. Ft. - Second Floor; 42,843 Cu. Ft.

● The exterior of this Tudor has interesting roof planes, delightful window treatment and recessed front entrance. The master suite with sitting room is one of the highlights of the interior.

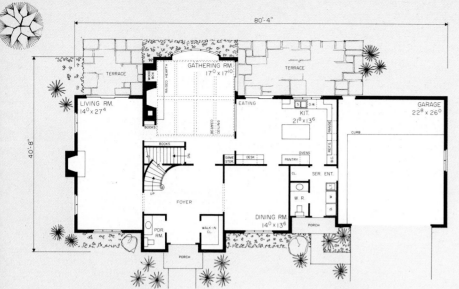

Design 302503

1,847 Sq. Ft. - First Floor
1,423 Sq. Ft. - Second Floor
50,671 Cu. Ft.

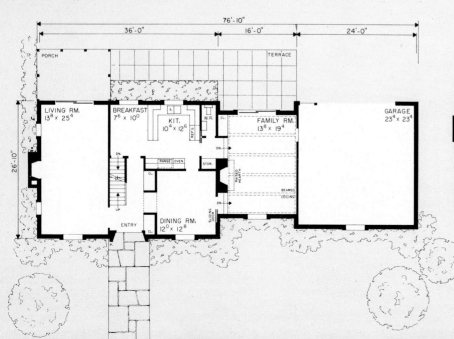

Design 301260

1,318 Sq. Ft. - First Floor
989 Sq. Ft. - Second Floor
31,787 Cu. Ft.

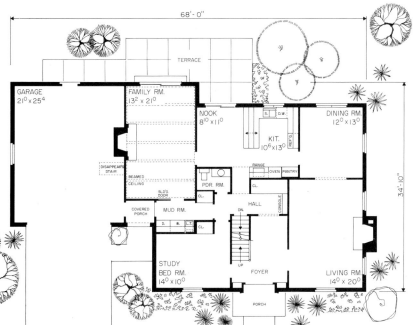

GARAGE
21⁰ x 25⁴

TERRACE

FAMILY RM.
13² x 21⁰

NOOK
8¹⁰ x 11⁰

DINING RM.
12⁰ x 13⁰

KIT.
10⁶ x 13⁰

DISAPPEARING STAIR

BEAMED CEILING

SLD'G DOOR

PDR. RM.

RANGE

OVEN PANTRY

COVERED PORCH

MUD RM.

HALL

CONSOLE

STUDY
BED RM.
14⁰ x 10⁰

DN.

UP

FOYER

LIVING RM.
14⁰ x 20⁰

PORCH

68'-0"

34'-10"

BED RM.
15⁴ x 11⁴

BED RM.
15⁸ x 11⁴

STORAGE

BATH

LIN.

DN.

BATH

SEAT

BED RM.
12⁴ x 10⁰

MASTER
BED RM.
17⁰ x 13⁰

Design 301774
1,574 Sq. Ft. - First Floor
1,124 Sq. Ft. - Second Floor
37,616 Cu. Ft.

Design 302192 1,884 Sq. Ft. - First Floor
1,521 Sq. Ft. - Second Floor; 58,380 Cu. Ft.

● This is surely a fine adaptation from the 18th-Century when formality and elegance were by-words. The authentic detailing of this design centers around the fine proportions, the dentils, the window symmetry, the front door and entranceway, the massive chimneys and the masonry work. The rear elevation retains all the grandeur exemplary of exquisite architecture. The appeal of this outstanding home does not end with its exterior elevations. Consider the formal living room with its corner fireplace. Also, the library with its wall of bookshelves and cabinets. Further, the dining room highlights corner china cabinets. Continue to study this elegant plan.

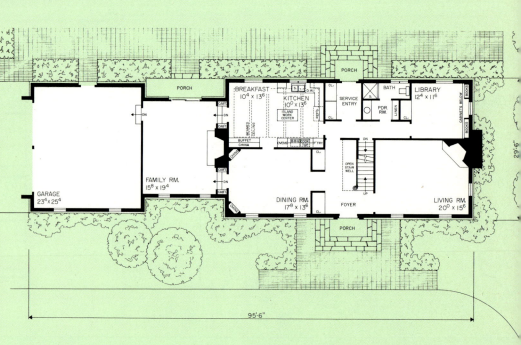

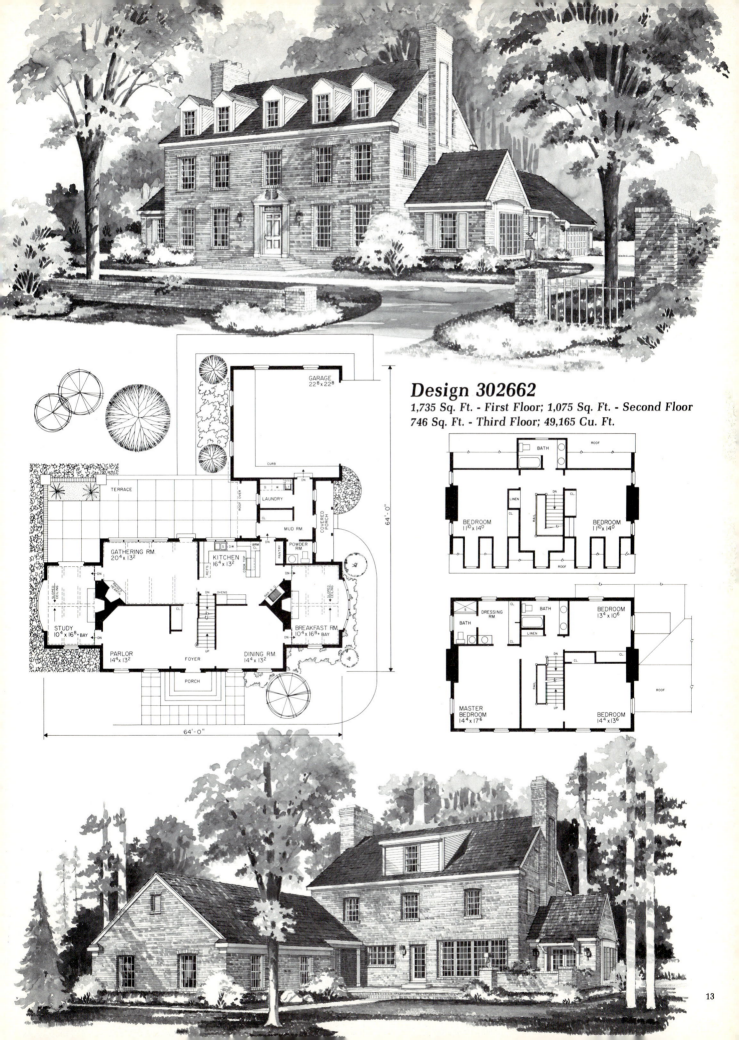

Design 302662

1,735 Sq. Ft. - First Floor; 1,075 Sq. Ft. - Second Floor
746 Sq. Ft. - Third Floor; 49,165 Cu. Ft.

GARAGE
22⁸ x 22⁸

TERRACE

LAUNDRY

MUD RM.

COVERED PORCH

GATHERING RM.
20⁴ x 13²

KITCHEN
16⁴ x 13²

PANTRY

POWDER RM.

STUDY
10⁴ x 16⁸ BAY

OVENS

PARLOR
14⁴ x 13²

FOYER

DINING RM.
14⁴ x 13²

BREAKFAST RM.
10⁴ x 16⁸ BAY

PORCH

UP

64'-0"

BATH

ROOF

LINEN

BEDROOM
11¹⁰ x 14⁰

BEDROOM
11¹⁰ x 14⁰

ROOF

DRESSING RM.

BATH

BATH

LINEN

BEDROOM
13⁴ x 10⁶

MASTER BEDROOM
14⁴ x 17⁶

BEDROOM
14⁴ x 13⁶

ROOF

13

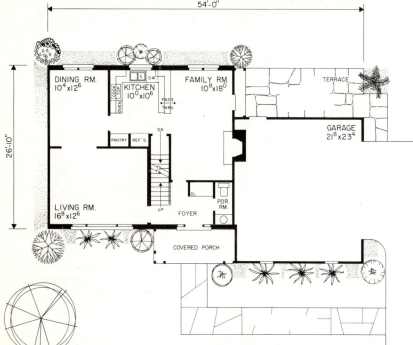

54'-0"

26'-10"

DINING RM.
10⁴x12⁶

KITCHEN
10⁰x10⁶

FAMILY RM.
10⁸x18⁰

TERRACE

GARAGE
21⁸x23⁴

PANTRY REF'G

DN

PASS THRU

LIVING RM.
16⁸x12⁶

CL.

PDR. RM.

UP

FOYER

COVERED PORCH

BEDROOM
10⁰x11⁰

BEDROOM
8⁶x10⁰

BEDROOM
10⁰x10⁰

CL.

CL.

ROOF

CL.

CL.

BATH

DN

LINEN

CL.

MASTER
BEDROOM
11⁴x13¹⁰

BATH

BEDROOM
10⁸x12⁴

ROOF

Design 301318
854 Sq. Ft. - First Floor
896 Sq. Ft. - Second Floor
24,420 Cu. Ft.

● Imagine! Five bedrooms, 2½ baths, informal family room, formal living and dining rooms, excellent kitchen, snack bar and a big two-car garage.

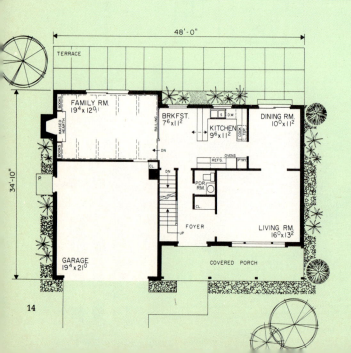

48'-0"

34'-10"

TERRACE

FAMILY RM.
19⁴x12⁹¹

BOOKS

RAISED HEARTH

BOOKS

BRKFST.
7⁶x11²

KITCHEN
9⁶x11²

DINING RM.
10⁰x11²

DN

CL.

OVENS

REF'G PTRY.

PDR RM

CL.

FOYER

UP

LIVING RM.
16⁰x13²

GARAGE
19⁴x21⁰

COVERED PORCH

BEDROOM
9⁴x9⁴

BATH

MASTER
BEDROOM
10⁰x15⁰

CL.

DN

CL.

BATH

CL.

LINEN

RAIL

DN

CL.

BEDROOM
10⁰x10⁰

BEDROOM
11⁴x10⁰

BATH

MASTER
BEDROOM
14⁸x11⁸

BATH

CL.

S

CL.

DN

RAIL

LINEN

BEDROOM
10⁰x10⁰

BEDROOM
11⁴x13⁴

Design 301956
990 Sq. Ft. - First Floor
728 Sq. Ft. - Second Floor
23,703 Cu. Ft.

● The blueprints for this home include details for both the three bedroom and four bedroom options. The first floor livability does not change.

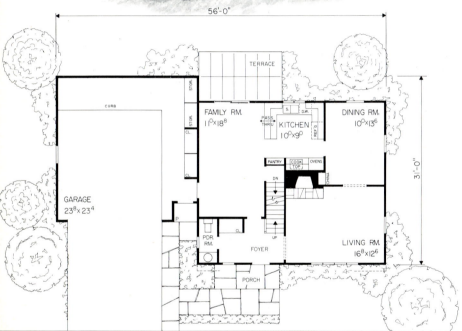

FAMILY RM.
11⁰x18⁸

KITCHEN
10⁰x9⁰

DINING RM.
10⁰x13⁶

PANTRY   COOK TOP   OVENS

LIVING RM.
16⁸x12⁶

FOYER

PDR. RM.

PORCH

GARAGE
23⁸x23⁴

TERRACE

56'-0"

31'-0"

Design 301719

864 Sq. Ft. - First Floor
896 Sq. Ft. - Second Floor
26,024 Cu. Ft.

BEDROOM
11⁰x10⁰

BEDROOM
10⁰x11⁴

WALK-IN CLOSET

MASTER BEDROOM
13⁴x13⁴

BEDROOM
11⁰x13⁸

WALK-IN CLOSET

BATH

● What an appealing low-cost Colonial adaptation. Most of the livability features generally found in the largest of homes are present to cater to family needs.

Design 302646 1,274 Sq. Ft. - First Floor
1,322 Sq. Ft. - Second Floor; 42,425 Cu. Ft.

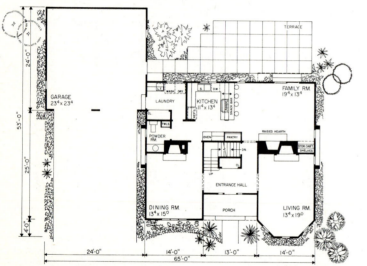

● What a stylish departure from today's usual architecture. This refreshing exterior may be referred to as Neo-Victorian. Its vertical lines, steep roofs and variety of gables remind one of the old Victorian houses of yesteryear. Inside, there is an efficiently working floor plan that is delightfully spacious.

Design 302647 2,104 Sq. Ft. - First Floor; 1,230 Sq. Ft. - Second Floor; 56,395 Cu. Ft.

● Another Neo-Victorian, and what an impressive and unique design it is. Observe the roof lines, the window treatment, the use of contrasting exterior materials and the arched, covered front entrance.

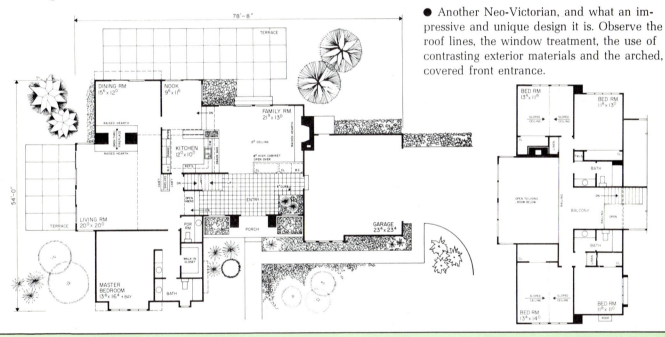

Design 302645 1,600 Sq. Ft. - First Floor; 1,305 Sq. Ft. - Second Floor
925 Sq. Ft. - Third Floor; 58,355 Cu. Ft.

● Reminiscent of the Gothic Victorian style of the mid-19th Century, this delightfully detailed, three-story house has a wrap-around veranda for summertime relaxing. The parlor and family room, each with fireplaces, provide excellent formal and informal living facilities. The third floor houses two more great areas plus bath.

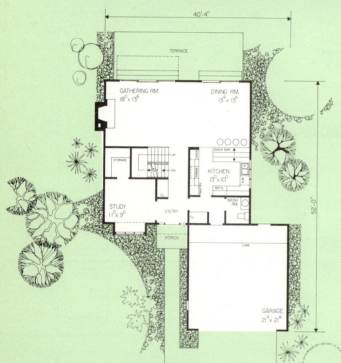

Design 302711 975 Sq. Ft. - First Floor
1,024 Sq. Ft. - Second Floor; 31,380 Cu. Ft.

● Special features! A complete master suite with a private balcony plus two more bedrooms and a bath upstairs. The first floor has a study with a storage closet. A convenient snack bar between kitchen and dining room. The kitchen offers many built-in appliances. Plus a gathering room and dining room that measures 31 feet wide. Note the curb area in the garage and fireplace in gathering room.

Design 302748
1,232 Sq. Ft. - First Floor
720 Sq. Ft. - Second Floor
27,550 Cu. Ft.

● This four bedroom contemporary will definitely have appeal for the entire family. The U-shaped kitchen-nook area with its built-in desk, adjacent laundry/wash room and service entrance will be very efficient for the busy kitchen activities. The living and family rooms are both sunken one step.

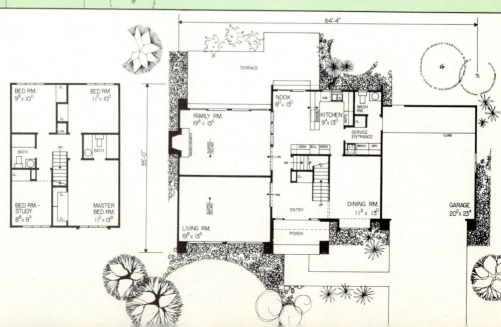

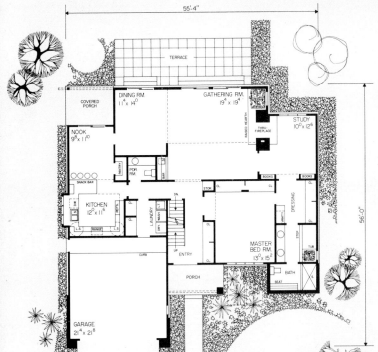

Design 302701 1,909 Sq. Ft. - First Floor
891 Sq. Ft. - Second Floor; 50,830 Cu. Ft.

● A snack bar in the kitchen! Plus a breakfast nook and formal dining room. Whether it's an elegant dinner party or a quick lunch, this home provides the right spot. There's a wet bar in the gathering room. Built-in bookcases in the study. And between these two rooms, a gracious fireplace. Three large bedrooms. Including a luxury master suite. Plus a balcony lounge overlooking gathering room below.

TERRACE

TERRACE

GATHERING RM.
17⁴ x 19⁴

DINING RM.
11⁰ x 13⁶

NOOK
9⁴ x 8⁶

MASTER
BED RM.
11⁸ x 15⁰

RAISED HEARTH

SEAT

PANTRY

BATH

LINEN

DRESSING RM.

TUB

VANITY

CL

WALK IN
CLOSET

RAIL

OPEN

UP   DN

DN

ENTRY
OPEN ABOVE

OPEN ABOVE

PDR.
RM.

CL

KITCHEN
10⁴ x 14¹⁰

DRY WASH

LAUNDRY

B.CL. OVENS REFG.

CURB

PORCH

DN

GARAGE
21⁸ x 21⁴

STORAGE

66'-8"

63'-4"

BALCONY

BED RM.
11⁸ x 13⁶

OPEN TO
GATHERING RM.
BELOW

SLOPED CEILING

BED RM.
11⁰ x 13⁶

OPEN

RAIL

DRESS.
RM.

BATH

VANITY

DN

UP

RAIL

OPEN TO
ENTRY BELOW

RAIL

OPEN

BATH

DRESS.
RM.

CL

Design 302729
1,590 Sq. Ft. - First Floor
756 Sq. Ft. - Second Floor
39,310 Cu. Ft.

● Entering this home will surely be a pleasure through the sheltered walk-way to the double front doors. And the pleasure and beauty does not stop there. The entry hall and sunken gathering room are open to the upstairs for added dimension.

There's even a built-in seat in the entry area. The kitchen-nook area is very efficient with its many built-ins and the adjacent laundry room. There is a fine indoor-outdoor living relationship in this design. Note the private terrace off the luxurious

master bedroom suite, a living terrace accessible from the gathering room, dining room and nook plus the balcony off the upstairs bedroom. Upstairs there is a total of two bedrooms, each having its own private bath and plenty of closets.

Design 302379 *1,525 Sq. Ft. - First Floor; 748 Sq. Ft. - Second Floor; 26,000 Cu. Ft.*

● A house that has "everything" may very well look just like this design. Its exterior is well-proportioned and impressive. Inside the inviting double front doors there are features galore. The living room and family room level are sunken. Separating these two rooms is a dramatic thru fireplace. A built-in bar, planter and beamed ceiling highlight the family room. Nearby is a full bath and a study which could be utilized as a fourth bedroom. The fine functioning kitchen has a pass-thru to the snack bar in the breakfast nook. The adjacent dining room overlooks the living room and has sliding doors to the covered porch. Upstairs three bedrooms, two baths and an outdoor balcony. Blueprints for this design include optional basement details.

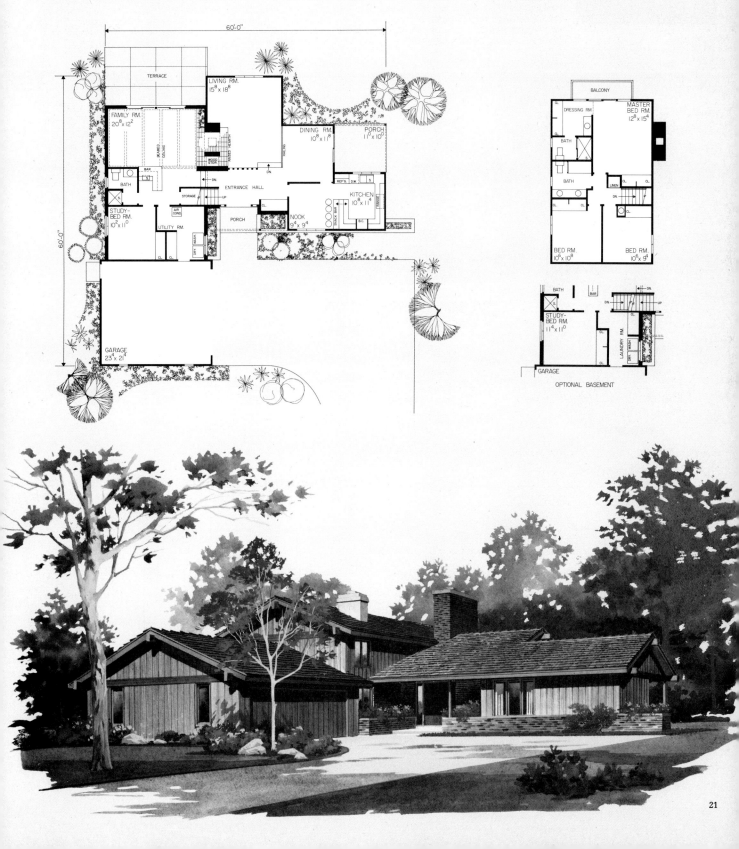

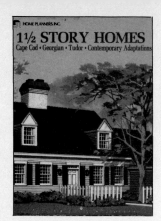

1½ STORY HOMES
Cape Cod • Georgian • Tudor • Contemporary Adaptations

THE 1½-STORY HOME . . .

like the full two-story home can be an economical one to build; for it utilizes upper level livability without requiring additional foundation or roof area. But, perhaps, the 1½-story home's most significant feature is its expandable living potential. With a couple of bedrooms often located on the first floor, the finishing-off of the upstairs can be delayed to a future date. This permits the modest 1½-story house to serve as an entry-level home for those building their first home. As family size increases and finances improve, the development of the second floor can then proceed.

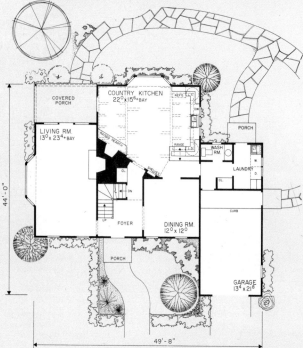

Design 302657 1,217 Sq. Ft. - First Floor
868 Sq. Ft. - Second Floor; 33,260 Cu. Ft.

● Deriving its design from the traditional Cape Cod style, this facade features clapboard siding, small-paned windows and a transom-lit entrance flanked by carriage lamps. A central chimney services two fireplaces, one in the country-kitchen and the other in the formal living room which is removed from the disturbing flow of traffic. The master suite is located to the left of the upstairs landing.

Design 301394

832 Sq. Ft. - First Floor
512 Sq. Ft. - Second Floor
19,385 Cu. Ft.

● The growing family with a restricted building budget will find this a great investment - a convenient living floor plan inside an attractive facade.

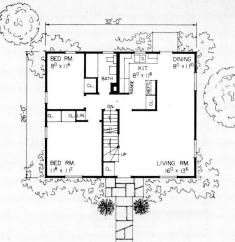

Design 302510

1,191 Sq. Ft. - First Floor
533 Sq. Ft. - Second Floor
27,500 Cu. Ft.

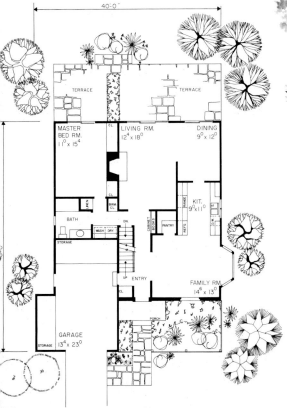

● The pleasant in-line kitchen is flanked by a separate dining room and a family room. The master bedroom is on the first floor with two more bedrooms upstairs.

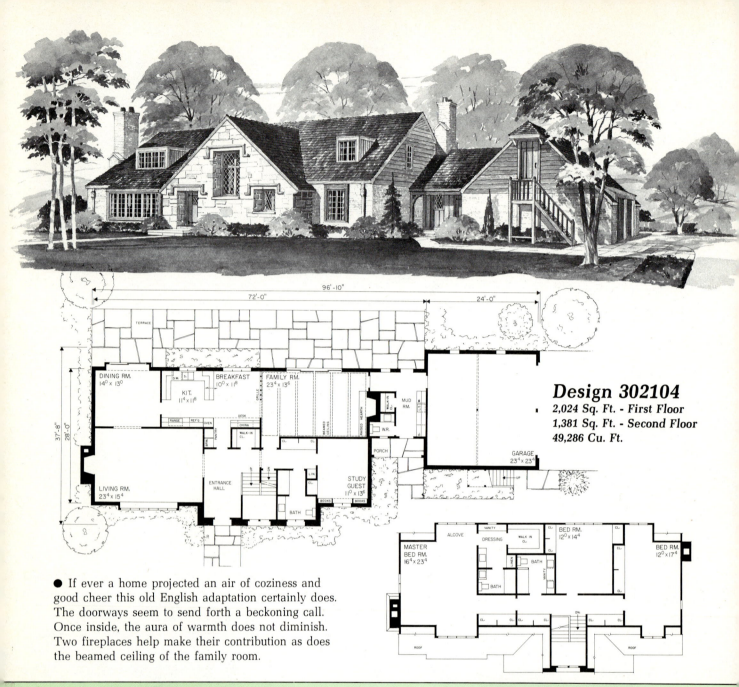

Design 302104

- **2,024 Sq. Ft. - First Floor**
- **1,381 Sq. Ft. - Second Floor**
- **49,286 Cu. Ft.**

● If ever a home projected an air of coziness and good cheer this old English adaptation certainly does. The doorways seem to send forth a beckoning call. Once inside, the aura of warmth does not diminish. Two fireplaces help make their contribution as does the beamed ceiling of the family room.

Design 301991

1,262 Sq. Ft. - First Floor
1,108 Sq. Ft. - Second Floor
31,073 Cu. Ft.

● Put yourself and your family in this English cottage adaptation and you'll all rejoice over your new home for many a year. The pride of owning and living in a home that is distinctive will be a constant source of satisfaction. Count the features that will serve your family well for years.

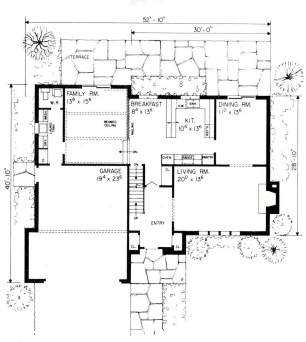

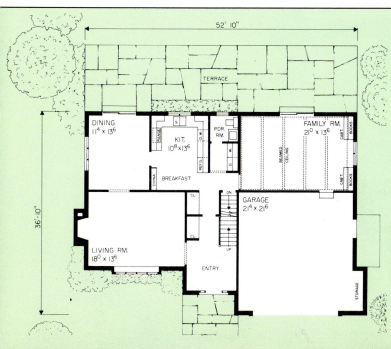

Design 302175
1,206 Sq. Ft. - First Floor
1,185 Sq. Ft. - Second Floor; 32,655 Cu. Ft.

● An English adaptation with all the amenities for gracious living. Note built-ins.

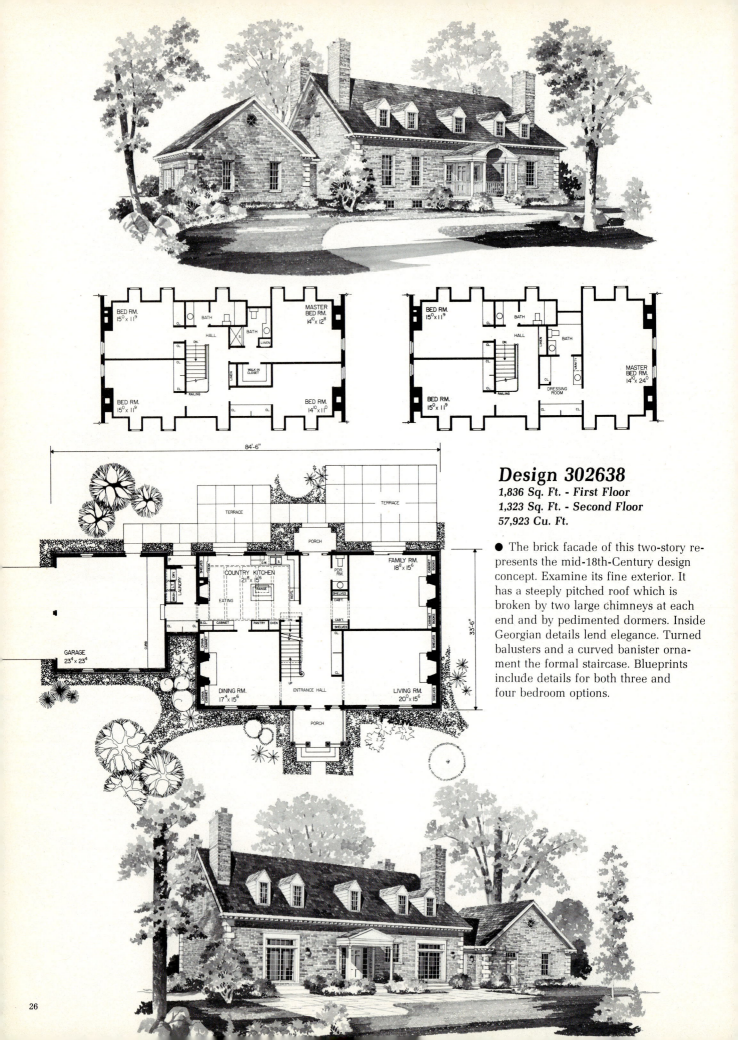

Design 302638
1,836 Sq. Ft. - First Floor
1,323 Sq. Ft. - Second Floor
57,923 Cu. Ft.

● The brick facade of this two-story represents the mid-18th-Century design concept. Examine its fine exterior. It has a steeply pitched roof which is broken by two large chimneys at each end and by pedimented dormers. Inside Georgian details lend elegance. Turned balusters and a curved banister ornament the formal staircase. Blueprints include details for both three and four bedroom options.

Design 302132

1,958 Sq. Ft. - First Floor
1,305 Sq. Ft. - Second Floor
51,428 Cu. Ft.

● Another Georgian adaptation with a great heritage dating back to 18th-Century America. Exquisite and symmetrical detailing set the character of this impressive home. Don't overlook such features as the two fireplaces, the laundry, the beamed ceiling, the built-in china cabinets and the oversized garage.

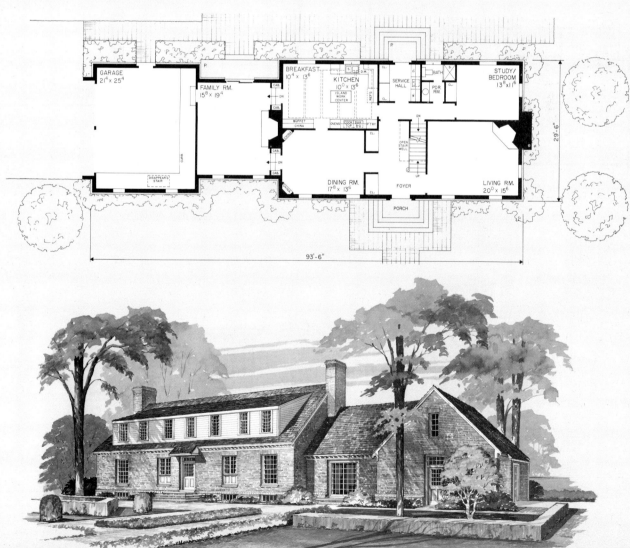

Design 301766 1,638 Sq. Ft. - First Floor
1,006 Sq. Ft. - Second Floor; 35,352 Cu. Ft.

● Here is a home that truly fits the description of traditional charm. The symmetry is, indeed, delightful. A certain magnetic aura seems to reach out with a whisper of welcome. Observe the spacious family-kitchen area, the study, the separate dining room and the extra bath.

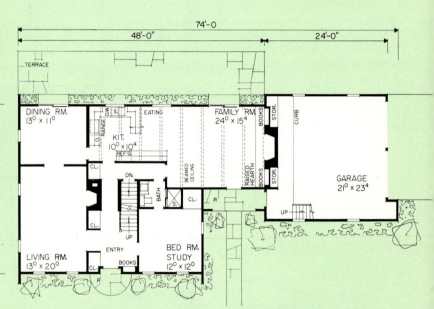

Design 302124
1,180 Sq. Ft. - First Floor
1,018 Sq. Ft. - Second Floor; 29,854 Cu. Ft.

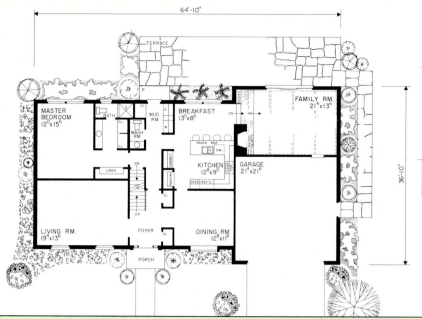

● This cozy home has over 2,600 square feet of livable floor area! And the manner in which this space is put to work to function conveniently for the large family is worth studying. Imagine five bedrooms, three full baths, living, dining and family rooms. Note large kitchen.

Design 301701 1,344 Sq. Ft. - First Floor; 948 Sq. Ft. - Second Floor; 33,952 Cu. Ft.

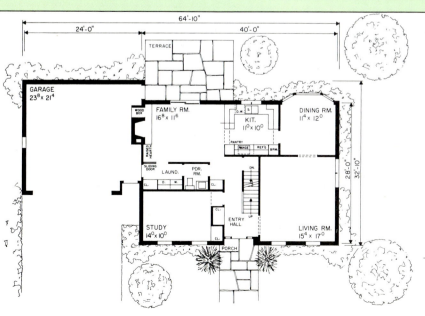

● Here is a home that truly fits the description of traditional charm. The symmetry is, indeed, delightful. A certain magnetic aura seems to reach out with a whisper of welcome. Observe the spacious family-kitchen area, the study, the separate dining room and the extra bath.

Design 302780

2,006 Sq. Ft. - First Floor
718 Sq. Ft. - Second Floor; 42,110 Cu. Ft.

● This 1½-story contemporary has more fine features than one can imagine. The livability is outstanding and can be appreciated by the whole family. Note the fine indoor-outdoor living relationships.

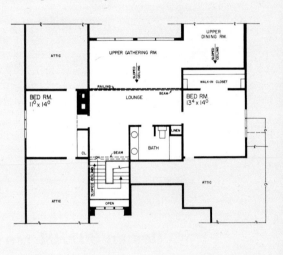

Design 302772

1,579 Sq. Ft. - First Floor
1,240 Sq. Ft. - Second Floor; 39,460 Cu. Ft.

● This four-bedroom two-story contemporary design is sure to suit your growing family needs. The rear U-shaped kitchen, flanked by the family and dining rooms, will be very efficient to the busy homemaker. Parents will enjoy all the convenience of the master bedroom suite.

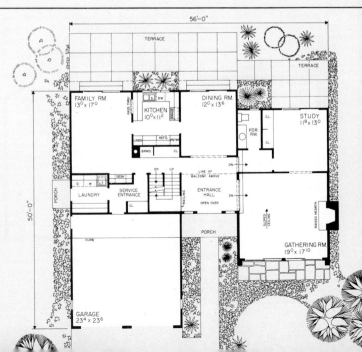

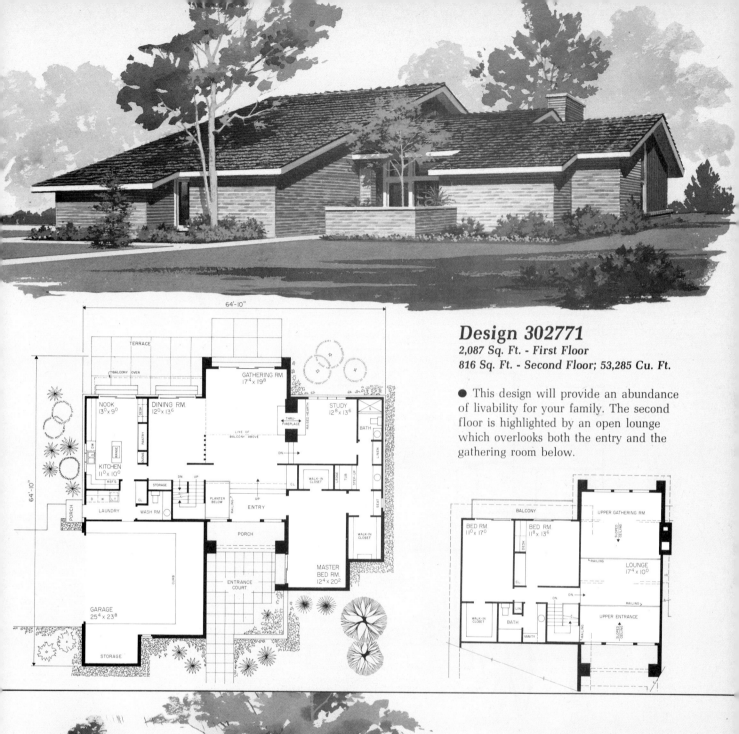

Design 302771

2,087 Sq. Ft. - First Floor
816 Sq. Ft. - Second Floor; 53,285 Cu. Ft.

● This design will provide an abundance of livability for your family. The second floor is highlighted by an open lounge which overlooks both the entry and the gathering room below.

TERRACE

BALCONY OVER

GATHERING RM.
17⁴ x 19⁸

NOOK
13⁰ x 9⁰

DINING RM.
12⁰ x 13⁶

STUDY
12⁸ x 13⁶

BATH

THRU
FIREPLACE

LINE OF
BALCONY ABOVE

KITCHEN
11⁰ x 10⁰

RANGE

PANTRY

OVEN

STORAGE

DN UP

DN

WALK-IN
CLOSET

TUB
STEP-UP

REF'G

CL

PLANTER
BELOW

UP

ENTRY

LAUNDRY

WASH RM.

PORCH

WALK-IN
CLOSET

CURB

PORCH

ENTRANCE
COURT

MASTER
BED RM.
12⁴ x 20²

GARAGE
25⁴ x 23⁸

STORAGE

64'-10"

64'-10"

BALCONY

UPPER GATHERING RM.

BED RM.
11⁰ x 17⁰

BED RM.
11⁸ x 13⁶

DESK

SLOPED
CEILING

RAILING

LOUNGE
17⁴ x 10⁰

CL

DN

RAILING

WALK-IN
CLOSET

BATH

DN

UPPER
ENTRANCE

VANITY

SLOPED
CEILING

Design 302820 2,261 Sq. Ft.; 46,830 Cu. Ft.

● A privacy wall around the courtyard with pool and trellised planter area is a gracious area by which to enter this one-story design. The Spanish flavor is accented by the grillework and the tiled roof. Interior livability has a great deal to offer. The front living room has slid-ing glass doors which open to the entrance court; the adjacent dining room features a bay window. Informal activities will be enjoyed in the rear family room. Its many features include a sloped, beamed ceiling, raised hearth fireplace, sliding glass doors to the terrace and a snack bar for those very informal meals. A laundry and powder room are adjacent to the U-shaped kitchen. The sleeping wing can remain quiet away from the plan's activity centers. Notice the three-car garage with an extra storage area.

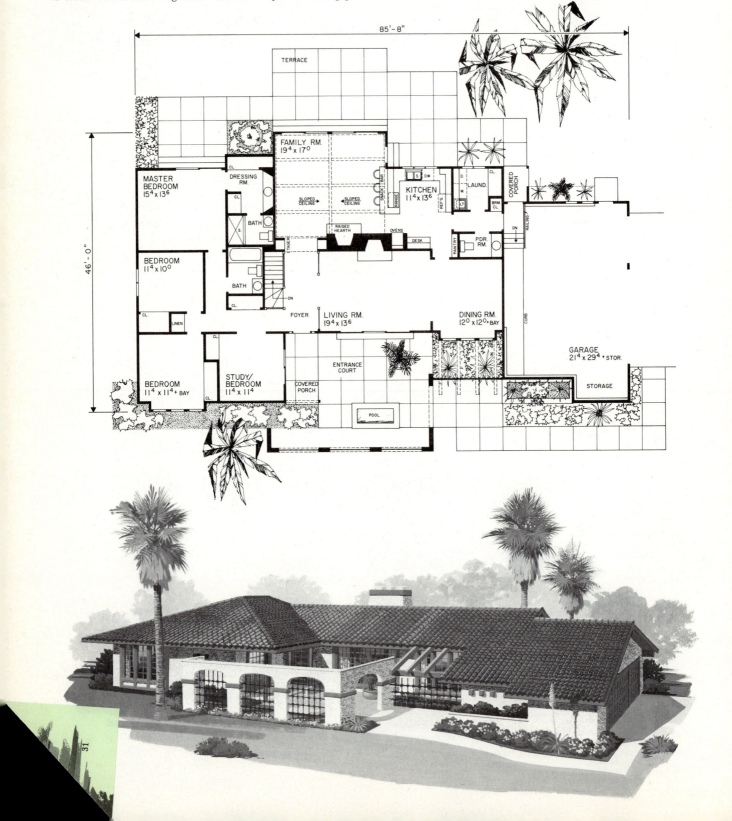

THE ONE-STORY HOME over 2000 Sq. Ft. . . . *has been*

regarded by many as the epitome of convenient living. Locating all of a family's living facilities on a single level eliminates the daily chore of ascending and descending stairs when sleeping facilities are situated on a second floor. Further, the one-story home over 2000 sq. ft. is large enough so that with proper floor planning a full measure of outstanding livability features can be provided. As described on pages 166 and 167, this Design Category Series book features Tudor, French, Spanish, Western, Contemporary exteriors. There are sections on country-estate and solar oriented designs.

Design 302857
2,982 Sq. Ft.; 60,930 Cu. Ft.

● Imagine yourself occupying this home! Study the outstanding master bedroom. You will be forever pleased by its many features. It has "his" and "her" baths each with a large walk-in closet, sliding glass doors to a private, side terrace (a great place to enjoy a morning cup of coffee) and an adjacent study. Notice that the two family bedrooms are separated from the master bedroom. This allows for total privacy both for the parents and the children. Continue to observe this plan. You will have no problem at all entertaining in the gathering room. Your party can flow to the adjacent balcony on a warm summer evening. The work center has been designed in an orderly fashion. The U-shaped kitchen utilizes the triangular work pattern, said to be the most efficient. Only a few steps away, you will be in the breakfast room, formal dining room, laundry or washroom. Take your time and study every last detail in this home plan.

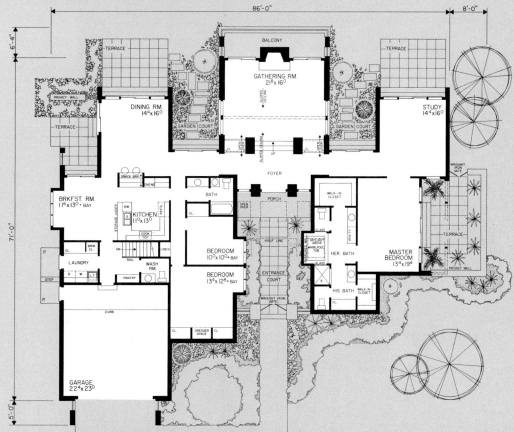

Design 301835
2,144 Sq. Ft.; 33,310 Cu. Ft.

● Cedar shakes and quarried natural stone, are the exterior materials which adorn this irregularly shaped traditional ranch home. Adding to the appeal of the exterior are the cut-up windows, the shutters, the pediment gable, the cupola and the double front doors. The detail of the garage door opening adds further interest. Inside, this favorite among floor plans, reflects all the features neccessary to provide complete livability for the large family. The sleeping zone is a 24' x 40' rectangle which contains four bedrooms and two full baths. A dressing room with a vanity and a wall of wardrobe storage highlights the master bedroom. Both the informal family room and the formal living room have a fireplace.

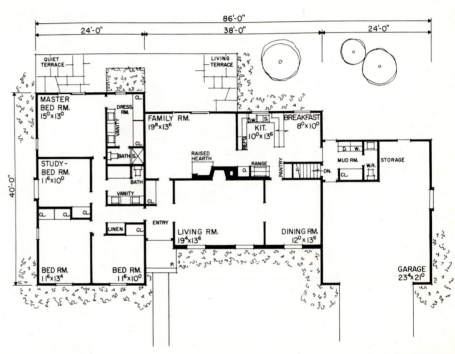

● Whatever the setting, here is a traditional, one story home that is truly impressive. Zoned in a most practical manner, the floor plan features an isolated bedroom wing, formal living and dining rooms and, across the rear of the house, the informal living areas.

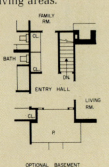

OPTIONAL BASEMENT

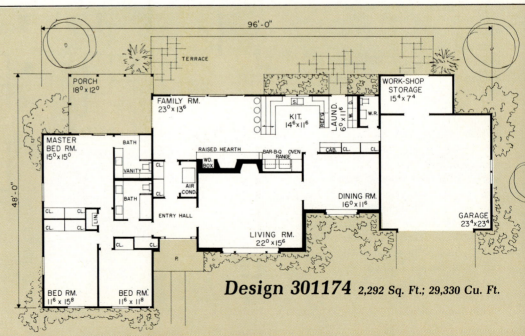

Design 301174 2,292 Sq. Ft.; 29,330 Cu. Ft.

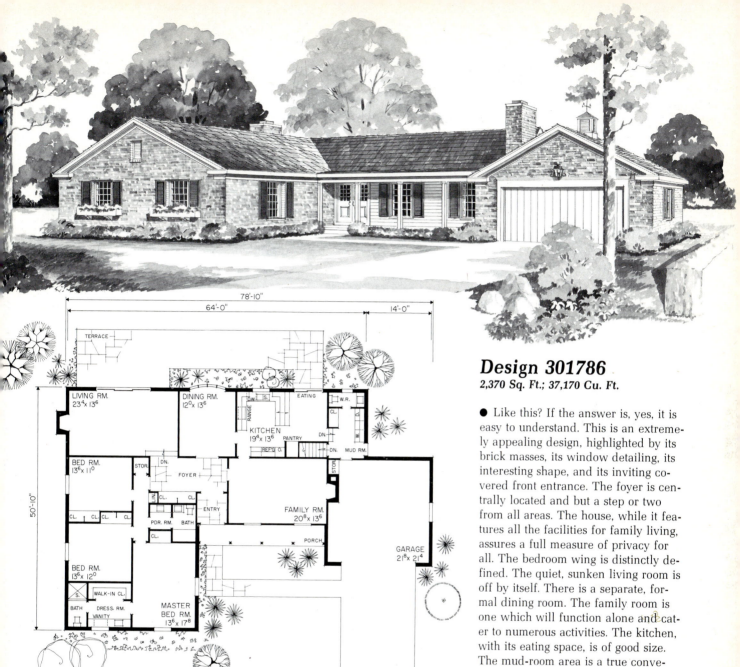

Floor plan dimensions: 78'-10" overall (64'-0" and 14'-0"), 50'-10" depth

TERRACE

LIVING RM.
23⁴ x 13⁶

DINING RM.
12⁰ x 13⁶

EATING

RANGE / DW. / S. / CL. / W.R.

KITCHEN
19⁴ x 13⁶

PANTRY

REF. / O. / DN. / MUD RM. / W / D

BED RM.
13⁶ x 11⁰

STOR. / DN. / FOYER

CL. / CL. / ENTRY

FAMILY RM.
20⁸ x 13⁶

PDR. RM. / BATH / CL.

PORCH

BED RM.
13⁶ x 12⁰

WALK-IN CL.

GARAGE
21⁸ x 21⁴

BATH / DRESS. RM. / VANITY / S.

MASTER
BED RM.
13⁶ x 17⁸

Design 301786
2,370 Sq. Ft.; 37,170 Cu. Ft.

● Like this? If the answer is, yes, it is easy to understand. This is an extremely appealing design, highlighted by its brick masses, its window detailing, its interesting shape, and its inviting covered front entrance. The foyer is centrally located and but a step or two from all areas. The house, while it features all the facilities for family living, assures a full measure of privacy for all. The bedroom wing is distinctly defined. The quiet, sunken living room is off by itself. There is a separate, formal dining room. The family room is one which will function alone and cater to numerous activities. The kitchen, with its eating space, is of good size. The mud-room area is a true convenient living feature.

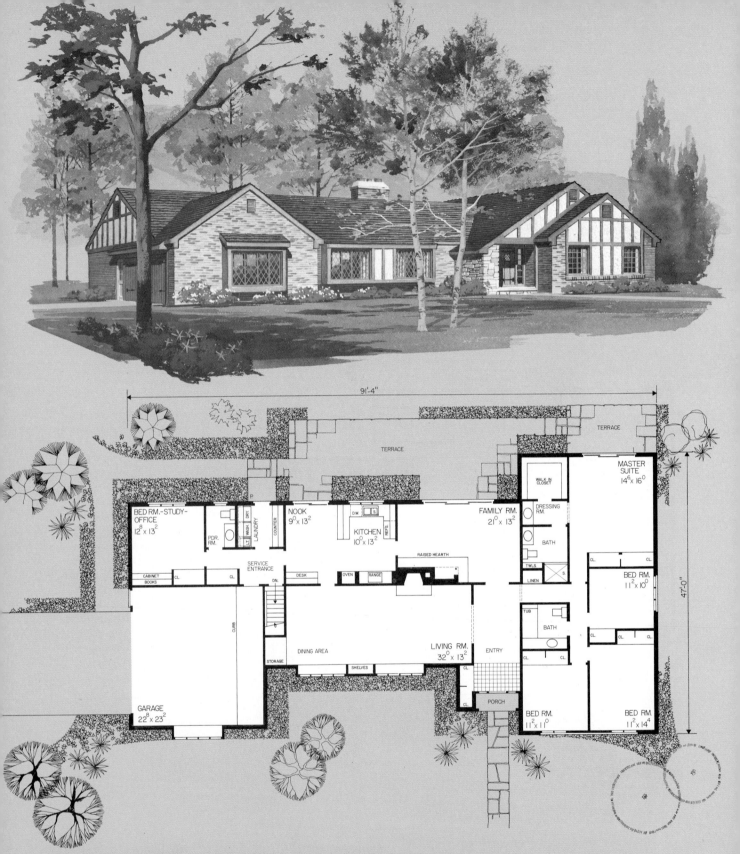

Design 302573 2,747 Sq. Ft.; 48,755 Cu. Ft.

● A Tudor ranch! Combining brick and wood for an elegant look. It has a living/dining room measuring 32' by 13', large indeed. It is fully appointed with a traditional fireplace and built-in shelves, flanked by diagonally paned windows. There's much more! There is a family room with a raised hearth fireplace and sliding glass doors that open onto the terrace. A U-shaped kitchen has lots of built-ins . . . a range, an oven, a desk. Plus a separate breakfast nook. The sleeping facilities consist of three family bedrooms plus an elegant master bedroom suite. A conveniently located laundry with a folding counter is in the service entrance. Adjacent to the laundry is a washroom. The corner of the plan has a study or make it a fifth bedroom if you prefer.

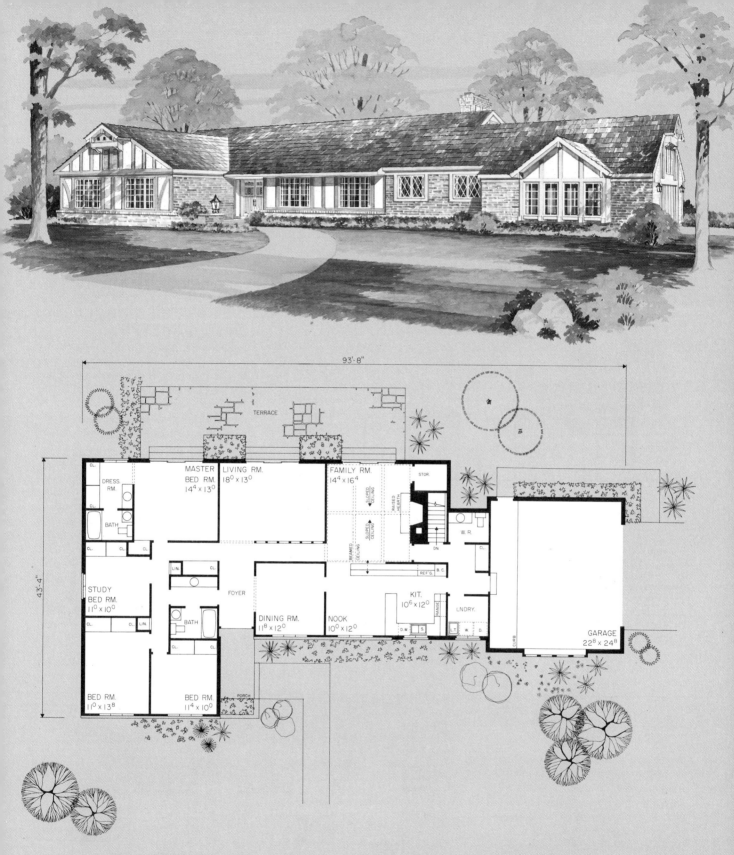

Design 302515 2,363 Sq. Ft.; 46,676 Cu. Ft.

● Another Tudor adaptation with all the appeal that is inherent in this design style. The brick veneer exterior is effectively complimented by the beam work, the stucco, and the window treatment. The carriage lamp perched on the planter wall adds a delightful touch as do the dovecotes of the bedroom wing and over the garage door. The livability of the interior is just great. The kitchen, nook, and dining room overlook the front yard. Around the corner from the kitchen is the laundry with an extra wash room not far away. Sloping, beamed ceiling and raised hearth fireplace are highlights of the family room. Like the living room and master bedroom it functions with rear terrace. Note vanity outside main bath. Stolid wood posts on 3 foot wall separate living room and hall.

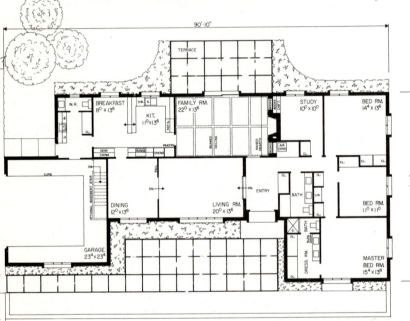

Design 302179
2,439 Sq. Ft.; 33,043 Cu. Ft.

● The formality of this French adaptation is a pleasing picture to behold. Wherever you may choose to build it, this one-story will most assuredly receive the accolades of passers-by. It is the outstanding proportion and the fine detail that make this a home of distinction. What's inside is every bit as delightful as what is outside. Your family will enjoy its three sizable bedrooms. The study will be a favorite haven for those who wish a period of peace and quiet. The sunken living room and the informal family room offer two large areas for family living. For eating there is the breakfast and separate dining room. Two baths and extra wash room serve the family well.

Design 302851
2,739 Sq. Ft.; 55,810 Cu. Ft.

● This spacious one-story has a classic Country French hip roof. The front entrance creates a charming entry. Beyond the covered porch is an octagonal foyer. A closet, shelves and powder room are contained in the foyer. All of the living areas overlook the rear yard. Sliding glass doors open each of these areas to the rear terrace. Their features include a fireplace in the living room, skylight in the dining room and a second set of sliding glass doors in the family room leading to a side covered porch. An island range and other built-ins are featured in the spacious, front kitchen.

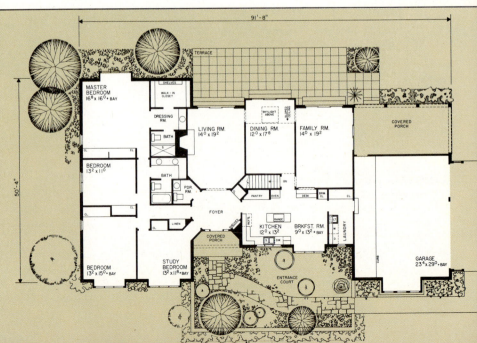

Design 301892
2,036 Sq. Ft.; 26,575 Cu. Ft.

● The romance of French Provincial is captured here by the hip-roof masses, the charm of the window detailing, the brick quoins at the corners, the delicate dentil work at the cornices, the massive centered chimney, and the recessed double front doors. The slightly raised entry court completes the picture. The basic floor plan is a favorite of many. And little wonder, for all areas work well together, while still maintaining a fine degree of separation of functions. The highlight of the interior, perhaps, will be the sunken living room. The family room, with its beamed ceiling, will not be far behind in its popularity. The separate dining room, mud room, efficient kitchen, complete the livability.

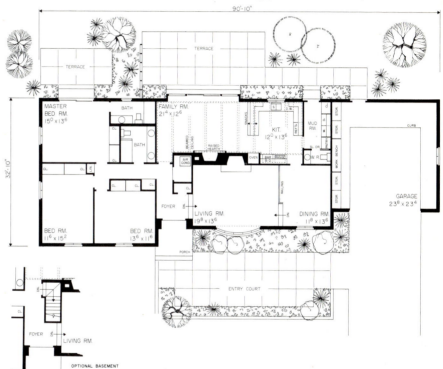

Design 302793 2,065 Sq. Ft.; 48,850 Cu. Ft.

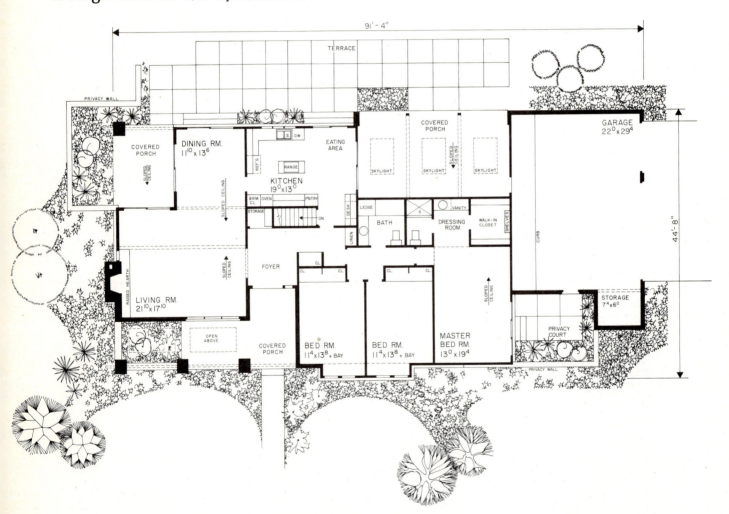

● Privacy will be enjoyed in this home both inside and out. The indoor-outdoor living relationships offered in this plan are outstanding. A covered porch at the entrance. A privacy court off the master bedroom divided from the front yard with a privacy wall. A covered porch serving both the living and dining rooms through sliding glass doors. Also utilizing a privacy wall. Another covered porch off the kitchen eating area. This one is the largest and has skylights above. Also a large rear terrace. The kitchen is efficient with eating space available, an island range and built-in desk. Storage space is abundant. Note storage area in the garage and its overall size. Three front bedrooms. Raised hearth fireplace in the living room.

Design 302790 2,075 Sq. Ft.; 45,630 Cu. Ft.

● Enter this contemporary hip-roofed home through the double front doors and immediately view the sloped ceilinged living room with fireplace. This room will be a sheer delight when it comes to formal entertaining. It has easy access to the kitchen and also a powder room nearby. The work area will be convenient. The kitchen has an island work center with snack bar. The laundry is adjacent to the service entrance and stairs leading to the basement. This area is planned to be a real "step saver". The sleeping wing consists of two family bedrooms, bath and master bedroom suite. Maybe the most attractive feature of this design is the rear covered porch with skylights above. It is accessible by way of sliding glass doors in the family/dining area, living room and master bedroom.

THE ONE-STORY HOME under 2000 Sq. Ft. . . . *presents the*

home designer with the challenge of just how much livability can be incorporated into houses with varying size restrictions. A study of plans in this square footage range is interesting, indeed. Obviously, as houses increase in size so should their livability potential. It may be reflected in larger rooms, more rooms or a combination of both. And, of course, it is possible for the smaller of two houses to have more rooms. An analysis of a family's housing needs must begin with the number and type of rooms it will require to assure the level of livability it wants to enjoy and can afford.

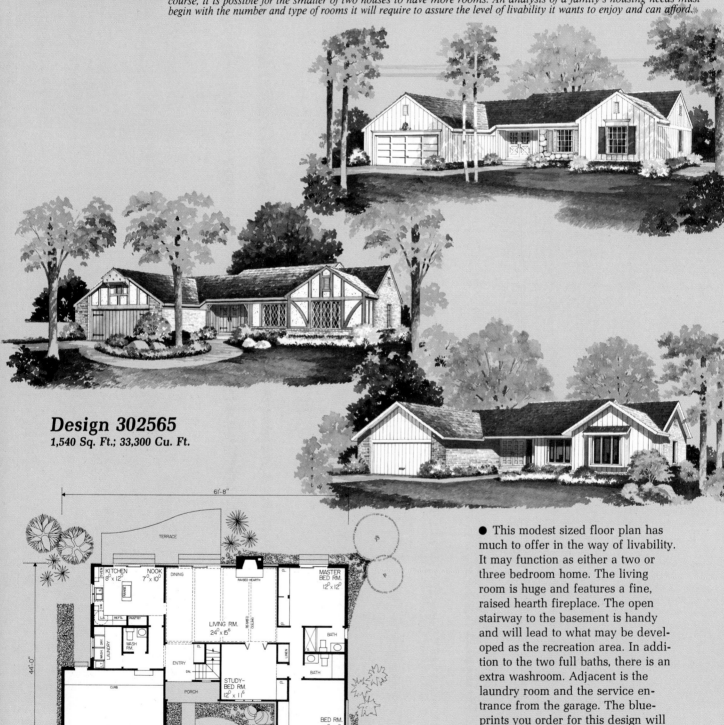

Design 302565
1,540 Sq. Ft.; 33,300 Cu. Ft.

● This modest sized floor plan has much to offer in the way of livability. It may function as either a two or three bedroom home. The living room is huge and features a fine, raised hearth fireplace. The open stairway to the basement is handy and will lead to what may be developed as the recreation area. In addition to the two full baths, there is an extra washroom. Adjacent is the laundry room and the service entrance from the garage. The blueprints you order for this design will show details for each of the three delightful elevations above. Which is your favorite? The Tudor, the Colonial or the Contemporary?

Design 302702
1,636 Sq. Ft.; 38,700 Cu. Ft.

● A rear living room with a sloping ceiling, built-in bookcases, a raised hearth fireplace and sliding glass doors to the rear living terrace. If desired, bi-fold doors permit this room to function with the adjacent study. Open railing next to the stairs to the basement recreation area fosters additional spaciousness. The kitchen has plenty of cabinet and cupboard space. It features informal eating space and is but a step or two from the separate dining room. Note side dining terrace. Each of the three rooms in the sleeping wing has direct access to outdoor living. The master bedroom highlights a huge walk-in wardrobe closet, dressing room with built-in vanity and private bath with large towel storage closet. Projecting the two-car garage with its twin doors to the front not only contributes to an interesting exterior, but reduces the size of the building site required for this home. A lot of living from 1,636 square feet.

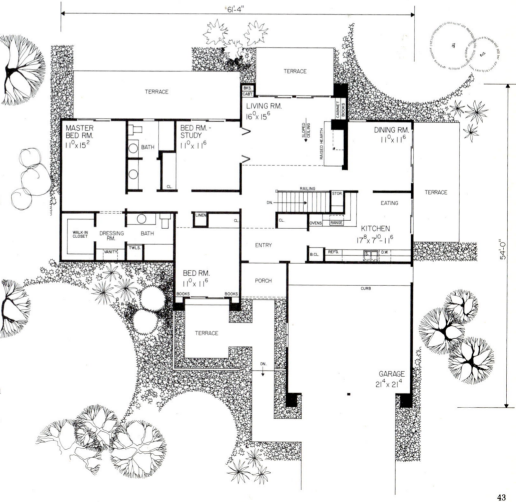

Design 302859
1,599 Sq. Ft.; 37,497 Cu. Ft.

● Incorporated into the extremely popular basic one-story floor plan is a super-insulated structure. This means that it has double exterior walls separated by R-33 insulation and a raised roof truss that insures ceiling insulation will extend to the outer wall. More popularity is shown in the always popular Tudor facade. Enter the home through the air-locked vestibule to the foyer. To the left is the sleeping area. To the right of the foyer is the breakfast room, kitchen and stairs to the basement. Viewing the rear yard are the gathering and dining rooms. Study the technical details described in the blueprints of the wall section so you can better understand this super-insulated house.

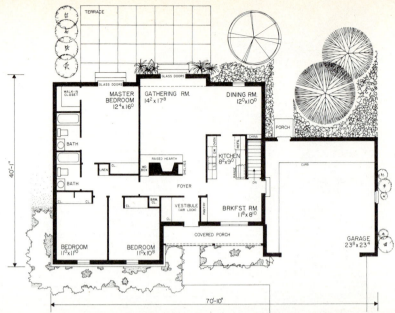

Design 301802
1,315 Sq. Ft.; 24,790 Cu. Ft.

● A small house which includes a full measure of big house livability features. The master bedroom has its extra wash room. In addition to the two bedrooms for the children, there is a study, or fourth bedroom. (This extra room offers the option to serve as a sewing, TV, music or even a guest room.) The living room is well situated and will not be bothered by cross-room traffic. The kitchen functions conveniently with the family-dining area. The stairs to the basement are just inside the entrance from the attached garage.

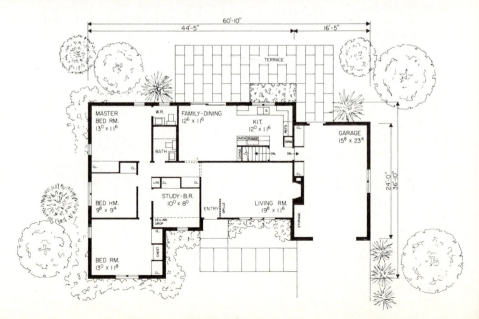

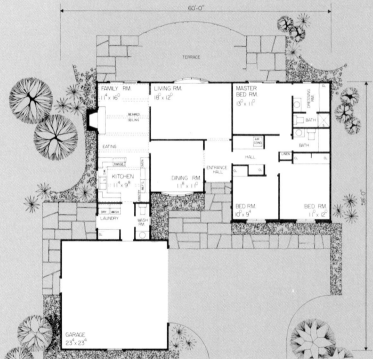

Design 302606
1,499 Sq. Ft.; 19,716 Cu. Ft.

● This modest sized house with its 1,499 square feet could hardly offer more in the way of exterior charm and interior livabiltiy. Measuring only 60 feet in width means it will not require a huge, expensive piece of property. The orientation of the garage and the front drive court are features which promote an economical use of property. In addition to the formal, separate living and dining rooms, there is the informal kitchen/family room area. Note the beamed ceiling, the fireplace, the sliding glass doors and the eating area of the family room.

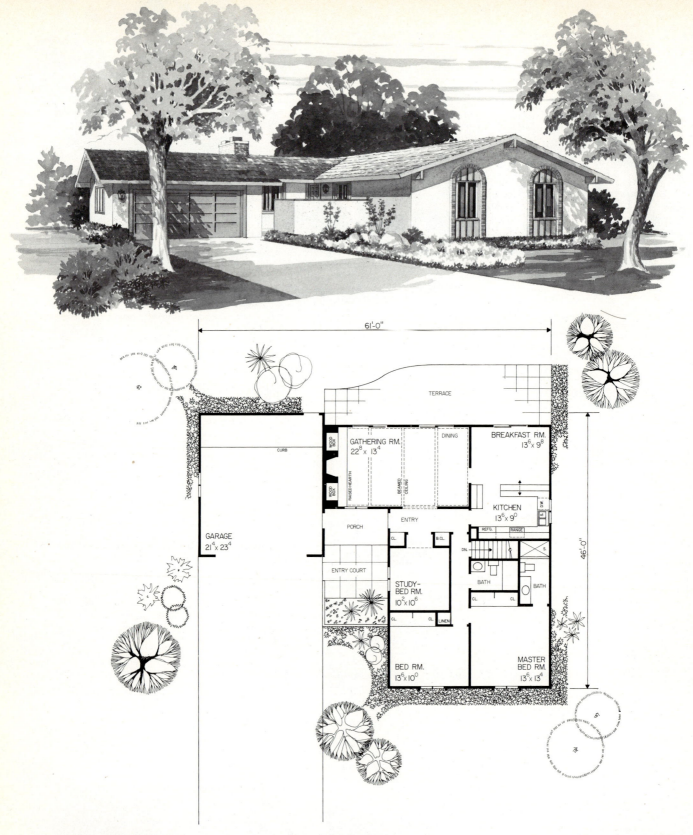

Design 302593 *1,391 Sq. Ft.; 28,781 Cu. Ft.*

● A fireplace wall! Including a raised hearth and two built-in wood boxes. A beamed ceiling, too. Inviting warmth in a spacious gathering room . . . more than 22' x 13' with ample space for a dining area. There's a sunny breakfast room, too, with sliding glass doors onto the terrace. And a pass-through from the kitchen. For efficiency, a U-shaped work area in the kitchen and lots of counter space. Two full baths. Three bedrooms! Including one with a private bath . . . and one suitable for use as a study, if that's your desire. This home is ideal for young families . . . equally perfect for those whose children are grown! It offers many of the attractive extras usually reserved for larger and more expensive designs. The appealing exterior will be appreciated.

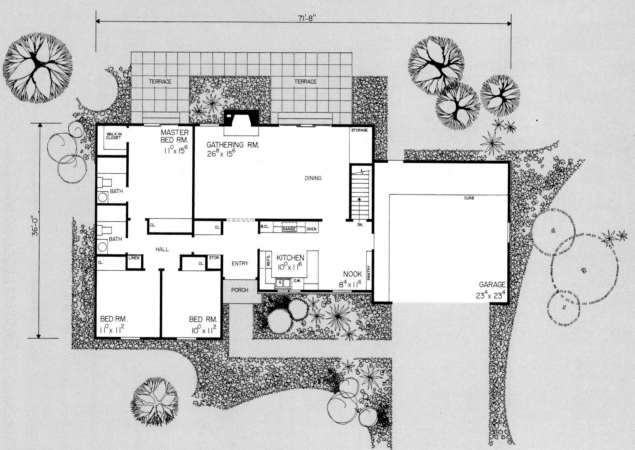

Design 302597 1,515 Sq. Ft.; 32,000 Cu. Ft.

● Whether it be a starter house you are after, or one in which to spend your retirement years, this pleasing frame home will provide a full measure of pride in ownership. The contrast of vertical and horizontal lines, the double front doors and the coach lamp post at the garage create an inviting exterior. The floor plan functions in an orderly and efficient manner. The 26 foot gathering room has a delightful view of the rear yard and will take care of those formal dining occasions. There are two full baths serving the three bedrooms. There are plenty of storage facilities, two sets of glass doors to the terraces, a fireplace in the gathering room, a basement and an attached two-car garage to act as a buffer against the wind. A delightful home, indeed.

Design 302802
1,729 Sq. Ft.; 42,640 Cu. Ft.

● The three exteriors shown at the left house the same, efficiently planned one-story floor plan shown below. Be sure to notice the design variations in the window placement and roof pitch. The Tudor design to the left is delightful. Half-timbered stucco and brick comprise the facade of this English Tudor variation of the plan. Note authentic bay window in the front bedroom.

Design 302803
1,679 Sq. Ft.; 36,755 Cu. Ft.

● Housed in varying facades, this floor plan is very efficient. The front foyer leads to each of the living areas. The sleeping area of two, or optional three, bedrooms is ready to serve the family. Then there is the gathering room. This room is highlighted by its size, 16 x 20 feet. A contemporary mix of fieldstone and vertical wood siding characterizes this exterior. The absence of columns or posts gives a modern look to the covered porch.

Design 302804
1,674 Sq. Ft.; 35,465 Cu. Ft.

● Stuccoed arches, multi-paned windows and a gracefully sloped roof accent the exterior of this Spanish-inspired design. Like the other two designs, the interior kitchen will efficiently serve the dining room, covered dining porch and breakfast room with great ease. Blueprints for all three designs include details for an optional non-basement plan.

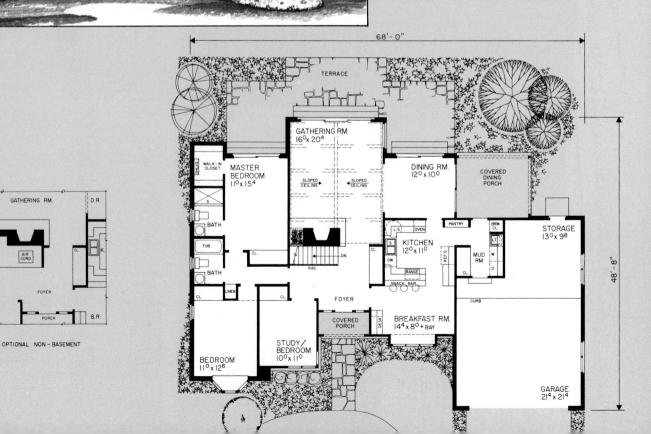

Design 302805
1,547 Sq. Ft.; 40,880 Cu. Ft.

● Three completely different exterior facades share one compact, practical and economical floor plan. The major design variations are roof pitch, window placement and garage openings. Each design will hold its own when comparing the three exteriors. The design to the right is a romantic stone-and-shingle cottage design. This design, along with the other two designs presented here, make outstanding one-story homes.

Design 302806
1,584 Sq. Ft.; 41,880 Cu. Ft.

● Even though these exteriors are extremely different in their styling and also have a few design variations, their floor plans are identical. Each will provide the family with a very livable plan. In this brick and half-timbered stucco Tudor version, like the other two, the living-dining room expands across the rear of the plan and has direct access to the skylite covered porch. Notice the built-in planter adjacent to the open staircase leading to the basement.

Design 302807
1,576 Sq. Ft.; 35,355 Cu. Ft.

● Along with the living-dining areas of the other two plans, this sleek contemporary styled home's breakfast room also will have a view of the covered porch. A desk, snack bar and mud room housing the laundry facilities are near the U-shaped kitchen. Clustering these work areas together is very convenient. The master bedroom has a private bath and walk-in closet.

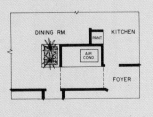

OPTIONAL NON-BASEMENT

Three Distinctively Styled Exteriors . . .

Design 302705 1,746 Sq. Ft.; 37,000 Cu. Ft.

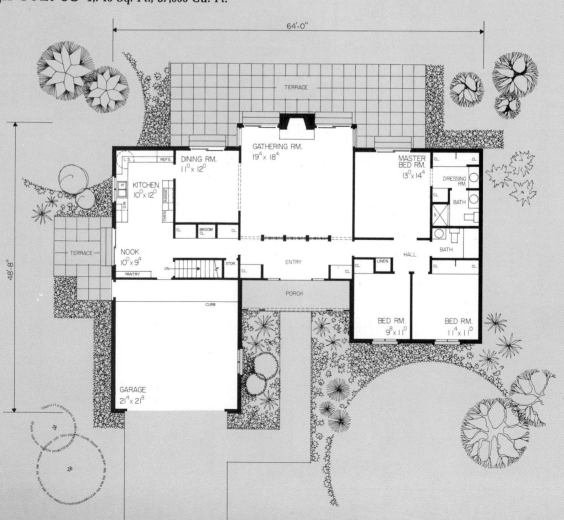

Design 302706 1,746 Sq. Ft.; 36,800 Cu. Ft.

. . . One Practical, Efficient Floor Plan

● Three different exteriors! But inside it's all the same livable house. Begin with the impressive entry hall . . . more than 19' long and offering double entry to the gathering room. Now the gathering room which is notable for its size and design. Notice how the fireplace is flanked by sliding glass doors leading to the terrace! That's unusual.

There's a formal dining room, too! The right spot for special birthday dinners as well as supper parties for friends. And an efficient kitchen that makes meal preparation easy whatever the occasion. Look for a built-in range and oven here . . . plus a bright dining nook with sliding doors to a second terrace. Three large bedrooms! All

located to give family members the utmost privacy. Including a master suite with a private dressing room, bath and a sliding glass door opening onto the main terrace. For blueprints of the hip-roof French adaptation on the opposite page order 302705. For the Contemporary version order 302706. The Colonial order 302704.

Design 302704 1,746 Sq. Ft.; 38,000 Cu. Ft.

Design 302737
1,796 Sq. Ft.; 43,240 Cu. Ft.

● You will be able to build this distinctive, modified U-shaped one-story home on a relatively narrow site. But, then, if you so wished, with the help of your architect and builder you may want to locate the garage to the side of the house. Inside, the living potential is just great. The interior U-shaped kitchen handily services the dining and family rooms and nook. A rear covered porch functions ideally with the family room while the formal living room has its own terrace. Three bedrooms and two baths highlight the sleeping zone (or make it two bedrooms and a study). Notice the strategic location of the wash room, laundry, two storage closets and the basement stairs.

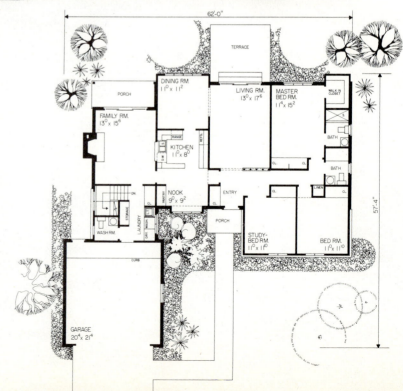

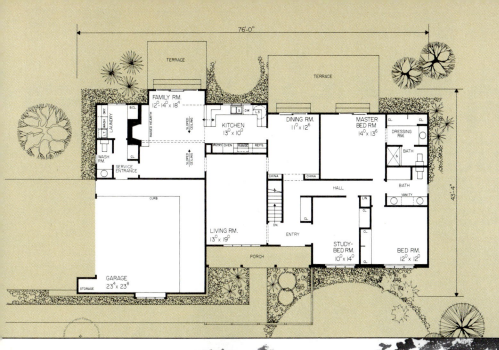

Design 302742
1,907 Sq. Ft.; 38,950 Cu. Ft.

● Colonial charm is expressed in this one-story design by the vertical siding, the post pillars, the cross fence, paned glass windows and the use of stone. A 19' wide living room, a sloped ceilinged family room with a raised hearth fireplace and its own terrace, a kitchen with many built-ins and a dining room with built-in china cabinets are just some of the highlights. The living terrace is accessible from the dining room and master bedroom. There are two more bedrooms and a full bath in addition to the master bedroom.

Design 302738
1,898 Sq. Ft.; 36,140 Cu. Ft.

● Impressive architectural work is indeed apparent in this three bedroom home. The three foot high entrance court wall, the high pitched roof and the paned glass windows all add to this home's appeal. It is also apparent that the floor plan is very efficient with the side U-shaped kitchen and nook with two pantry closets, the rear dining and gathering rooms and the three (or make it two with a study) bedrooms and two baths of the sleeping wing. Indoor-outdoor living also will be enjoyed in this home with a dining terrace off the nook and a living terrace off the gathering room and master bedroom. Note the fireplace in the gathering room and bay window in dining room.

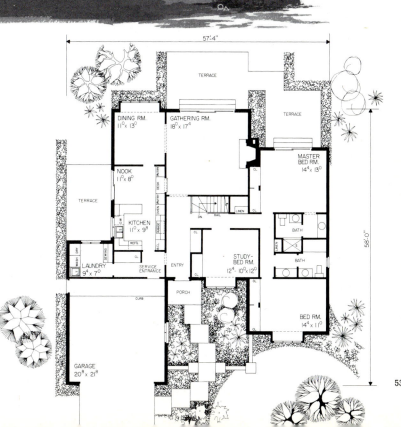

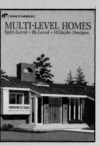

THE MULTI-LEVEL HOME . . . *can take many forms and be*

classified in varying categories. As defined in Home Planners' portfolio, the multi-level home can be a bi-level, a split-level, or a hillside design. Bi-level houses can be of the split-level foyer type or the lower entry type with the main living on the upper level. The split-level can be a tri-level or quad-level including basement. The levels are generally split side-to-side or front-to-back. Split-levels also can be a variety of irregularly placed living levels. Hillside houses usually have their lower levels exposed to the rear, front or sides.

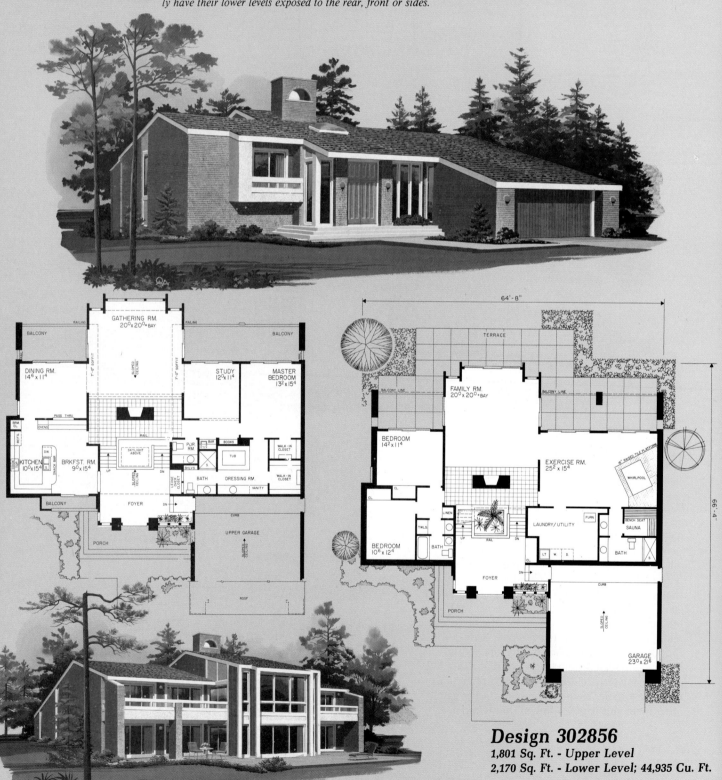

Design 302856

1,801 Sq. Ft. - Upper Level

2,170 Sq. Ft. - Lower Level; 44,935 Cu. Ft.

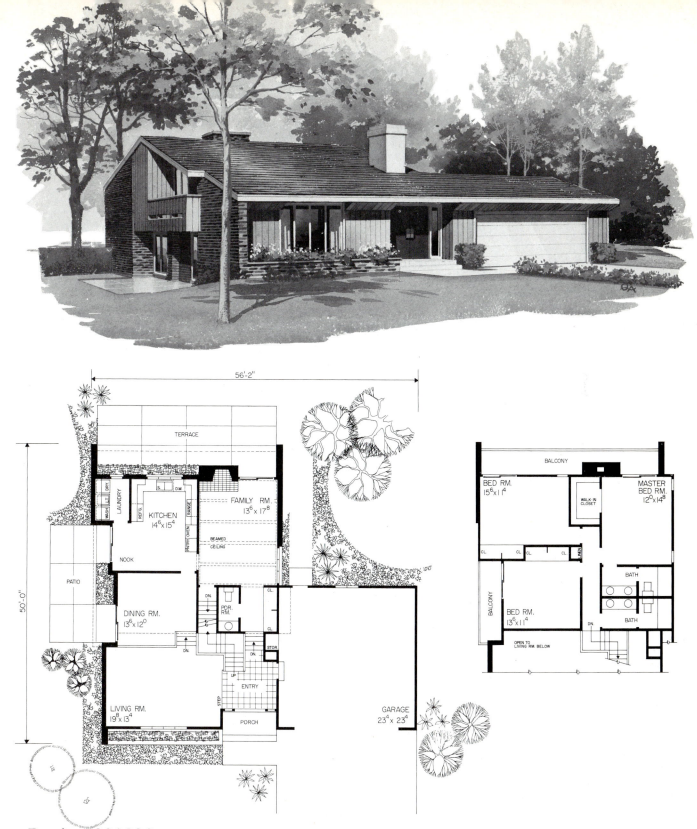

Design 302393 392 Sq. Ft. - Entry Level; 841 Sq. Ft. - Upper Level; 848 Sq. Ft. - Lower Level; 24,980 Cu. Ft.

● For those with a flair for something refreshingly contemporary both inside and out. This modest sized multi-level has a unique exterior and an equally interesting interior. The low-pitched, wide-overhanging roof protects the inviting double front doors and the large picture window. The raised planter and the side balcony add an extra measure of appeal. Inside, the living patterns will be delightful! The formal living room will look down into the dining room. Like the front entry, the living room has direct access to the lower level. The kitchen is efficient and spacious enough to accommodate an informal breakfast eating area. The laundry room is nearby. The all-purpose family room has beamed ceiling, fireplace and sliding glass doors to rear terrace. The angular, open stairwell to the upper level is dramatic, indeed. Notice how each bedroom has direct access to an outdoor balcony.

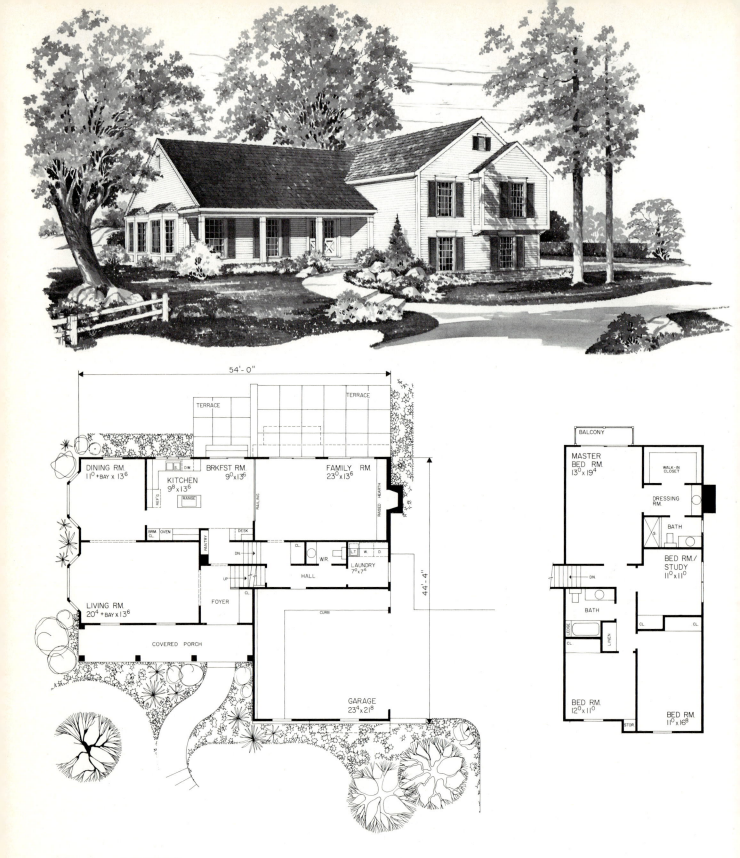

Labels within floor plan:

TERRACE

TERRACE

BALCONY

DINING RM.
11⁰ +BAY x 13⁶

KITCHEN
9⁸ x13⁶
RANGE

BRKFST RM.
9⁰ x13⁶

FAMILY RM.
23⁰ x 13⁶

RAISED HEARTH

MASTER BED RM.
13⁰ x 19⁴

WALK-IN CLOSET

DRESSING RM.

BRM. CL. OVEN

DESK

PANTRY

BATH

DN

CL.

W.R.

LT W D

LAUNDRY
7⁰ x 7⁶

BED RM./ STUDY
11⁰ x 11⁰

UP

HALL

BATH

LINEN

LIVING RM.
20⁴ +BAY x 13⁶

FOYER

CL.

DN

CL.

CL.

FOYER

CURB

LEDGE

CL.

COVERED PORCH

BED RM.
12⁰ x 11⁰

BED RM.
11⁰ x 16⁸

GARAGE
23⁴ x 21⁸

STOR.

54'-0"

44'-4"

Design 302786 *871 Sq. Ft. - Main Level; 1,132 Sq. Ft. - Upper Level; 528 Sq. Ft. - Lower Level; 44,000 Cu. Ft.*

● A bay window in each the formal living room and dining room. A great interior and exterior design feature to attract attention to this tri-level home. The exterior also is enhanced by a covered front porch to further the

Colonial charm. The interior livability is outstanding, too. An abundance of built-ins in the kitchen create an efficient work center. Features include an island range, pantry, broom closet, desk and breakfast room with

sliding glass doors to the rear terrace. The lower level houses the informal family room, wash room and laundry. Further access is available to the outdoors by the family room to the terrace and laundry room to the side yard.

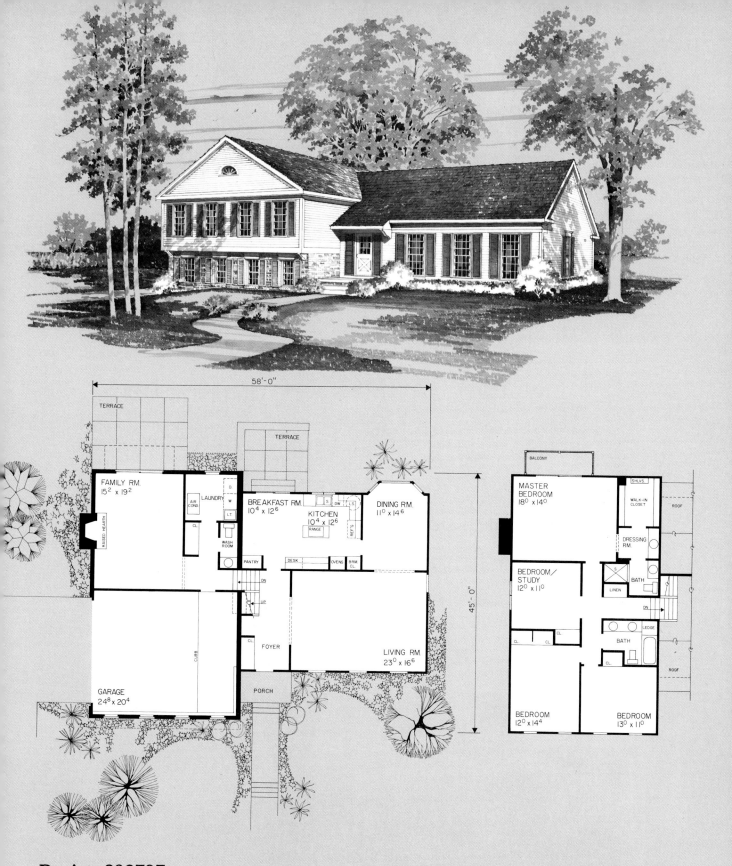

Design 302787 976 Sq. Ft. - Main Level; 1,118 Sq. Ft. - Upper Level; 524 Sq. Ft. - Lower Level; 36,110 Cu. Ft.

● Three level living! Main, upper and lower levels to serve you and your family with great ease. Start from the bottom and work your way up. Family room with raised hearth fireplace, laundry and wash room on the lower level. Formal living and dining rooms, kitchen and breakfast room on the main level. Stop and take note at the efficiency of the kitchen with its many outstanding extras. The upper level houses the three bedrooms, study (or fourth bedroom if you prefer) and two baths. This design has really stacked up its livability to serve its occupants to their best advantage. This design has great interior livability and exterior charm.

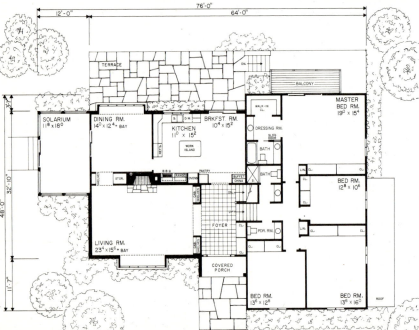

Design 302254

1,220 Sq. Ft. - Main Level
1,344 Sq. Ft. - Upper Level
659 Sq. Ft. - Lower Level
56,706 Cu. Ft.

● Tudor charm is deftly exemplified by this outstanding four level design. The window treatment, the heavy timber work and the chimney pots help set the character of this home. Contributing an extra measure of appeal is the detailing of the delightful solarium. The garden view of this home is equally appealing. The upper level balcony looks down onto the two terraces. The covered front entry leads to the spacious formal entrance hall with its slate floor. . .

Design 302243

1,274 Sq. Ft. - Main Level; 960 Sq. Ft. - Upper Level
936 Sq. Ft. - Lower Level; 42,478 Cu. Ft.

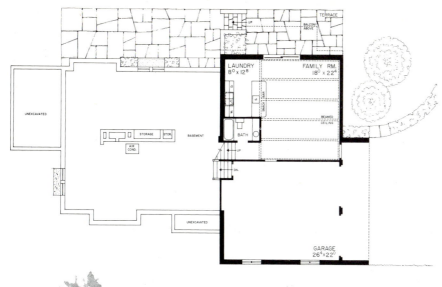

. . . Straight ahead is the kitchen and nook. The open planning of this area results in a fine feeling of spaciousness. Both living and dining rooms are wonderfully large. Each room highlights a big bay window. Notice the built-in units. Upstairs there are four bedrooms, two full baths and a powder room. Count the closets. The lower level is reserved for the all-purpose room, the separate laundry and a third full bath. The garage is adjacent. A fourth level is a basement with an abundance of space for storage and hobbies.

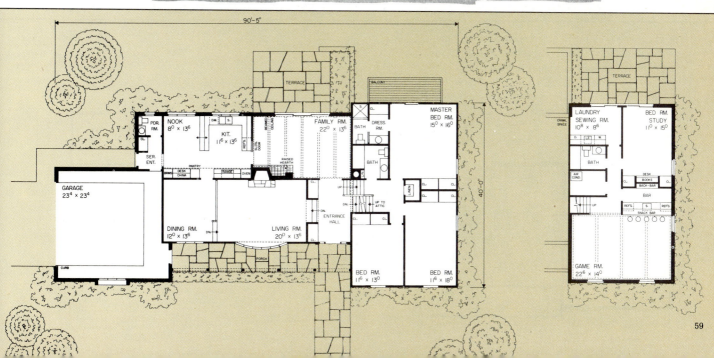

● Projecting over the lower level in Garrison Colonial style is the upper level containing three bedrooms a compartmented bath with twin lavatories and two handy linen closets. The main level consists of an L-shaped kitchen with convenient eating space, a formal dining room with sliding glass doors to the terrace and a sizable living room. On the lower level there is access to the outdoors, a spacious family room and a laundry-washroom area.

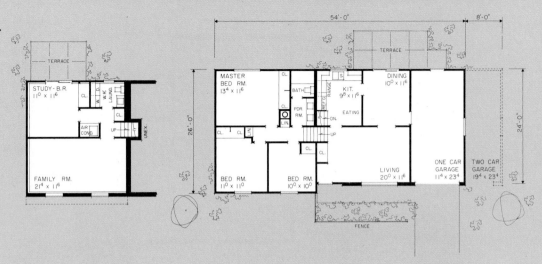

● Here are four levels just waiting for the opportunity to serve the living requirements of the active family. The traditional appeal of the exterior will be difficult to beat. Observe the window treatment, the double front doors, the covered front porch and the wrought iron work.

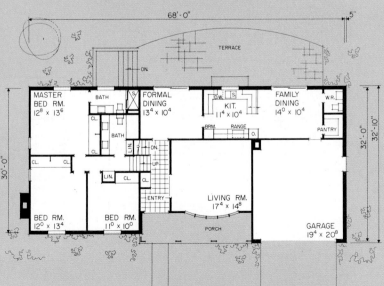

Design 301308 496 Sq. Ft. - Main Level; 572 Sq. Ft. - Upper Level; 537 Sq. Ft. - Lower Level; 16,024 Cu. Ft.

Design 301981

784 Sq. Ft. - Main Level; 912 Sq. Ft. - Upper Level
336 Sq. Ft. - Lower Level; 26,618 Cu. Ft.

● Here are three multi-level designs which are ideal for those who wish to build on a relatively narrow site. These split-levels have delightful exteriors and each offers exceptional family livability. Formal and informal areas are in each along with efficiently planned work centers. Outdoor areas are easily accessible from various rooms in these plans. Note that two of the upper level plans even have balconies.

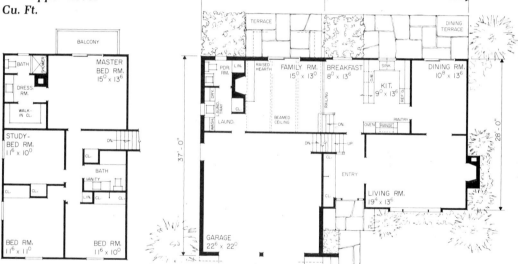

Design 301768 844 Sq. Ft. - Main Level; 740 Sq. Ft. - Upper Level; 740 Sq. Ft. - Lower Level; 29,455 Cu. Ft.

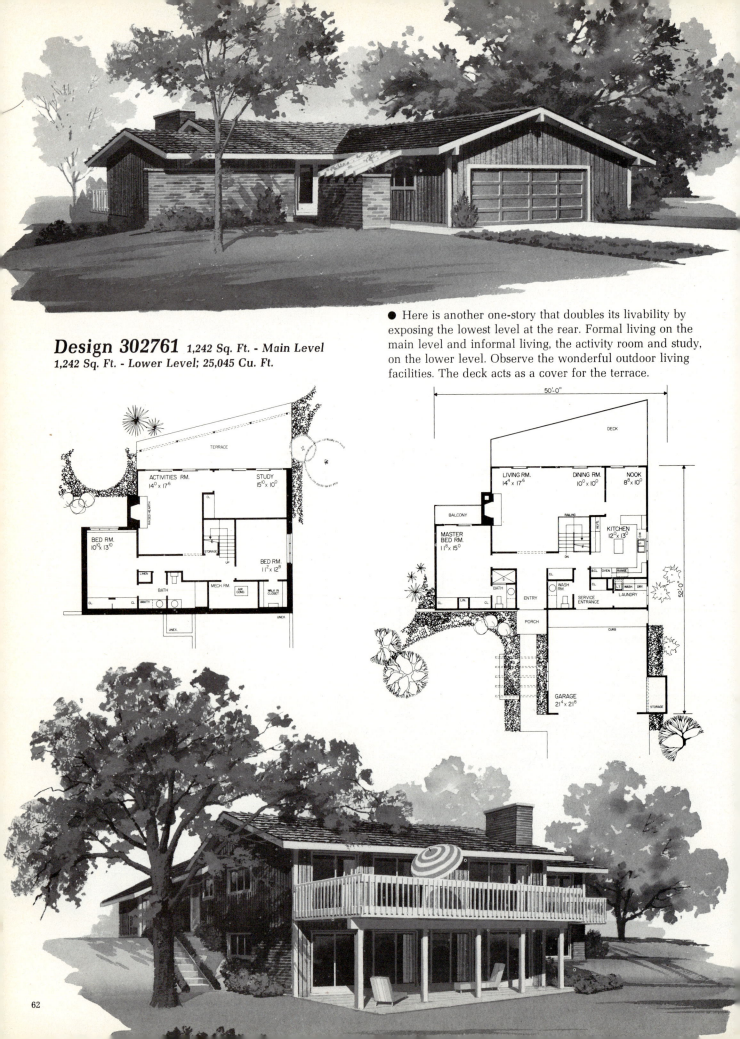

Design 302761 1,242 Sq. Ft. - Main Level
1,242 Sq. Ft. - Lower Level; 25,045 Cu. Ft.

● Here is another one-story that doubles its livability by exposing the lowest level at the rear. Formal living on the main level and informal living, the activity room and study, on the lower level. Observe the wonderful outdoor living facilities. The deck acts as a cover for the terrace.

TERRACE

ACTIVITIES RM.
14⁰ x 17⁶

STUDY
15⁰ x 10⁰

CL.

BED RM.
10⁰ x 13⁰

STORAGE

UP

BED RM.
11² x 12⁸

LINEN

BATH

MECH. RM.

AIR COND.

WALK IN CLOSET

CL.   VANITY   CL.

UNEX.

UNEX.

50'-0"

DECK

LIVING RM.
14⁴ x 17⁶

DINING RM.
10⁰ x 10⁰

NOOK
8⁸ x 10⁰

BALCONY

RAILING

REF'S.

KITCHEN
12⁰ x 13⁰

MASTER BED RM.
11⁸ x 15⁰

DN.

OVEN   RANGE

BATH

CL.

WASH RM.

BCL.

CL.   LT   WASH   DRY.

LIN.   CL.   CL.

ENTRY

SERVICE ENTRANCE

LAUNDRY

PORCH

CURB

GARAGE
21⁴ x 21⁸

STORAGE

52'-0"

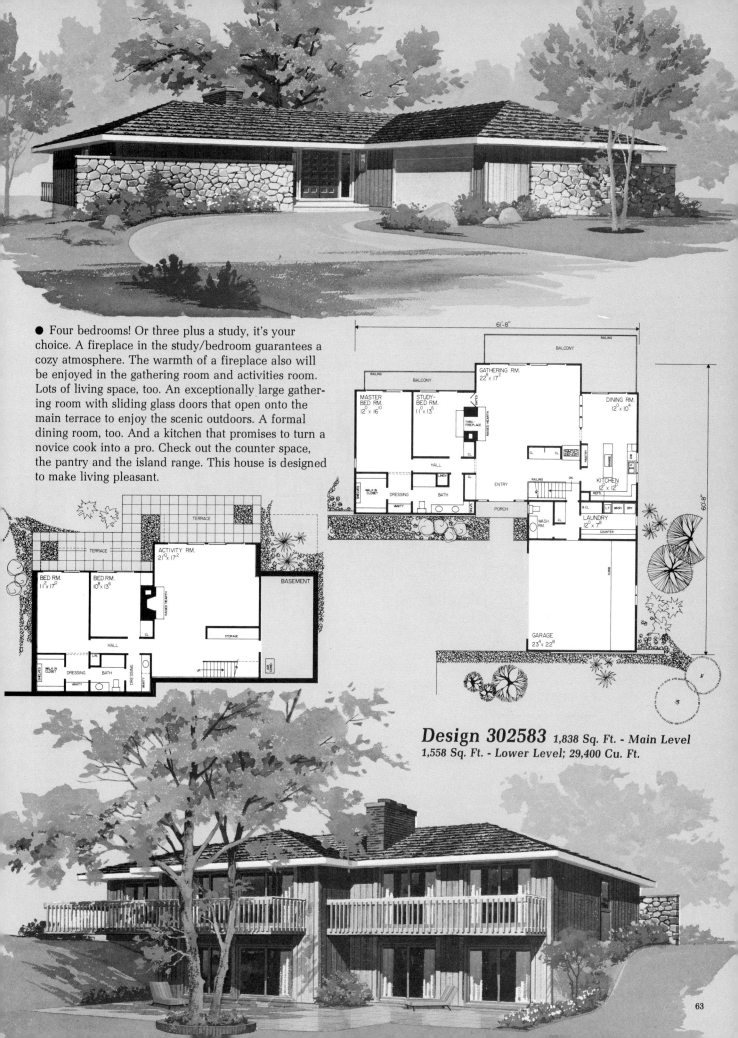

● Four bedrooms! Or three plus a study, it's your choice. A fireplace in the study/bedroom guarantees a cozy atmosphere. The warmth of a fireplace also will be enjoyed in the gathering room and activities room. Lots of living space, too. An exceptionally large gathering room with sliding glass doors that open onto the main terrace to enjoy the scenic outdoors. A formal dining room, too. And a kitchen that promises to turn a novice cook into a pro. Check out the counter space, the pantry and the island range. This house is designed to make living pleasant.

Design 302583 1,838 Sq. Ft. - Main Level
1,558 Sq. Ft. - Lower Level; 29,400 Cu. Ft.

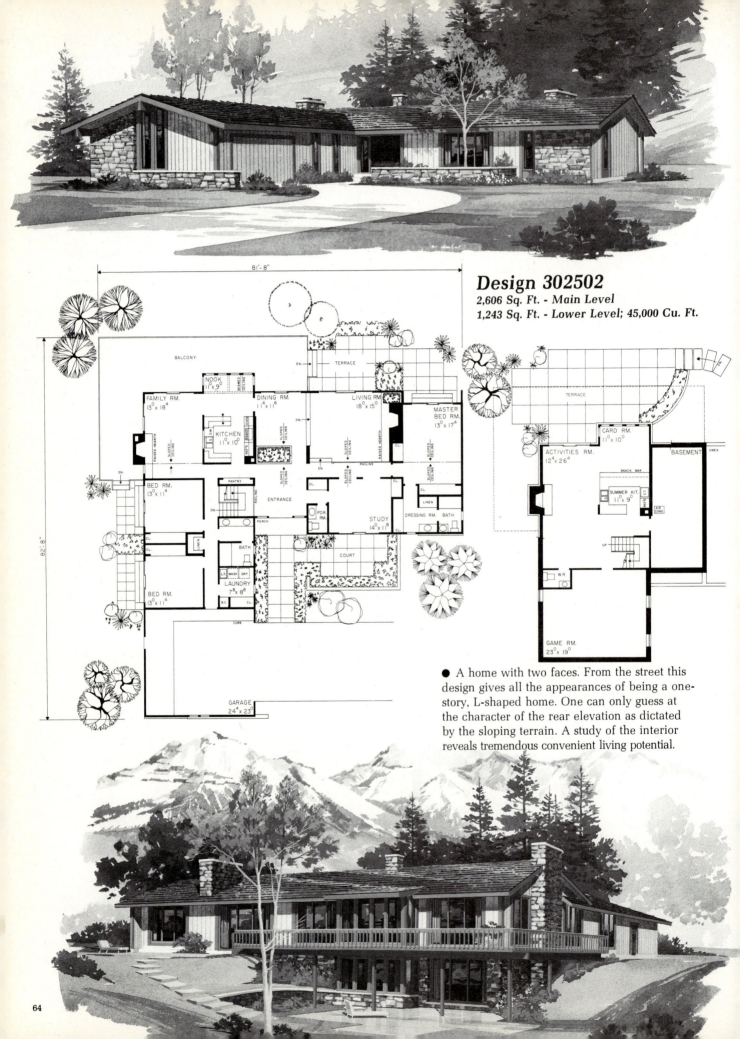

Design 302502
2,606 Sq. Ft. - Main Level
1,243 Sq. Ft. - Lower Level; 45,000 Cu. Ft.

● A home with two faces. From the street this design gives all the appearances of being a one-story, L-shaped home. One can only guess at the character of the rear elevation as dictated by the sloping terrain. A study of the interior reveals tremendous convenient living potential.

Main Level labels: BALCONY · TERRACE · NOOK 11" x 9" · FAMILY RM. 13⁰ x 18⁴ · DINING RM. 11⁴ x 11⁶ · LIVING RM. 18⁰ x 15⁰ · MASTER BED RM. 13⁰ x 17⁴ · KITCHEN 11⁰ x 10⁰ · BED RM. 13⁰ x 11⁴ · PANTRY · ENTRANCE · PDR. RM. · LINEN · STUDY 14⁰ x 11⁸ · DRESSING RM. · BATH · PORCH · BATH · COURT · BED RM. 13⁰ x 11⁴ · LAUNDRY 7⁸ x 8⁸ · CURB · GARAGE 24⁴ x 23⁰

Lower Level labels: TERRACE · CARD RM. 11⁰ x 10⁰ · BASEMENT · ACTIVITIES RM. 12⁴ x 26⁰ · SNACK BAR · SUMMER KIT. 11⁰ x 9⁰ · AIR COND. · UNEX. · W R · UP · GAME RM. 23⁰ x 19⁰

Dimensions: 81'-8" · 82'-8"

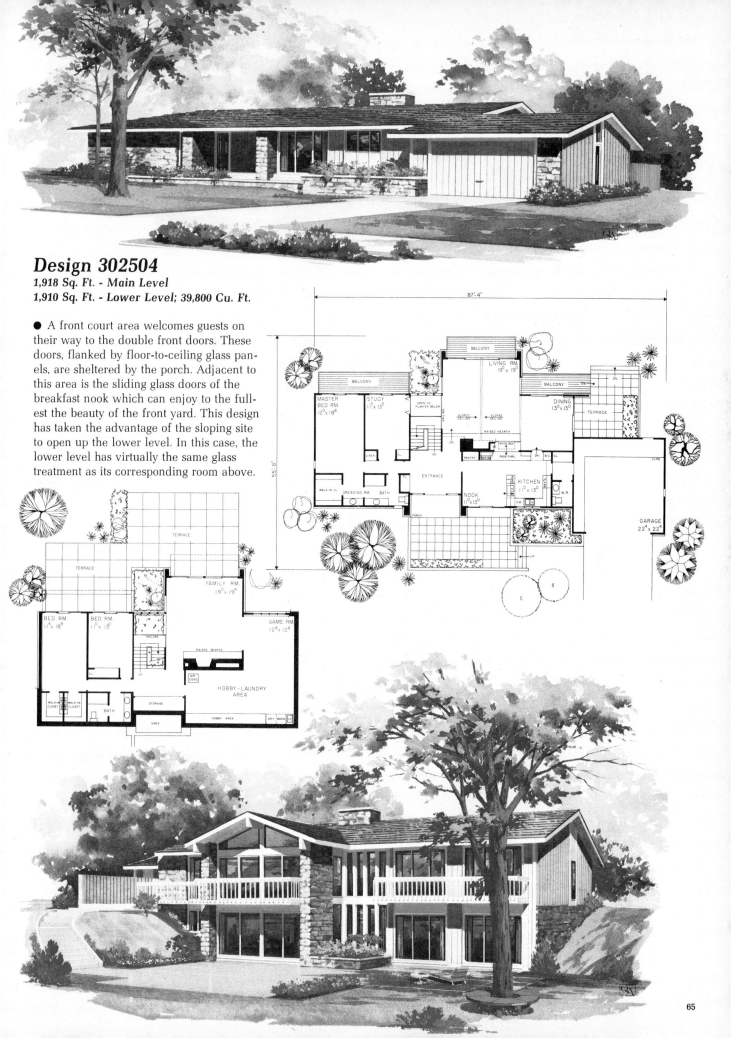

Design 302504

1,918 Sq. Ft. - Main Level
1,910 Sq. Ft. - Lower Level; 39,800 Cu. Ft.

● A front court area welcomes guests on their way to the double front doors. These doors, flanked by floor-to-ceiling glass panels, are sheltered by the porch. Adjacent to this area is the sliding glass doors of the breakfast nook which can enjoy to the fullest the beauty of the front yard. This design has taken the advantage of the sloping site to open up the lower level. In this case, the lower level has virtually the same glass treatment as its corresponding room above.

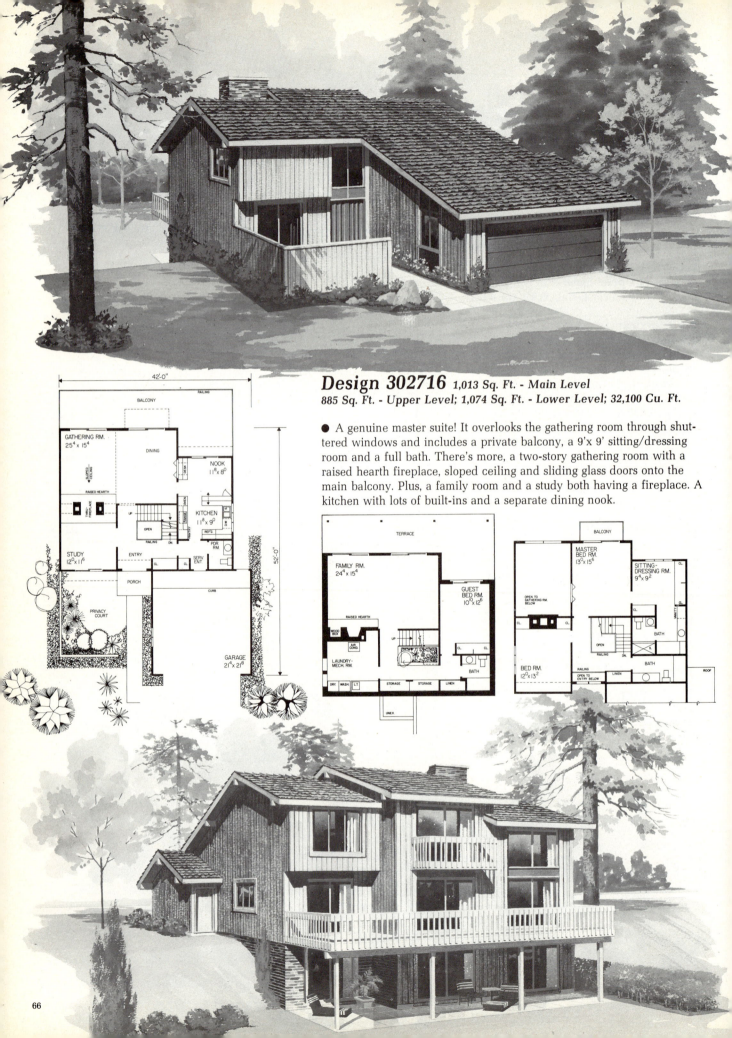

Design 302716 1,013 Sq. Ft. - Main Level
885 Sq. Ft. - Upper Level; 1,074 Sq. Ft. - Lower Level; 32,100 Cu. Ft.

● A genuine master suite! It overlooks the gathering room through shuttered windows and includes a private balcony, a 9'x 9' sitting/dressing room and a full bath. There's more, a two-story gathering room with a raised hearth fireplace, sloped ceiling and sliding glass doors onto the main balcony. Plus, a family room and a study both having a fireplace. A kitchen with lots of built-ins and a separate dining nook.

Design 302844 1,882 Sq. Ft. - Upper Level
1,168 Sq. Ft. - Lower Level; 37,860 Cu. Ft.

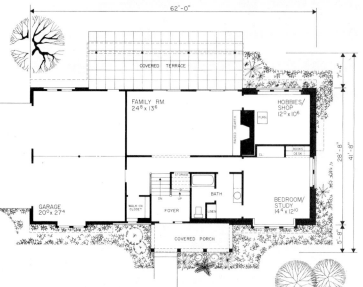

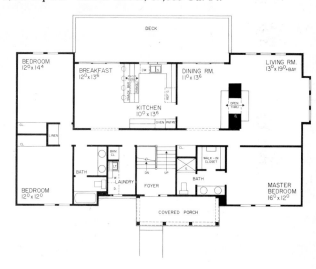

● Bi-level living will be enjoyed to the fullest in this Tudor design. The split-foyer type design will be very efficient for the active family. Three bedrooms are on the upper level, a fourth on the lower level.

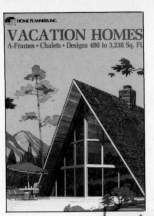

THE VACATION HOME . . .

has been designed to deliver informal, leisure living patterns. Its exterior represents a break from conventionally styled facades. Admittedly, one can call the most conventional of houses his vacation home. However, the vacation home is popularly thought of as one which provides the average family with something new in living patterns that is not to be experienced on a day-to-day basis in its primary residence. This type of house also offers the opportunity to express one's flair for distinctive exterior design. Informal indoor-outdoor living relationships are an important ingredient in successful leisure living.

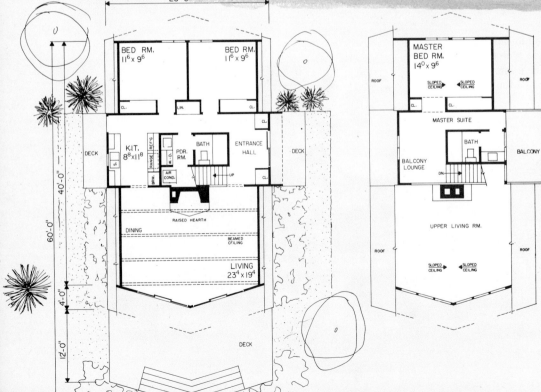

Design 302431

1,057 Sq. Ft. - First Floor
406 Sq. Ft. - Second Floor
15,230 Cu. Ft.

● A favorite everywhere – the A-frame vacation home. Its popularity is easily discernible at first glance. The stately appearance is enhanced by the soaring roof lines and the dramatic glass areas. Inside, the breathtaking beauty of outstanding architectural detailing also is apparent. The high ceiling of the living room slopes and has exposed beams. The second floor master suite is a great feature. Observe the raised hearth fireplace and the outdoor balcony.

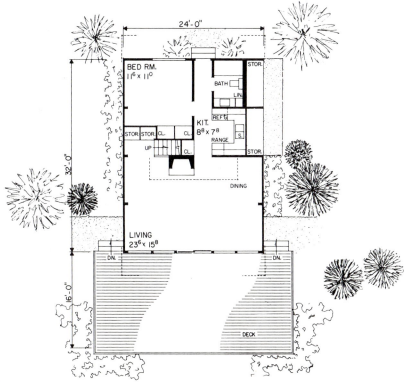

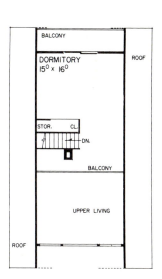

Design 301406

776 Sq. Ft. - First Floor
300 Sq. Ft. - Second Floor; 8,536 Cu. Ft.

● A spacious 23 foot by 15 foot living room is really something to talk about. And when it has a high, vaulted ceiling and a complete wall of windows it is even more noteworthy. Because of the wonderful glass area the livability of the living room seems to spill right out onto the huge wood deck. In addition to the bedroom downstairs, there is the sizable dormitory upstairs for sleeping quite a crew. Sliding glass doors open onto the outdoor balcony from the dormitory. Don't miss the fireplace, the efficient kitchen and the numerous storage facilities. The outside storage units are accessible from just below the roof line and are great for all the recreational equipment. Don't be without the exceptional wood deck. It will make a vital contribution to your outdoor vacation enjoyment.

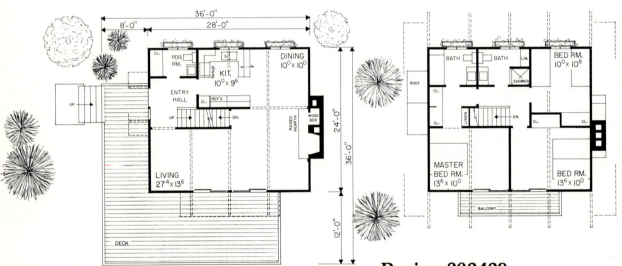

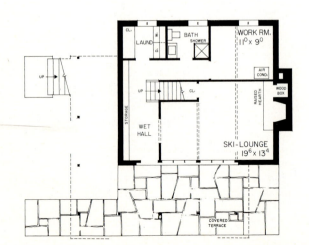

Design 302429
672 Sq. Ft. - Main Level; 672 Sq. Ft. - Upper Level
672 Sq. Ft. - Lower Level; 19,152 Cu. Ft.

● A ski lodge with a Swiss chalet character. If you are a skier, you know that all the fun is not restricted to schussing the slopes. A great portion of the pleasure is found in the living accommodations and the pursuant merriment fostered by good fellowship. As for the specific features which will surely contribute to everyone's off-the-slopes fun consider: the outdoor deck, balcony and covered terrace; the ski lounge; the two fireplaces; and the huge L-shaped living and dining room area. The three bedrooms are of good size and with bunk beds will sleep quite a crew. Note the wet hall for skis, the all important work room and the laundry.

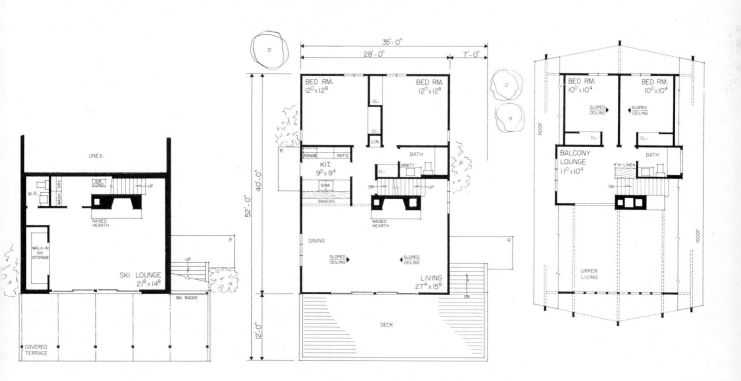

Design 301475 *1,120 Sq. Ft. - Main Level; 522 Sq. Ft. - Upper Level; 616 Sq. Ft. - Lower Level; 24,406 Cu. Ft.*

● Skiers take notice! This vacation home tells an exciting story of activity - and people. Whether you build this design to function as your ski lodge, or to serve your family and friends during the summer months, it will perform ideally. It would take little imagination to envision this second home overlooking your lakeshore site with the grownups sunning themselves on the deck while the children play on the terrace. Whatever the season or the location, visualize how your family will enjoy the many hours spent in this delightful chalet adaptation.

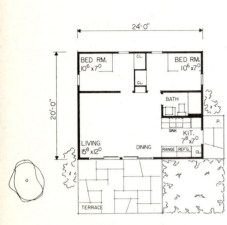

Design 301486
480 Sq. Ft.; 4,118 Cu. Ft.

● You'll be anxious to start building this delightful little vacation home. Whether you do-it-yourself, or engage professional help, you will not have to wait long for its completion.

Design 302425
1,106 Sq. Ft.; 14,599 Cu. Ft.

● You'll adjust to living in this vacation cottage with the greatest of ease. And forevermore the by-word will be, "fun". Imagine, a thirty-one foot living room with access to a large deck!

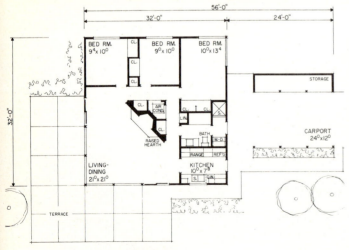

Design 301449
1,024 Sq. Ft.; 11,264 Cu. Ft.

● If yours is a preference for a vacation home with a distinctive flair, then you need not look any further. Here is a simple and economically built 32 foot rectangle to meet your needs.

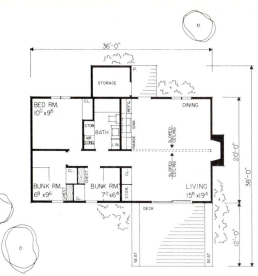

Design 301488
720 Sq. Ft.; 8,518 Cu. Ft.

● The kids won't be able to move into this vacation retreat soon enough. Two bunk rooms plus another bedroom for Mom and Dad. Open-planned living area. A real leisure-time home.

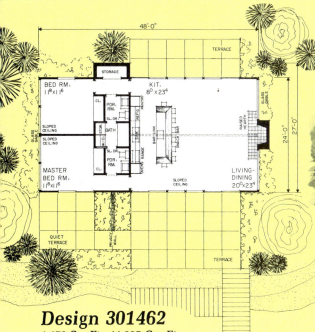

Design 301462
1,176 Sq. Ft.; 11,995 Cu. Ft.

● A second home with the informal living message readily apparent both inside and out. The zoning of this home is indeed most interesting – and practical, too. Study the plan carefully.

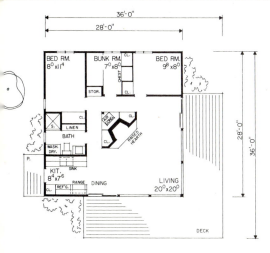

Design 301485
784 Sq. Ft.; 10,192 Cu. Ft.

● Here's a perfect 28 foot square that will surely open up new dimensions in living for its occupants. A fine, lower budget version of 301449 on the opposing page yet retaining many of the fine qualities.

Design 302417 1,520 Sq. Ft.; 19,952 Cu. Ft.

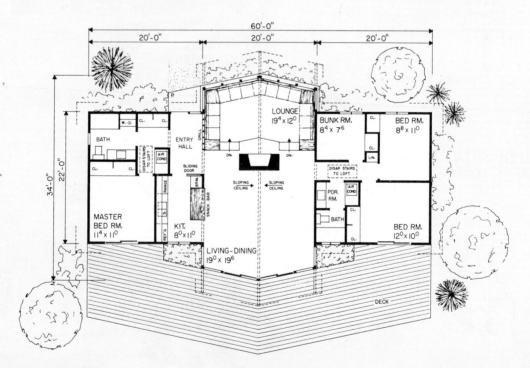

● Have you ever seen a vacation home design that is anything quite like this one? Probably not. The picturesque exterior is dominated by a projecting gable with its wide overhanging roof acting as a dramatic sun visor for the wonderfully large glass area below.

Effectively balancing this 20 foot center section are two 20 foot wings. Inside, and below the high, sloping, beamed ceiling is the huge living area. In addition to the living-dining area, there is the spacious sunken lounge. This pleasant area has a built-in seat-

ing arrangement and a cozy fireplace. The kitchen is efficient and handy to the snack bar and dining area. The parents' and children's sleeping areas are separated and each has a full bath. The large deck is accessible from sliding glass doors.

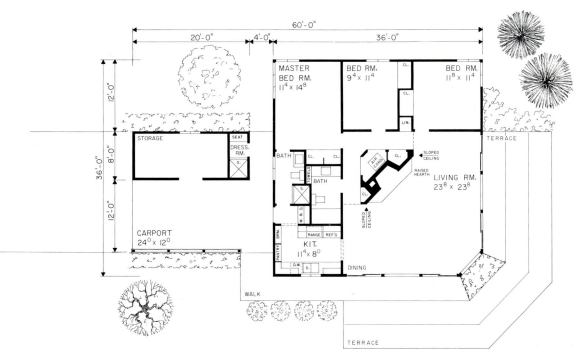

Design 302457 *1,288 Sq. Ft.; 13,730 Cu. Ft.*

● Leisure living will indeed be graciously experienced in this hip-roofed second home. Except for the clipped corner, it is a perfect square measuring 36 x 36 feet. The 23 foot square living room enjoys a great view of the surrounding environment by virtue of the expanses of glass. The wide overhanging roof affords protection from the sun. The "open planning" adds to the spaciousness of the interior. The focal point is the raised hearth fireplace. The three bedrooms are served by two full baths which are also accessible to other areas. The kitchen, looking out upon the water, will be a delight in which to work. Observe the carport, the big bulk storage room and the dressing room with its stall shower. What great planning for a leisure-time second home.

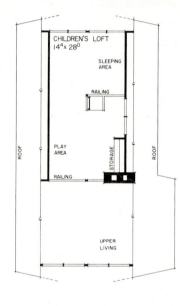

Design 301459
1,056 Sq. Ft. - First Floor
400 Sq. Ft. - Second Floor
17,504 Cu. Ft.

● There is a heap of vacation living awaiting the gang that descends upon this smart looking chalet adaptation. If you have a narrow site, this design will be of extra interest to you. Should one of your requirements be an abundance of sleeping facilities, you'd hardly do better in such an economically built design. There are three bedrooms downstairs. A ladder leads to the second floor loft. The children will love the idea of sleeping here. In addition, there is a play area which looks down into the first floor living room. A great vacation home.

Design 302427
784 Sq. Ft. - First Floor
504 Sq. Ft. - Second Floor
13,485 Cu. Ft.

● If ever a design had "vacation home" written all over it, this one has! Perhaps the most carefree characteristic of all is the second floor balcony which looks down into the wood deck. This balcony provides the outdoor living facility for the big master bedroom. Also occupying the second floor is the three-bunk dormitory. The use of bunks would be a fine utilization of this space. Panels through the knee walls give access to an abundant storage area. Downstairs there is yet another bedroom, a full bath and a 27 foot living room.

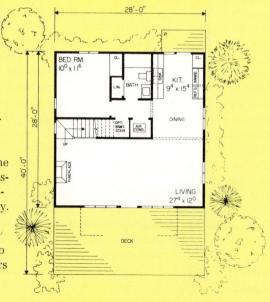

Design 301424

672 Sq. Ft. - First Floor
256 Sq. Ft. - Second Floor
8,736 Cu. Ft.

● This chalet-type vacation home with its steep, overhanging roof, will catch the eye of even the most casual onlooker. It is designed to be completely livable whether the season be for swimming or skiing. The dormitory of the upper level will sleep many vacationers, while the two bedrooms of the first floor provide the more convenient and conventional sleeping facilities. The upper level overlooks the living and dining area with its beamed ceiling. The lower level provides everything that one would want for vacation living.

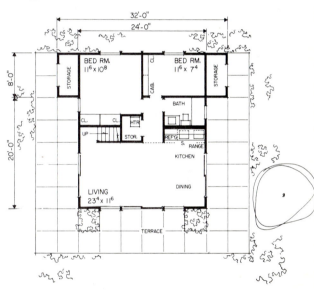

Design 302439 1,312 Sq. Ft.; 17,673 Cu. Ft.

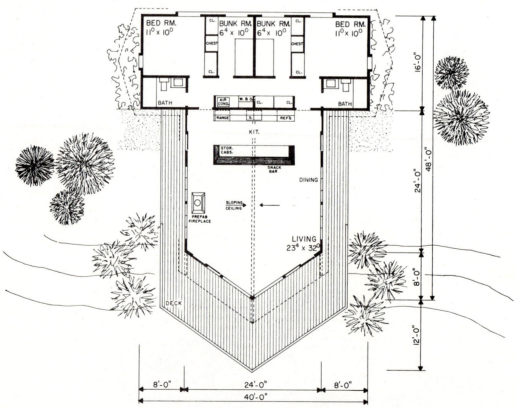

● A wonderfully organized plan with an exterior that will surely command the attention of each and every passer-by. And what will catch the eye? Certainly the roof lines and the pointed glass gable end wall will be noticed immediately. The delightful deck will be quickly noticed, too. Inside a visitor will be thrilled by the spaciousness of the huge living room. The ceilings slope upward to the exposed ridge beam. A free-standing fireplace will make its contribution to a cheerful atmosphere. The kitchen is separated from the living area by a three foot high snack bar with cupboards below servicing the kitchen. What could improve upon the sleeping zone when it has two bedrooms, two bunk rooms, two full baths, two built-in chests and fine closet space?

Design 302485 1,108 Sq. Ft. - Main Level
983 Sq. Ft. - Lower Level; 21,530 Cu. Ft.

● This hillside vacation home gives the appearance of being a one-story from the road. However, since it is built off the edge of a slope, the rear exterior is a full two-story structure. Notice the projecting deck and how it shelters the terrace. Each of the generous glass areas is protected from the summer sun by the overhangs and the extended walls. The clerestory windows of the front exterior provide natural light to the center of the plan.

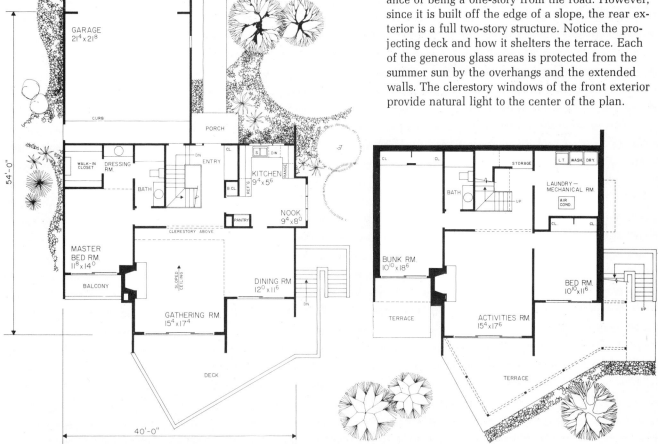

Design 302488 1,113 Sq. Ft. - First Floor; 543 Sq. Ft. - Second Floor; 36,055 Cu. Ft.

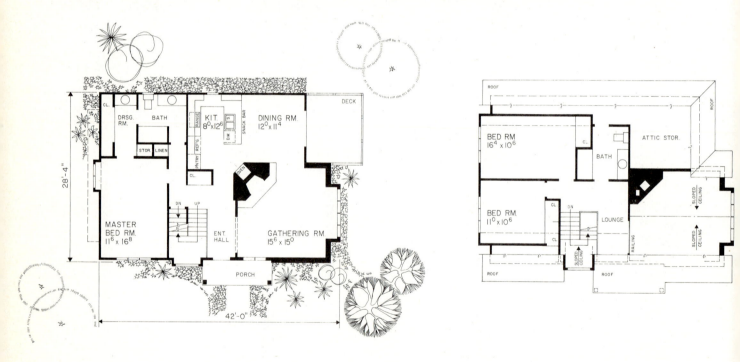

● A cozy cottage for the young at heart! Whether called upon to serve the young active family as a leisure-time retreat at the lake, or the retired couple as a quiet haven in later years, this charming design will perform well. As a year round second home, the up-stairs with its two sizable bedrooms, full bath and lounge area looking down into the gathering room below, will ideally accommodate the younger generation. When called upon to function as a retirement home, the second floor will cater to the visiting family members and friends. Also, it will be available for use as a home office, study, sewing room, music area, the pursuit of hobbies, etc. Of course, as an efficient, economical home for the young, growing family, this design will function well.

THE EXTERIOR STYLE SERIES . . .

represents a highly selective grouping of designs from the Home Planners' portfolio edited in four distinctive plan books. The four major style categories are Early American, Contemporary, English Tudor and Spanish & Western. These books are delightfully edited for those who wish to review home plans with their favorite exterior styling. This series is ideal for those who want to compare the unique appeal of various pleasing facades with the many different types of houses - one, 1½ and two-story, and multi-levels. Also noteworthy is how these styles adapt to varying house sizes.

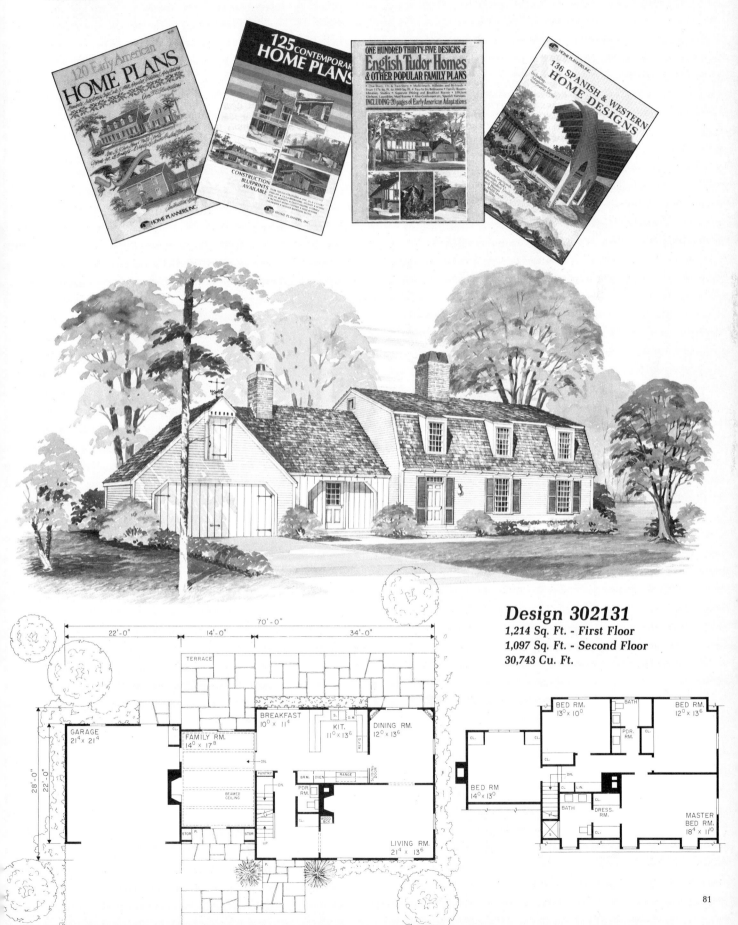

Design 302131
1,214 Sq. Ft. - First Floor
1,097 Sq. Ft. - Second Floor
30,743 Cu. Ft.

THE EARLY AMERICAN HOME . . .

whatever its antecedents, has a highly identifiable warmth and charm all its own. This image is achieved by such features as pleasing exterior proportions, small-paned windows, shutters, period oriented front entry and door treatment, dramatic columns, massive chimneys, brick quoins at the corners, pediment gables, dentil-work, wood drops, bay windows, cupolas, dovecotes, carriage lamps and horizontal clapboard siding. These features effectively can be adapted to the one, 1½, two-story and multi-level house configuration to project the delightfully traditional image we regard so highly today. Note the up-to-date floor plans.

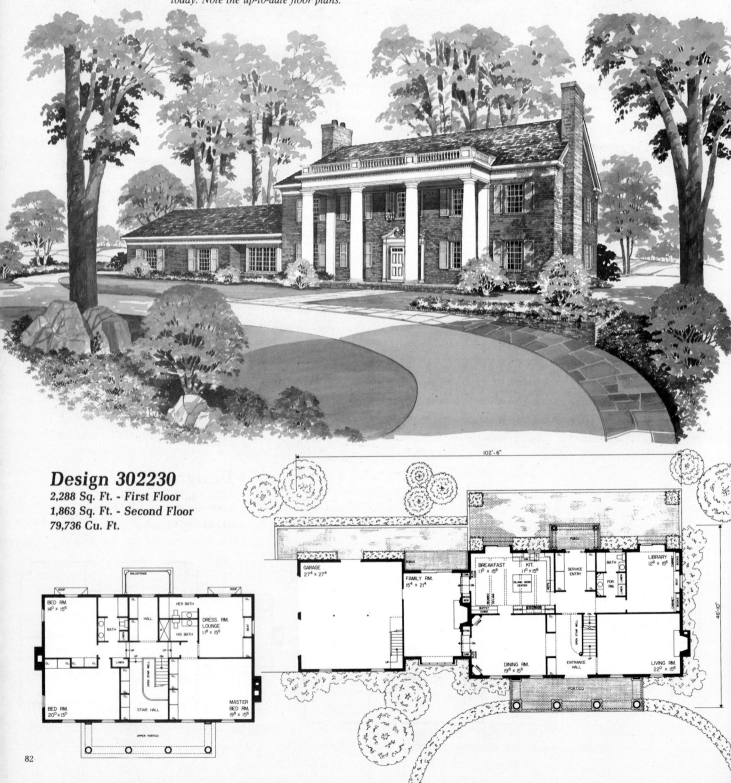

Design 302230

2,288 Sq. Ft. - First Floor
1,863 Sq. Ft. - Second Floor
79,736 Cu. Ft.

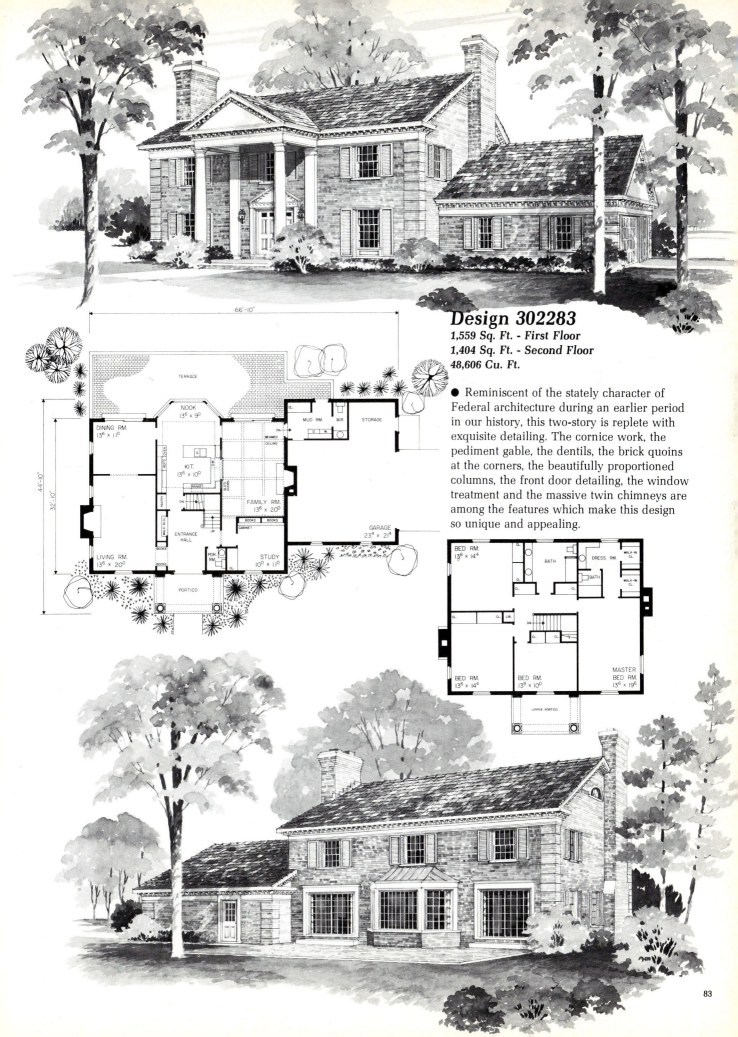

Design 302283
1,559 Sq. Ft. - First Floor
1,404 Sq. Ft. - Second Floor
48,606 Cu. Ft.

● Reminiscent of the stately character of Federal architecture during an earlier period in our history, this two-story is replete with exquisite detailing. The cornice work, the pediment gable, the dentils, the brick quoins at the corners, the beautifully proportioned columns, the front door detailing, the window treatment and the massive twin chimneys are among the features which make this design so unique and appealing.

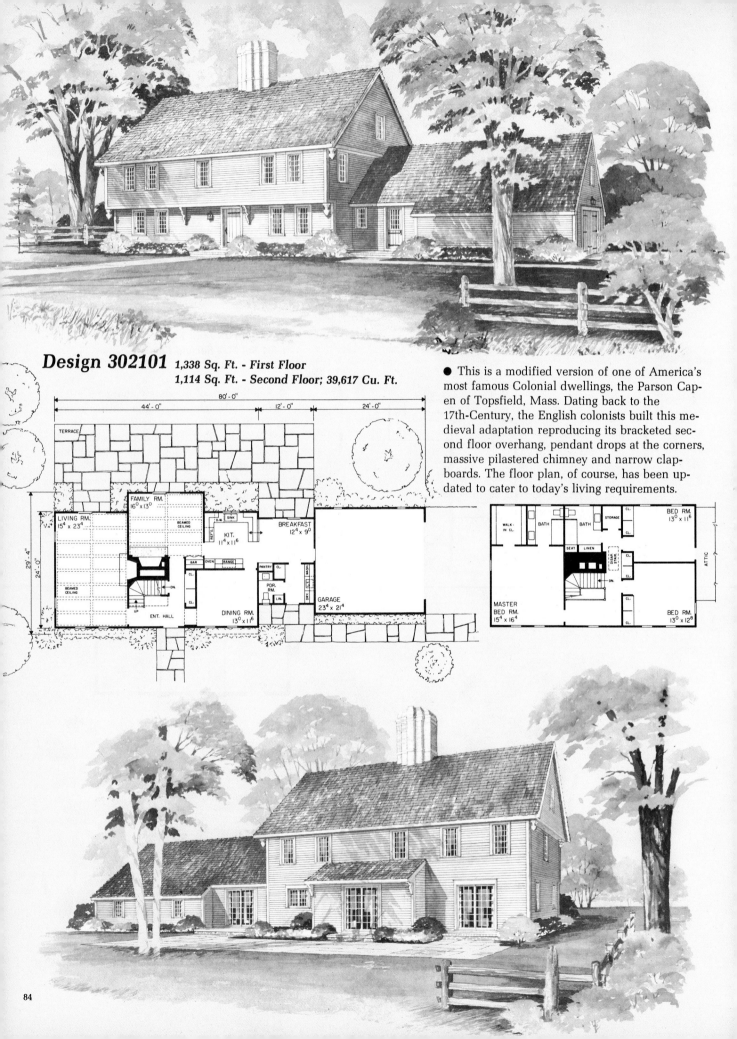

Design 302101
1,338 Sq. Ft. - First Floor
1,114 Sq. Ft. - Second Floor; 39,617 Cu. Ft.

● This is a modified version of one of America's most famous Colonial dwellings, the Parson Capen of Topsfield, Mass. Dating back to the 17th-Century, the English colonists built this medieval adaptation reproducing its bracketed second floor overhang, pendant drops at the corners, massive pilastered chimney and narrow clapboards. The floor plan, of course, has been updated to cater to today's living requirements.

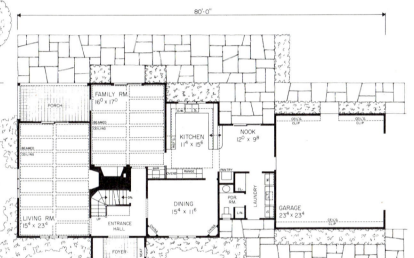

Design 302191

1,553 Sq. Ft. - First Floor
1,197 Sq. Ft. - Second Floor
47,906 Cu. Ft.

● This exquisite house reproduces the architectural details from the 17th-Century. Medieval and Tudor influences, brought to the New World by the first English colonists, distinguish this adaptation. The interior has been designed to serve today's active family.

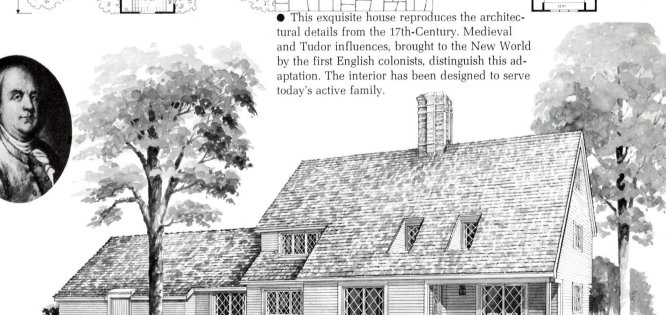

Design 301829
1,800 Sq. Ft.; 32,236 Cu. Ft.

● All the charm of a traditional heritage is wrapped up in this U-shaped home with its narrow, horizontal siding, delightful window treatment, and high pitched roof. The massive center chimney, the bay window, and the double front doors are plus features. Inside, the living potential is outstanding. The sleeping wing is self-contained and has four bedrooms and two baths. The large family and living rooms permit the divergent age groups in the family to enjoy themselves to the fullest. The breakfast and dining rooms allow for the experience of flexible eating patterns. The efficient kitchen and convenient laundry mean much to the housewife.

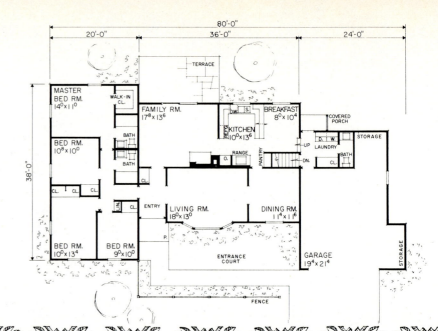

Design 301980
1,901 Sq. Ft.; 36,240 Cu. Ft.

● Planned for easy living, the livability patterns of the active family will be pleasant ones, indeed. All the elements are present to assure a wonderful family life. The impressive exterior is enhanced by the recessed front entrance area with its covered porch. The center entry results in a convenient and efficient flow of traffic. A secondary entrance leads from the covered side porch, or the garage, into the first floor laundry. Note the powder room nearby. Imagine, each of the three main living areas - the family, dining and living rooms - look out upon the rear yard.

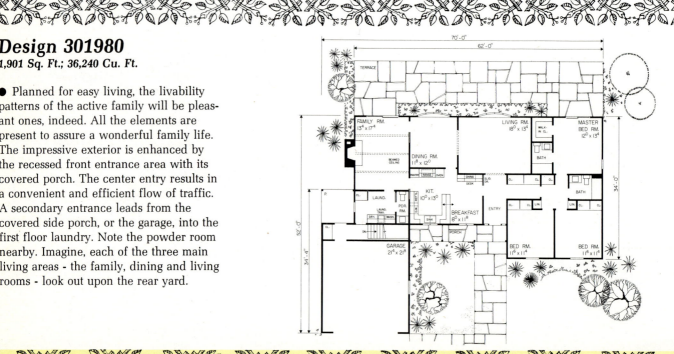

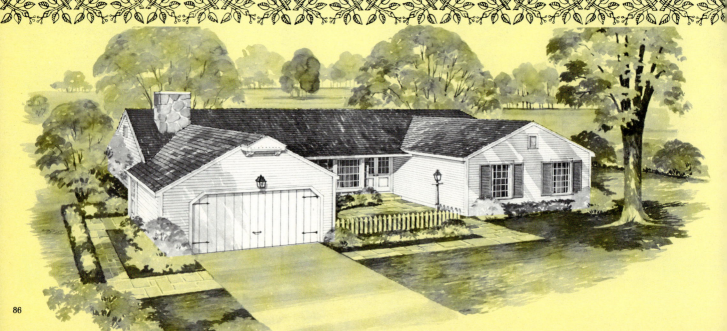

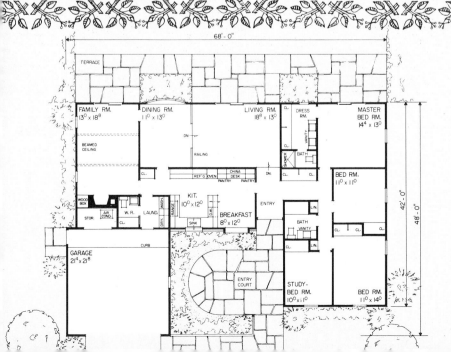

Floor plan labels:

- TERRACE
- FAMILY RM. 13⁰ x 18⁸
- DINING RM. 11⁰ x 13⁰
- LIVING RM. 18⁸ x 13⁰
- DRESS RM.
- MASTER BED RM. 14⁴ x 13⁰
- BEAMED CEILING
- BATH
- SHOWER
- REF'G OVEN
- CHINA DESK
- PANTRY
- BED RM. 11⁰ x 11⁰
- KIT. 10⁰ x 12⁰
- WOOD BOX
- AIR COND.
- STOR.
- W.R.
- LAUND.
- DRY RANGE
- SINK
- BREAKFAST 8⁰ x 12⁰
- ENTRY
- BATH VANITY
- GARAGE 21⁴ x 21⁸
- CURB
- ENTRY COURT
- STUDY-BED RM. 10⁰ x 11⁰
- BED RM. 11⁰ x 14⁰
- 68'-0"
- 42'-0"
- 48'-0"

Design 301950
2,076 Sq. Ft.; 27,520 Cu. Ft.

● If you were to count the various reasons that will surely cause excitement over the prospect of moving into this home, you would certainly be able to compile a long list. You might head your list with the grace and charm of the front exterior. You'd certainly have to comment on the delightful entry court, the picket fence and lamppost, and the recessed front entrance. Comments about the interior obviously would begin with the listing of such features as: spaciousness galore; sunken living room; separate dining room; beamed ceiling family room; excellent kitchen with pass-thru to breakfast room; two full baths, plus extra washroom, etc.

Design 301977 896 Sq. Ft. - Main Level; 884 Sq. Ft. - Upper Level; 896 Sq. Ft. - Lower level; 36,718 Cu. Ft.

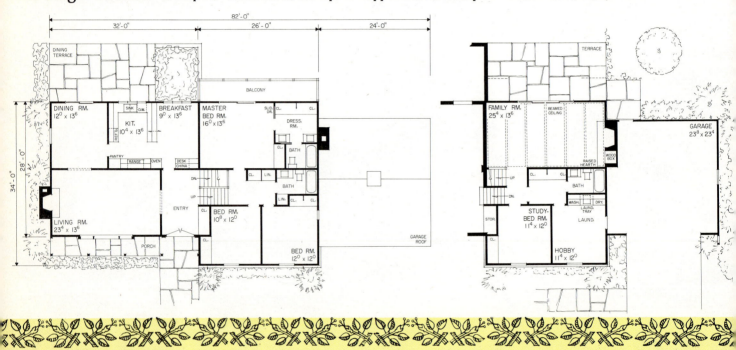

Design 302216

1,183 Sq. Ft. - Main Level; 1,344 Sq. Ft. - Upper Level
659 Sq. Ft. - Lower Level; 51,856 Cu. Ft.

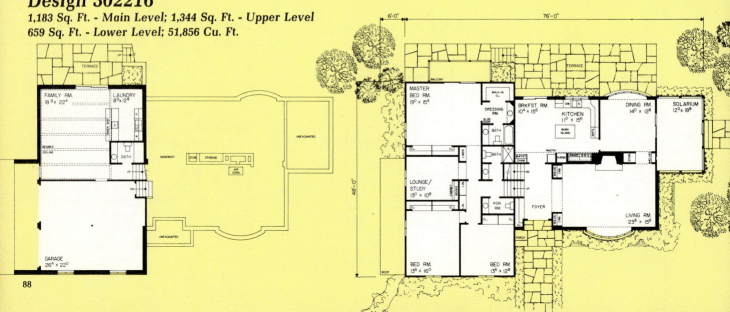

Design 302125 728 Sq. Ft. - Main Level; 672 Sq. Ft. - Upper Level; 656 Sq. Ft. - Lower Level; 28,315 Cu. Ft.

Design 302658

1,218 Sq. Ft. - First Floor
764 Sq. Ft. - Second Floor; 29,690 Cu. Ft.

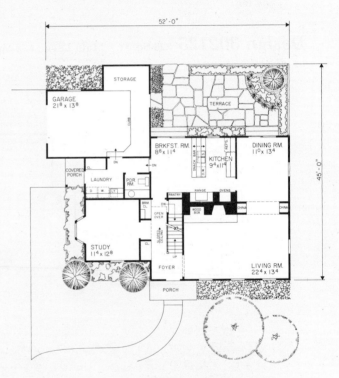

● Traditional charm of yesteryear is exemplified delightfully in this one-and-a-half story home. The garage has been conveniently tucked away in the rear of the house which makes this design ideal for a corner lot. Interior livability has been planned for efficient living. The front living room is large and features a fireplace with wood box. The laundry area is accessible by way of both the garage and a side covered porch. Enter the rear terrace from both eating areas, the formal dining room and the informal breakfast room.

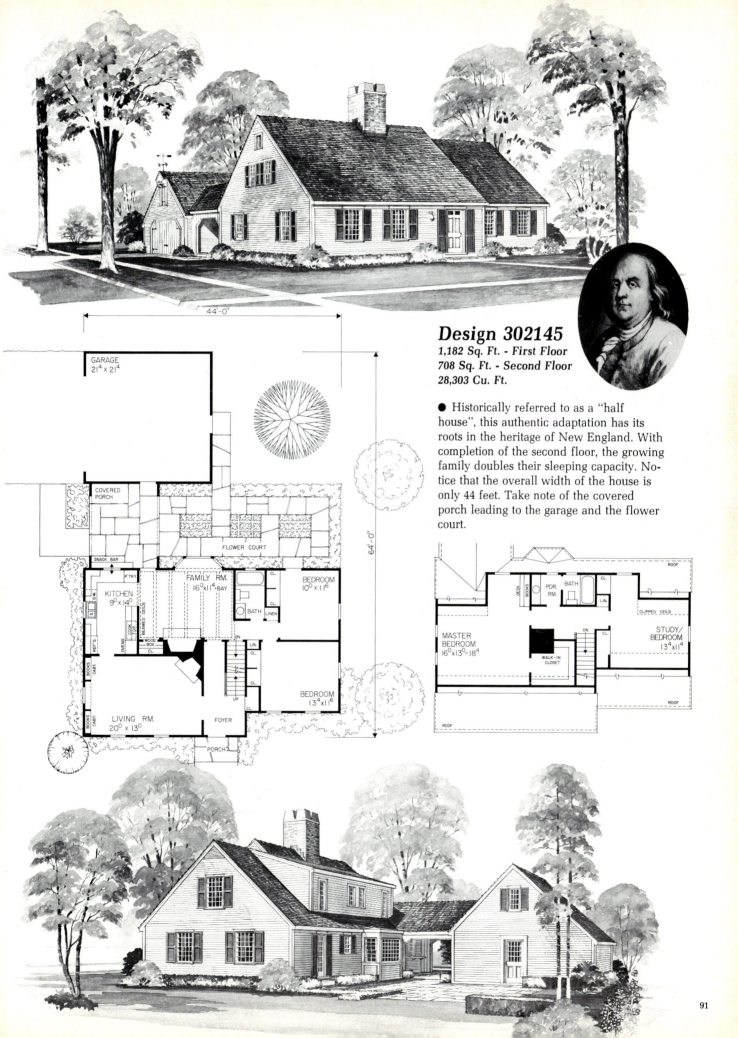

44'-0"

GARAGE
21⁴ x 21⁴

COVERED
PORCH

FLOWER COURT

SNACK BAR

KITCHEN
9⁰ x 14⁰

P'TRY

FAMILY RM.
16⁰ x 11⁴ BAY

BEDROOM
10⁰ x 11⁶

BATH

LINEN

CL.

REF'G.

COOK TOP

OVENS

BEAMED CEIL'G

WOOD BOX

CL.

BOOKS
CABT.

BOOKS
CABT.

LIVING RM.
20⁰ x 13⁰

FOYER

BEDROOM
13⁴ x 11⁶

LIN.

CL.

UP

DN

PORCH

64'-0"

MASTER
BEDROOM
16⁰ x 13⁰-18⁴

DESK

BOOKS

PDR.
RM.

BATH

CL.

LIN.

WALK-IN
CLOSET

DN

CL.

STUDY/
BEDROOM
13⁴ x 11⁴

CLIPPED CEIL'G.

ROOF

ROOF

ROOF

Design 302145
1,182 Sq. Ft. - First Floor
708 Sq. Ft. - Second Floor
28,303 Cu. Ft.

● Historically referred to as a "half house", this authentic adaptation has its roots in the heritage of New England. With completion of the second floor, the growing family doubles their sleeping capacity. Notice that the overall width of the house is only 44 feet. Take note of the covered porch leading to the garage and the flower court.

THE CONTEMPORARY HOME . . . *can be the most*

dramatic and eye-catching of exterior styles. Its forms can be almost boundless. Whether geometric, rectangular, angular, or irregular in shape, the contemporary styled house can result in new, exciting, yet practical, living patterns. The designs featured in this book include one, 1½, two-story and multi-level designs for a wide variety of building budgets. As the floor plans shown here reflect, contemporary livability can, indeed, be delightfully different. Note the open planning, second floor lounges, interior balconies, sunken living areas, sloping ceilings, etc.

Design 302781
2,132 Sq. Ft. - First Floor
1,156 Sq. Ft. - Second Floor
47,365 Cu. Ft.

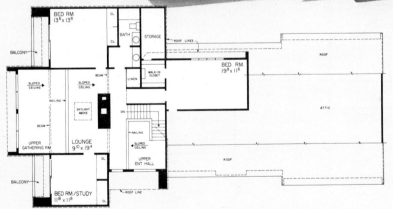

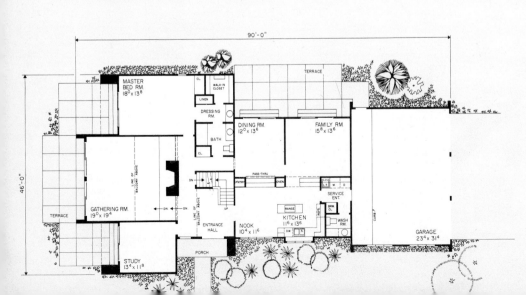

● This beautifully designed two-story could be considered a dream house of a lifetime. The exterior is sure to catch the eye of anyone who takes sight of its unique construction. The front kitchen features an island range, adjacent breakfast nook and pass-thru to formal dining room. The master bedroom suite with its privacy and convenience on the first floor has a spacious walk-in closet and dressing room. The side terrace is accessible through sliding glass doors from the master bedroom, gathering room and study. The second floor has three bedrooms and storage space galore. Also notice the lounge which has a sloped ceiling and a skylight above. This delightful area looks down into the gathering room. The outdoor balconies overlook the wrap-around terrace. Surely an outstanding trend house for decades to come.

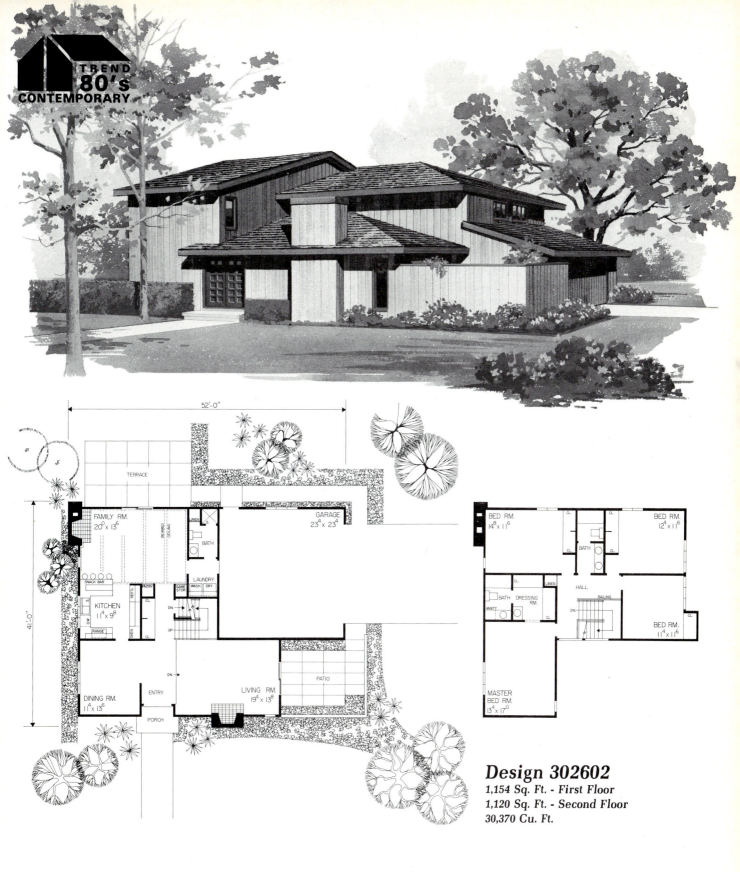

52'-0"

41'-0"

TERRACE

FAMILY RM.
20⁴ x 13⁶

GARAGE
23' x 23⁴

BATH

SNACK BAR

LAUNDRY
WASH DRY

KITCHEN
11⁴ x 9⁸

ENTRY

GAME
STOR.

RANGE

DINING RM.
11⁴ x 13⁶

ENTRY

LIVING RM.
19⁴ x 13⁸

PATIO

PORCH

BED RM.
14⁸ x 11⁶

BED RM.
12⁴ x 11⁶

BATH

BATH

DRESSING
RM.

HALL

RAILING

VANITY

BED RM.
11⁴ x 11⁶

MASTER
BED RM.
13⁴ x 17⁰

Design 302602

1,154 Sq. Ft. - First Floor
1,120 Sq. Ft. - Second Floor
30,370 Cu. Ft.

● Varying roof planes, wide overhangs, interestingly shaped blank wall areas and patterned double front doors provide the distinguishing characteristics of this refreshing, contemporary two-story design. The extension of the front wall results in an enclosed, private outdoor patio area accesssible from the living room. Inside the compact plan there is a fine feeling of spaciousness. The living area features open planning. The U-shaped kitchen is but a step or two from the dining room and the family room. There is a snack bar, laundry area, full bath with stall shower, pantry and game storage, and two fireplaces located on the first floor. Upstairs, four good-sized bedrooms, two baths, a dressing room and plenty of closets.

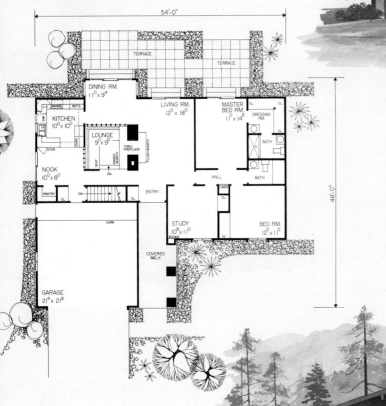

Design 302703
1,445 Sq. Ft.; 30,300 Cu. Ft.

● This modified, hip-roofed contemporary design will be the answer for those who want
something both practical, yet different, inside
and out. The covered front walk sets the stage for
entering a modest sized home with tremendous
livability. The focal point will be the pleasant
conversation lounge. It is sunken, partially open
to the other living areas and shares the enjoyment of the thru-fireplace with the living room.

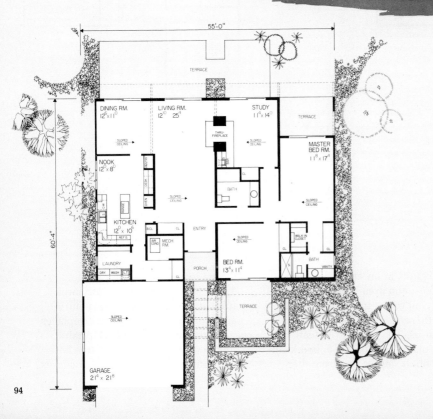

Design 302754
1,844 Sq. Ft.; 26,615 Cu. Ft.

● This really is a most dramatic and refreshing contemporary home. The slope of its
wide overhanging roofs is carried right indoors to provide an extra measure of spaciousness. The U-shaped privacy wall of the
front entrance area provides an appealing
outdoor living spot. The rectangular floor
plan will be economical to build. Notice the
efficient use of space and how it all makes
its contribution to outstanding livability.

Design 302753
1,539 Sq. Ft.; 31,910 Cu. Ft.

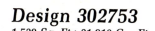

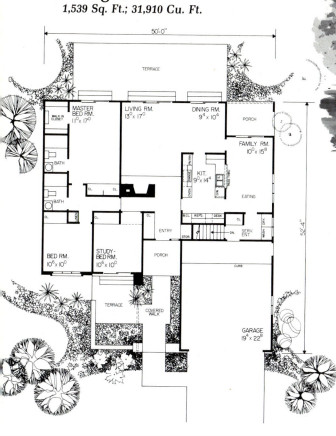

● In this day and age of expensive building sites, projecting the attached garage from the front line of the house makes a lot of economic sense. It also lends itself to interesting roof lines and plan configurations. Here, a pleasing covered walkway to the front door results. A privacy wall adds an extra measure of design appeal and provides a sheltered terrace for the study/bedroom. An excellent plan.

Design 302744
1,381 Sq. Ft.; 17,530 Cu. Ft.

● Here is a practical and an attractive contemporary home for that narrow building site. It is designed for efficiency with the small family or retired couple in mind. Sloping ceilings foster an extra measure of spaciousness. In addition to the master bedroom, there is the study that can also serve as the second bedroom or as an occasional guest room. Note raised hearth fireplace, snack bar, U-shaped kitchen, laundry, etc.

Design 302343 3,110 Sq. Ft.; 51,758 Cu. Ft.

● If yours is a growing active family the chances are good that they will want their new home to relate to the outdoors. This distinctive design puts a premium on private outdoor living. And you don't have to install a swim- ming pool to get the most enjoyment from this home. Developing this area as a garden court will provide the in- door living areas with a breathtaking awareness of nature's beauty. Notice the fine zoning of the plan and how each area has its sliding glass doors to provide an unrestricted view. Three bedrooms plus study are serviced by three baths. The family and gathering rooms provide two great living areas. The kitchen is most efficient.

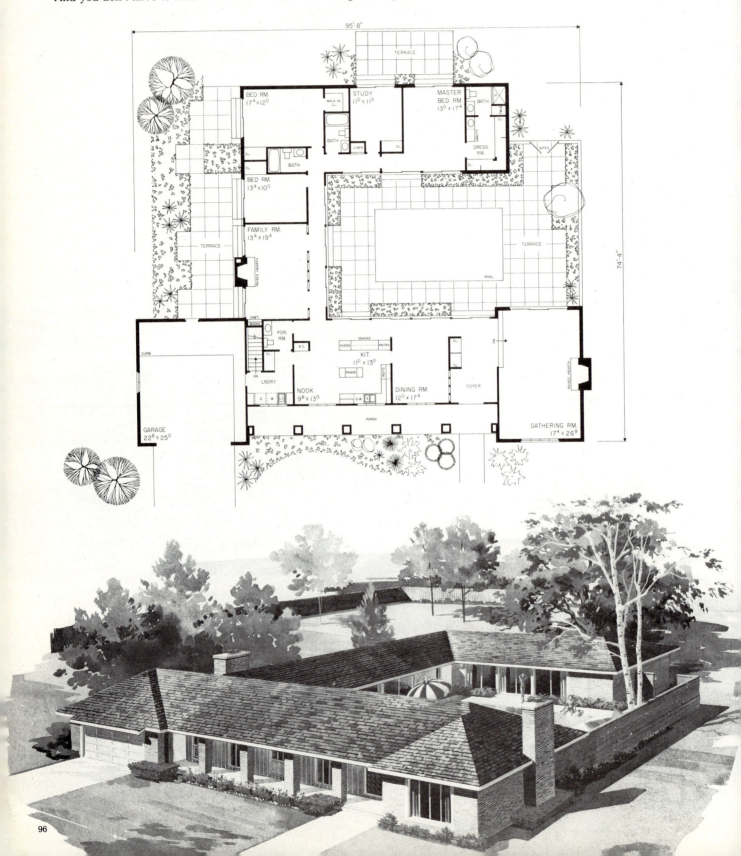

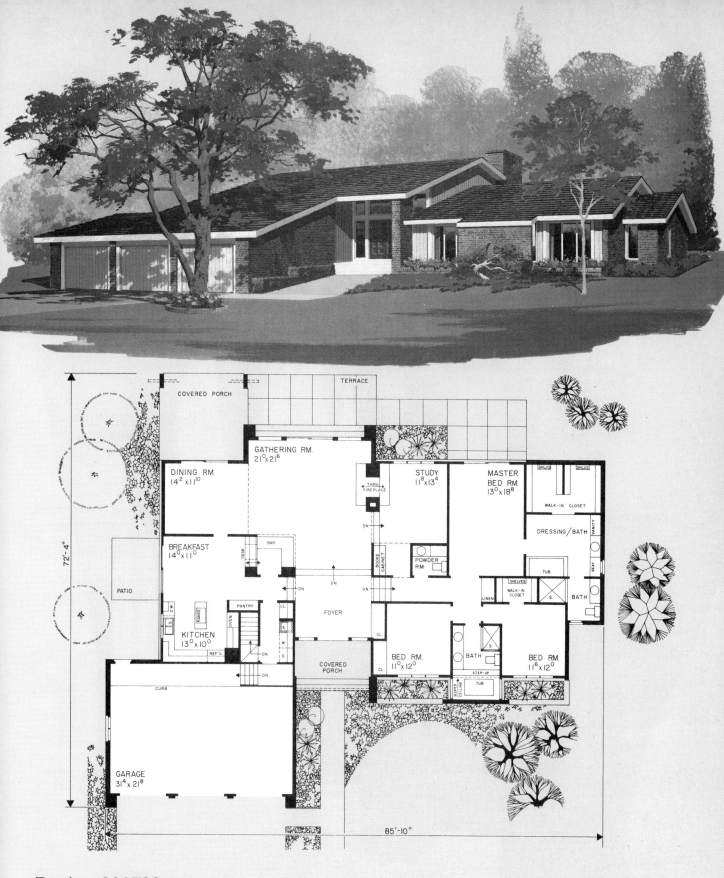

Design 302789 2,732 Sq. Ft.; 54,935 Cu. Ft.

● An attached three car garage! What a fantastic feature of this three bedroom contemporary design. And there's more. As one walks up the steps to the covered porch and through the double front doors the charm of this design will be overwhelming. Inside, a large foyer greets all visitors and leads them to each of the three areas, each down a few steps. The living area has a large gathering room with fireplace and a study adjacent on one side and the formal dining room on the other. The work center has an efficient kitchen with island range, breakfast room, laundry and built-in desk and bar. Then there is the sleeping area. Note the raised tub with sloped ceiling.

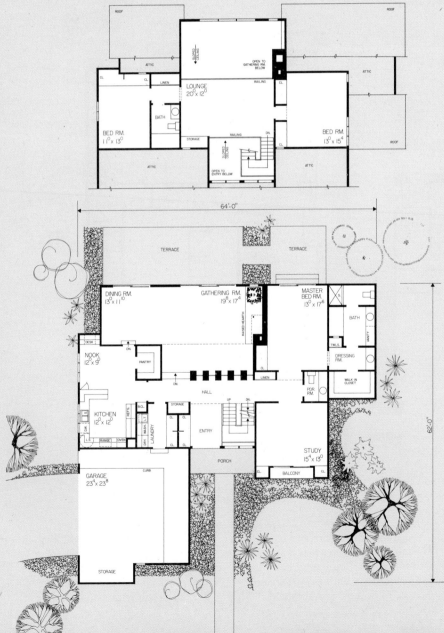

Design 302708

2,108 Sq. Ft. - First Floor
824 Sq. Ft. - Second Floor
52,170 Cu. Ft.

● Here is a one-and-a-half story home whose exterior is distinctive. It has a contemporary feeling, yet it retains some of the fine design features and proportions of traditional exteriors. Inside the appealing double front doors there is livability galore. The sunken rear living-dining area is delightfully spacious and is looked down into from the second floor lounge. The open end fireplace, with its raised hearth and planter, is another focal point. The master bedroom features a fine compartmented bath with both shower and tub. The study is just a couple steps away. The U-shaped kitchen is outstanding. Notice the pantry and laundry. Upstairs provides children with their own sleeping, studying and TV quarters. Absolutely a great design! Study all the fine details closely with your family.

ROOF

ATTIC

BED RM.
11⁰ x 13⁶

BED RM.
10⁰ x 10²

CL.
BATH

TWLS.

LINEN

ATTIC

CEILING CLIP

CL.

CL.

DN

ROOF

UPPER ENTRANCE

BED RM.
11⁴ x 12⁰

CEILING CLIP

LOUNGE
19⁰ x 9⁶

RAILING

SLOPED CEILING

ATTIC

ROOF

ROOF

UPPER GATHERING RM.

SLOPED CEILING

ROOF

Design 302782

2,060 Sq. Ft. - First Floor
897 Sq. Ft. - Second Floor
47,750 Cu. Ft.

● What makes this such a distinctive four bedroom design? Let's list some of the features. This plan includes great formal and informal living for the family at home or when entertaining guests. The formal gathering room and informal family room share a dramatic raised hearth fireplace. Other features of the sunken gathering room include: high, sloped ceilings, built-in planter and sliding glass doors to the front entrance court. The kitchen has a snack bar, many built-ins, a pass-thru to dining room and easy access to the large laundry/washroom. The master bedroom suite is located on the main level for added privacy and convenience. There's even a study with a built-in bar. The upper level has three more bedrooms, a bath and a lounge looking down into the gathering room.

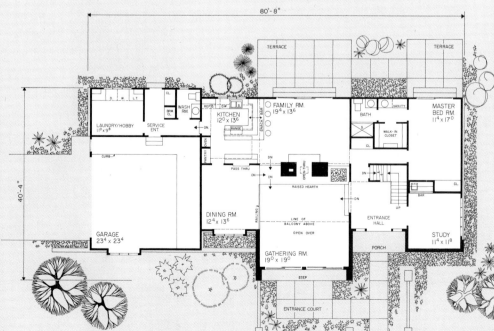

80'-8"

40'-4"

TERRACE

TERRACE

LAUNDRY/HOBBY
11⁰ x 9⁸

D. W. L.

CL.

WASH RM.

BRM CL

REFG

G.W.

FAMILY RM.
19⁴ x 13⁶

VANITY

BATH

MASTER BED RM.
11⁴ x 17⁰

SERVICE ENT.

KITCHEN
12⁰ x 13⁶

SNACK BAR

RANGE

DN

WALK-IN CLOSET

CURB

PANTRY

OVEN

PASS THRU

OPEN-THRU

DN

DN

S.

CL

DN

BAR

GARAGE
23⁴ x 23⁴

DINING RM.
12⁴ x 13⁶

RAISED HEARTH

DN

UP

RAILING

LINE OF BALCONY ABOVE

OPEN OVER

ENTRANCE HALL

STUDY
11⁴ x 11⁸

CL

GATHERING RM.
19⁰ x 19⁰

PORCH

STEP

ENTRANCE COURT

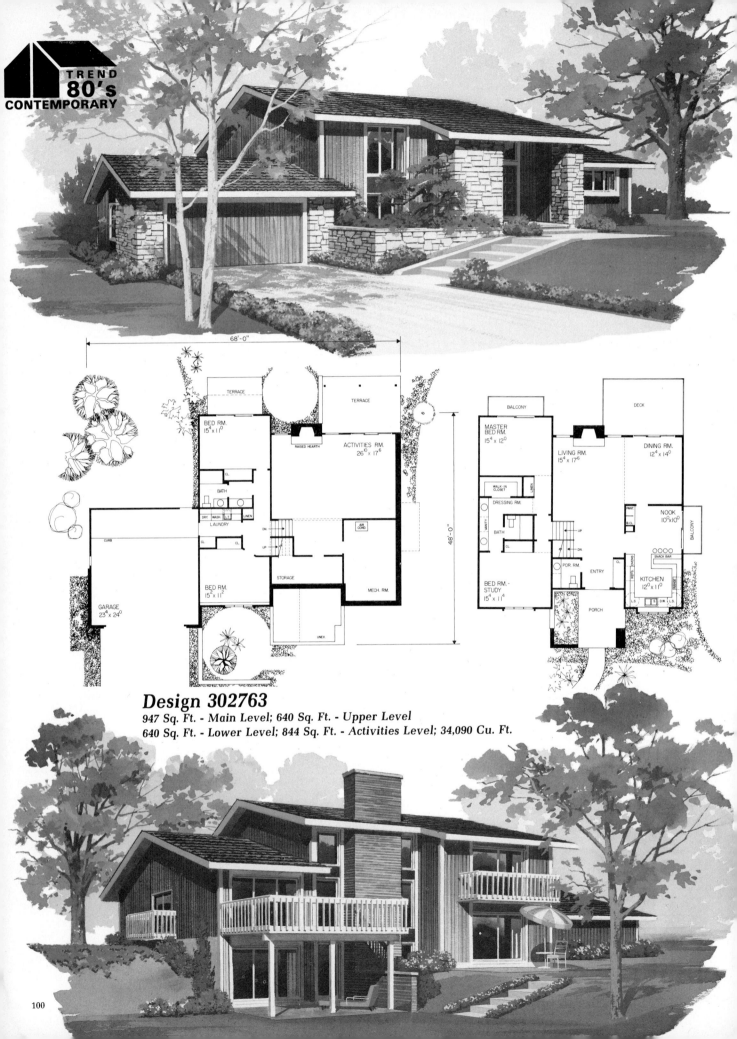

68'-0"

TERRACE

TERRACE

BED RM.
15⁴ x 11⁰

ACTIVITIES RM.
26¹⁰ x 17⁶

CL.

BATH

RAISED HEARTH

DRY. WASH. LT. LINEN

LAUNDRY

AIR.
COND.

CURB

DN.

CL. CL.

48'-0"

UP.

STORAGE

BED RM.
15² x 11²

MECH. RM.

GARAGE
23⁴ x 24⁰

UNEX.

BALCONY

DECK

MASTER
BED RM.
15⁴ x 12⁰

LIVING RM.
15⁴ x 17⁶

DINING RM.
12⁴ x 14⁰

WALK-IN
CLOSET

LINEN

PAINT

B.CL.

NOOK
10⁰ x 10⁰

DRESSING RM.

VANITY

BATH

CL.

UP.

DN.

REFG. OVENS

SNACK BAR

BALCONY

PDR. RM.

ENTRY

CL.

KITCHEN
12⁰ x 11⁰

BED RM. -
STUDY
15⁴ x 11⁴

PORCH

L.S.

S

D.W.

L.S.

Design 302763
947 Sq. Ft. - Main Level; 640 Sq. Ft. - Upper Level
640 Sq. Ft. - Lower Level; 844 Sq. Ft. - Activities Level; 34,090 Cu. Ft.

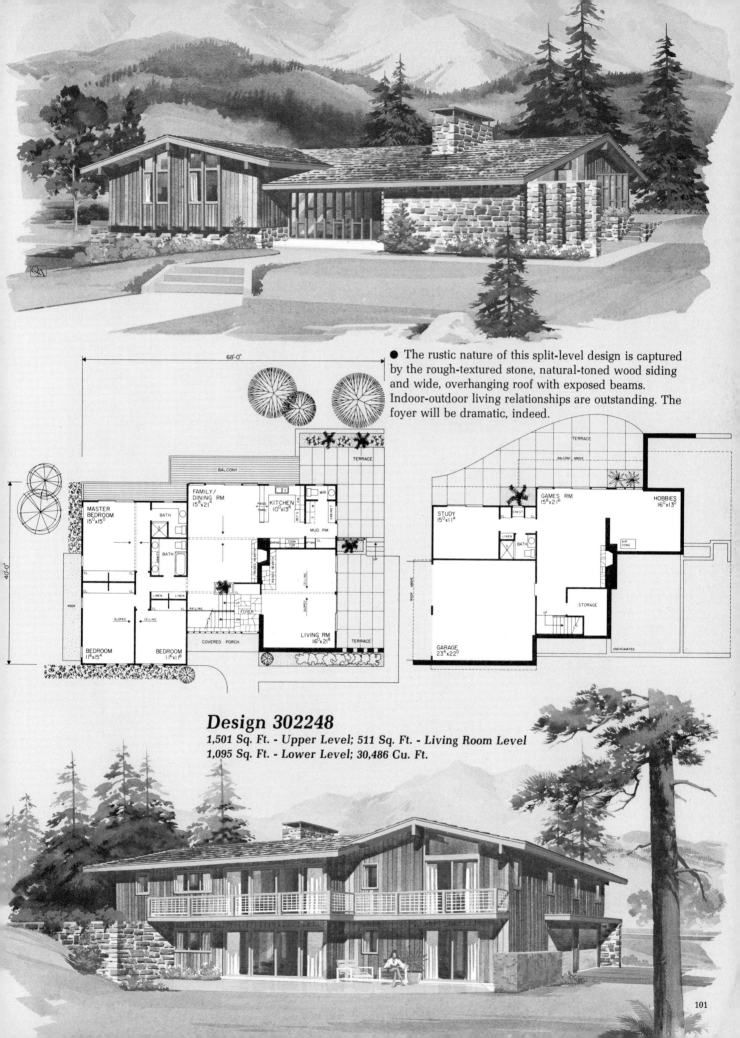

● The rustic nature of this split-level design is captured by the rough-textured stone, natural-toned wood siding and wide, overhanging roof with exposed beams. Indoor-outdoor living relationships are outstanding. The foyer will be dramatic, indeed.

Design 302248

1,501 Sq. Ft. - Upper Level; 511 Sq. Ft. - Living Room Level
1,095 Sq. Ft. - Lower Level; 30,486 Cu. Ft.

THE ENGLISH TUDOR STYLE . . .

has enjoyed a rebirth in popularity in recent years. This Tudor term of reference has, however, become an accepted misnomer. This style with its simulated half-timber work, stucco, diamonded paned windows, peaked roofs and sculptured chimneys was originally identified with Elizabethan architecture. As shown here, and as featured in the English Tudor Homes book, this style adapts to the one, 1½, two-story and multi-level house in a most pleasing fashion. Separate dining rooms, breakfast rooms, living and family rooms, studies and spacious foyers allow for flexible and formal living patterns.

Design 302855

1,372 Sq. Ft. - First Floor
1,245 Sq. Ft. - Second Floor
44,495 Cu. Ft.

● This elegant Tudor house is perfect for the family who wants to move-up in living area, style and luxury. As you enter this home you will find a large living room with a fireplace on your right. Adjacent, the formal dining room has easy access to both the living room and the kitchen. The kitchen/breakfast room has an open plan and access to the rear terrace. Sunken a few steps, the spacious family room is highlighted with a fireplace and access to the rear, covered porch. Note the optional planning of the garage storage area. Plan this area according to the needs of your family. Upstairs, your family will enjoy three bedrooms and a full bath, along with a spacious master bedroom suite. Truly a house that will bring many years of pleasure to your family.

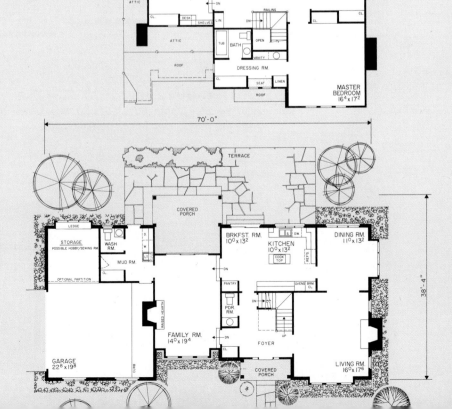

Design 302854

1,261 Sq. Ft. - First Floor
950 Sq. Ft. - Second Floor
36,820 Cu. Ft.

● The flair of old England has been captured in this outstanding one-and-a-half story design. Interior livability will efficiently serve the various needs of all family members. The first floor offers both formal and informal areas along with the work centers. Note some of the various features which include a wet-bar in the dining room, the kitchen's snack bar, first floor laundry and rear covered porch to mention a few. Accommodations for sleeping will be found on the second floor. Don't miss the uniqueness of the lounge/nursery area which is attached to the master bedroom.

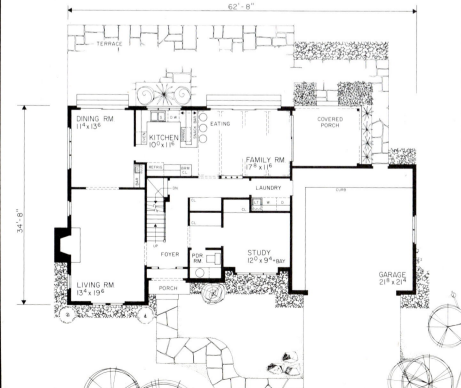

CLASSIC TUDOR DESIGNS

Design 302128
1,152 Sq. Ft. - First Floor
896 Sq. Ft. - Second Floor
30,707 Cu. Ft.

● Here is proof that your restricted building budget can return to you wonderfully pleasing design and loads of livability. This is an English Tudor adaptation that will surely become your subdivision's favorite facade. Its mark of individuality is obvious to all.

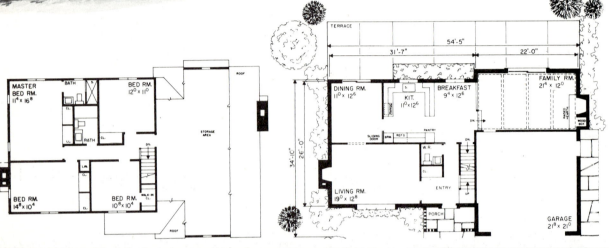

Design 302525
919 Sq. Ft. - First Floor
1,019 Sq. Ft. - Second Floor
29,200 Cu. Ft.

● Here is an economically built home that abounds with convenient living potential. In addition to the great upstairs sleeping facilities, there is a downstairs study. You may wish to call it a TV, sewing, or guest room. Blueprints include optional, hip roof French adaptation.

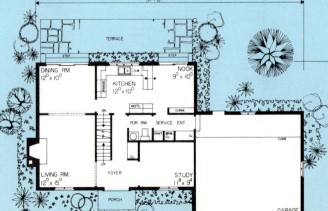

104

Design 302366 1,078 Sq. Ft. - First Floor
880 Sq. Ft. - Second Floor; 27,242 Cu. Ft.

● This is but one of the three exteriors that go with this outstanding floor plan. Blueprints include details for two other traditional exteriors, each with a hip roof. The interior includes all the features of a much more luxurious home. It will fit a relatively small site.

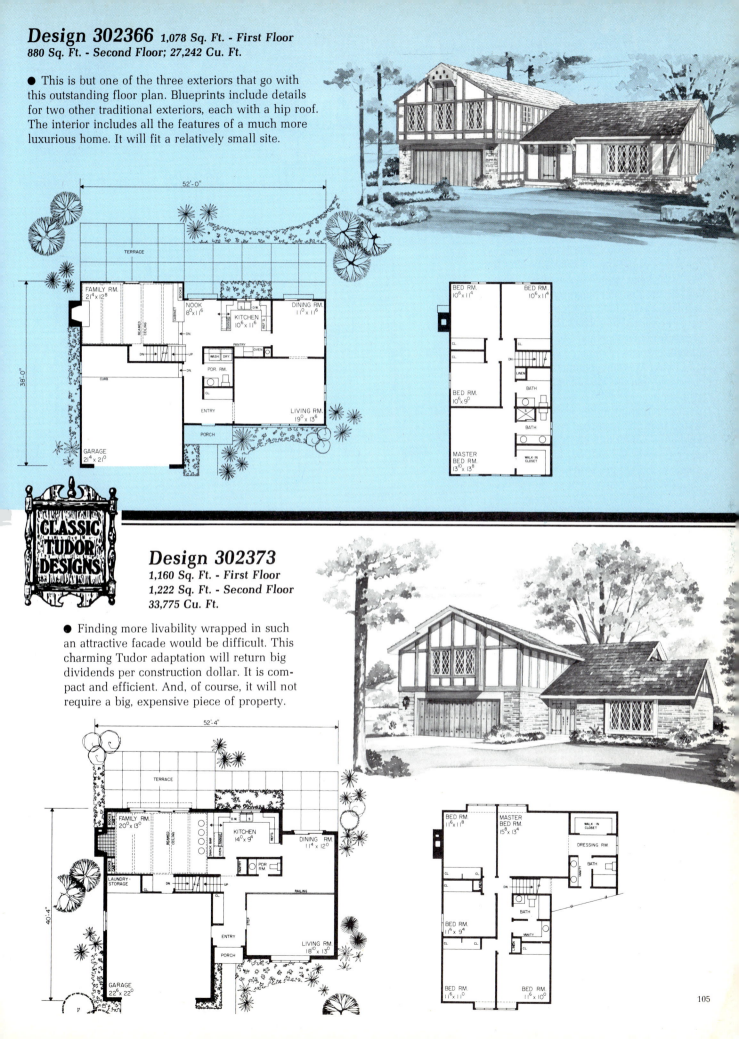

CLASSIC TUDOR DESIGNS

Design 302373
1,160 Sq. Ft. - First Floor
1,222 Sq. Ft. - Second Floor
33,775 Cu. Ft.

● Finding more livability wrapped in such an attractive facade would be difficult. This charming Tudor adaptation will return big dividends per construction dollar. It is compact and efficient. And, of course, it will not require a big, expensive piece of property.

Classic Tudor Designs

Design 302129 2,057 Sq. Ft.; 36,970 Cu. Ft.

● Here are four delightful Tudor adaptations. Their exterior charm is matched by the outstanding interior livability. The four bedroom home above is zoned for convenient living. The sleeping area, with its two full baths and plenty of closets, will have a lot of privacy. The formal living and dining rooms function together and may be completely by-passed when desired. The informal living areas are grouped together and overlook the rear yard. The family room with its beamed ceiling is but a step from the kitchen and through sliding glass doors, a step from the terrace. The U-shaped kitchen is handy to both the breakfast and dining rooms. A first floor laundry and extra washroom are strategically located for your everyday convenience.

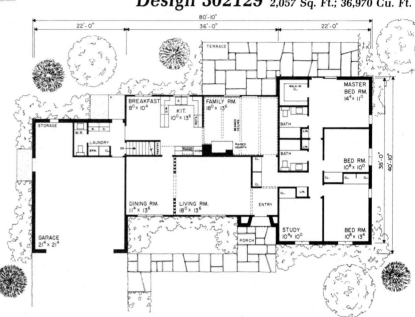

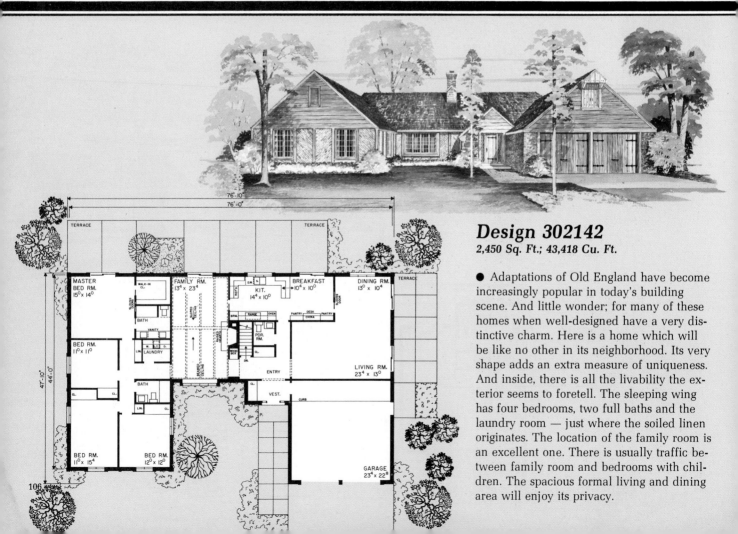

Design 302142
2,450 Sq. Ft.; 43,418 Cu. Ft.

● Adaptations of Old England have become increasingly popular in today's building scene. And little wonder; for many of these homes when well-designed have a very distinctive charm. Here is a home which will be like no other in its neighborhood. Its very shape adds an extra measure of uniqueness. And inside, there is all the livability the exterior seems to foretell. The sleeping wing has four bedrooms, two full baths and the laundry room — just where the soiled linen originates. The location of the family room is an excellent one. There is usually traffic between family room and bedrooms with children. The spacious formal living and dining area will enjoy its privacy.

CLASSIC TUDOR DESIGNS

Design 301989 2,282 Sq. Ft.; 41,831 Cu. Ft.

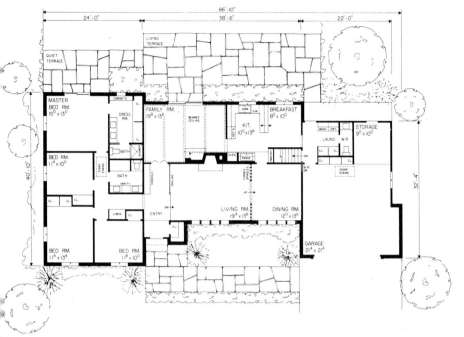

● This is high style reminiscent of Old England with a plan as contemporary as today and tomorrow. There is, indeed, a feeling of coziness that emanates from the ground-hugging qualities of this picturesque home. Inside, there is livability galore. There's the four bedroom, two bath sleeping wing with a dressing room as a bonus. There's the sunken living room and the separate dining room to function as the family's formal living area. Then, overlooking the rear yard, there's the informal living area with its beamed ceiling family room and wonderful kitchen with its adjacent breakfast room. As a positive plus to outstanding livability, there's the handy first floor laundry with its washroom. Don't miss the storage room.

Design 302318
2,029 Sq. Ft.; 31,021 Cu. Ft.

● Warmth and charm are characteristics of the Tudor adaptations. This modest sized home, with its twin front-facing gabled roofs, represents a great investment. While it will be an exciting and refreshing addition to any neighborhood, its appeal will never grow old. The covered front entrance opens to the center foyer. Traffic patterns flow in an orderly and efficient manner to the three main zones — formal dining; sleeping and informal living. The sunken living room with its fireplace is separated from the dining room by an attractive trellis divider. A second fireplace, along with beamed ceiling and sliding glass doors, highlights the family room. Note snack bar, mud room, two full baths and optional basement.

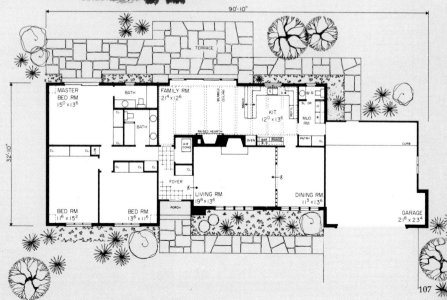

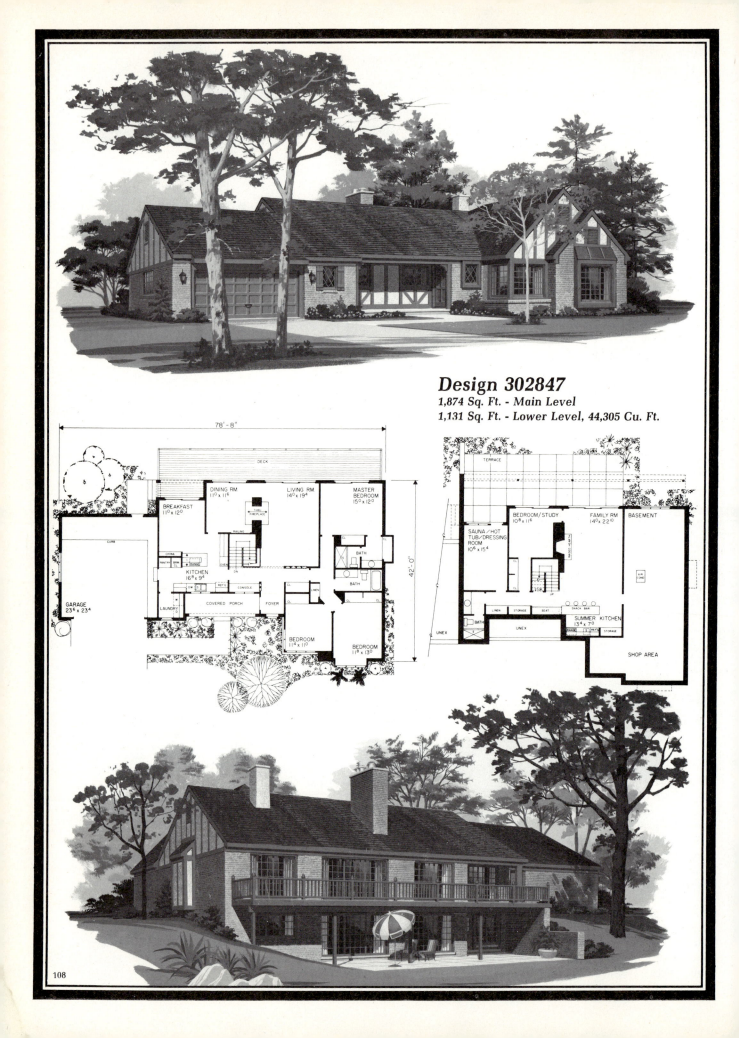

Design 302847
1,874 Sq. Ft. - Main Level
1,131 Sq. Ft. - Lower Level, 44,305 Cu. Ft.

78'-8"

42'-0"

DECK

DINING RM.
11⁰ x 11⁶

LIVING RM.
14⁰ x 19⁴

MASTER BEDROOM
15⁰ x 12⁰

BREAKFAST
11⁰ x 12⁰

THRU FIREPLACE

RAILING

BATH

CHINA

PANTRY BRM CL

OVEN DN

CL

BATH

KITCHEN
16⁸ x 9⁴

RANGE

CURB

REF'S

CONSOLE

CL

LINEN

DW

GARAGE
23⁶ x 23⁴

LAUNDRY

COVERED PORCH

FOYER

CL

CL CL

BEDROOM
11⁴ x 11⁰

BEDROOM
11⁸ x 13⁰

TERRACE

BEDROOM/STUDY
10⁸ x 11⁶

FAMILY RM.
14⁰ x 22¹⁰

BASEMENT

SAUNA/HOT TUB/DRESSING ROOM
10⁶ x 15⁴

RAISED HEARTH

CL

CL

AIR COND

UP

UNEX

BATH

LINEN

STORAGE

SEAT

SNACK BAR

SUMMER KITCHEN
13⁴ x 7⁰

UNEX

RANGE

STORAGE

SHOP AREA

Design 302218 *889 Sq. Ft. - Main Level; 960 Sq. Ft. - Upper Level; 936 Sq. Ft. Lower Level; 33,865 Cu. Ft.*

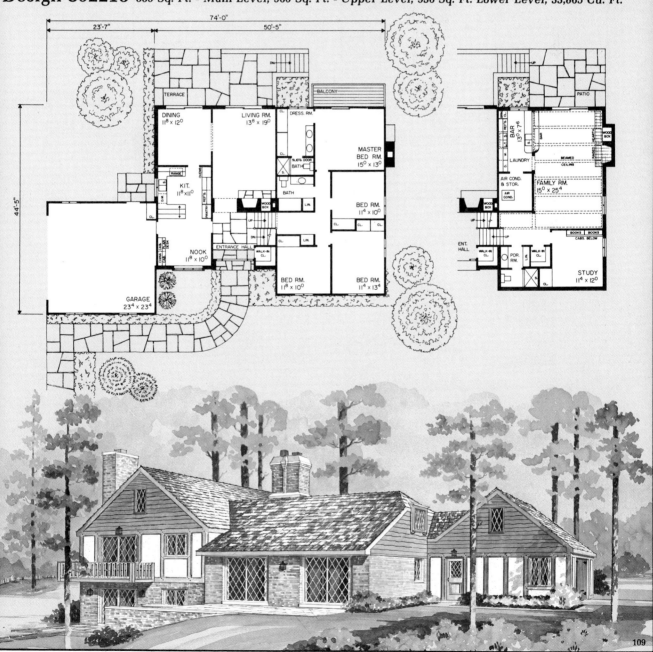

Design 302674 *1,922 Sq. Ft. - First Floor; 890 Sq. Ft. - Second Floor; 37,411 Cu. Ft.*

● This charming Tudor will captivate you with its many fine features. It has flexibility in its site orientation. For example: either the front door or the garage doors can face the street. The choice is yours. Notice the livability on the first floor. A large, open kitchen and breakfast room function nicely with the large, formal dining room and the laundry and washroom on the other side. The breakfast room has sliding glass doors leading to the covered porch for outdoor dining. Other first floor features include: a rear living room with sliding glass doors to the terrace, a sunken family room with a fireplace and built-in bookshelves, a powder room an d a large master bedroom. The master bedroom offers a dressing room, bath and more sliding glass doors that open to a private terrace. Upstairs three more bedrooms and a bath will be found. Obviously a delightful home, ideal for move-up buyers who want a more spacious and luxurious house.

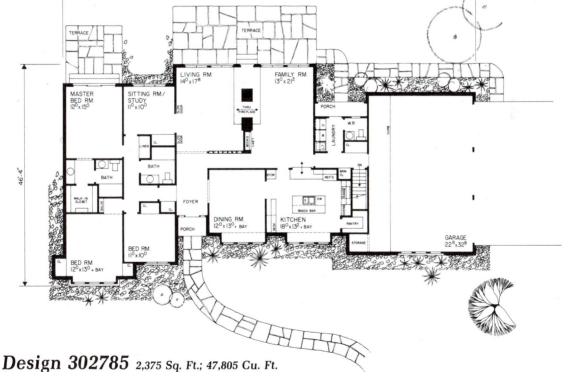

Design 302785 2,375 Sq. Ft.; 47,805 Cu. Ft.

● Exceptional Tudor design! Passersby will take a second glance at this fine home. And the interior is just as pleasing. As one enters the foyer and looks around, the plan will speak for itself in the areas of convenience and efficiency. Cross room traffic will be avoided. There is a hall leading to each of the three bedrooms and study of the sleeping wing and another leading to the living room, family room, kitchen and laundry with washroom. The formal dining room can be entered from both the foyer and the kitchen. Efficiency will be the by-word when describing the kitchen. Note the features: a built-in desk, pantry, island snack bar with sink and pass-thru to the family room. The fireplace will be enjoyed in the living and family rooms.

SPANISH AND WESTERN STYLES . . . *have be-*

come a favorite wherever built. Their facades and configurations offer a high degree of variety. Whether designed for the open space of the prairie or the sloping sites of the hillside areas, these designs put an emphasis on indoor-outdoor living relationships. Functional terraces, enclosed courtyards, balconies and decks cater to the West's inherent desire to enjoy the great outdoors. Identifying characteristics found in adaptations of these styles include wide-overhanging, low pitched roofs, exposed rafter tails, tile roofing, stucco exteriors, vertical board and batten siding, stonework, wrought iron work and massive patterned doors.

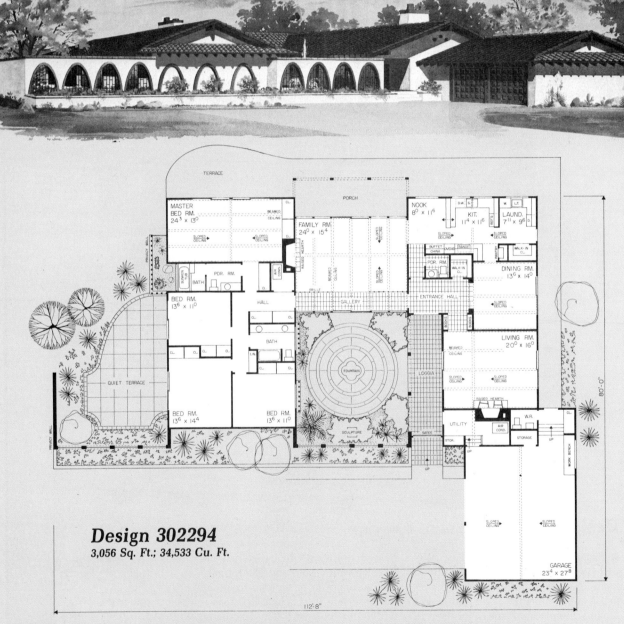

Design 302294
3,056 Sq. Ft.; 34,533 Cu. Ft.

● Here is a Western Ranch with an authentic Spanish flavor. Striking a note of distinction, the arched privacy walls provide a fine backdrop for the long, raised planter. The low-pitched roof features tile and has a wide overhang with exposed rafter tails. The interior is wonderfully zoned. The all-purpose family room is flanked by the sleeping wing and the living wing. Study each area carefully. The planning is excellent and the features are many. Indoor-outdoor integration is outstanding.

Design 301783 *2,412 Sq. Ft. - First Floor; 640 Sq. Ft. - Second Floor; 36,026 Cu. Ft.*

● Large families, take notice! Here is an impressive design that is not only going to be fun to live in, but to look at, as well. Interesting roof levels with exposed rafters and wide overhangs contribute to the appeal. A big en-

trance court, screened from the street by a masonry wall, heightens the drama of the front exterior. The 27 foot living room is captivating. It can function through sliding glass doors with either the front court or the side terrace.

Eating patterns can be flexible with the extra space in the kitchen, a formal dining room and a dining terrace. Study the outstanding master bedroom suite on the second floor. Sloping ceilings hightlight the first floor.

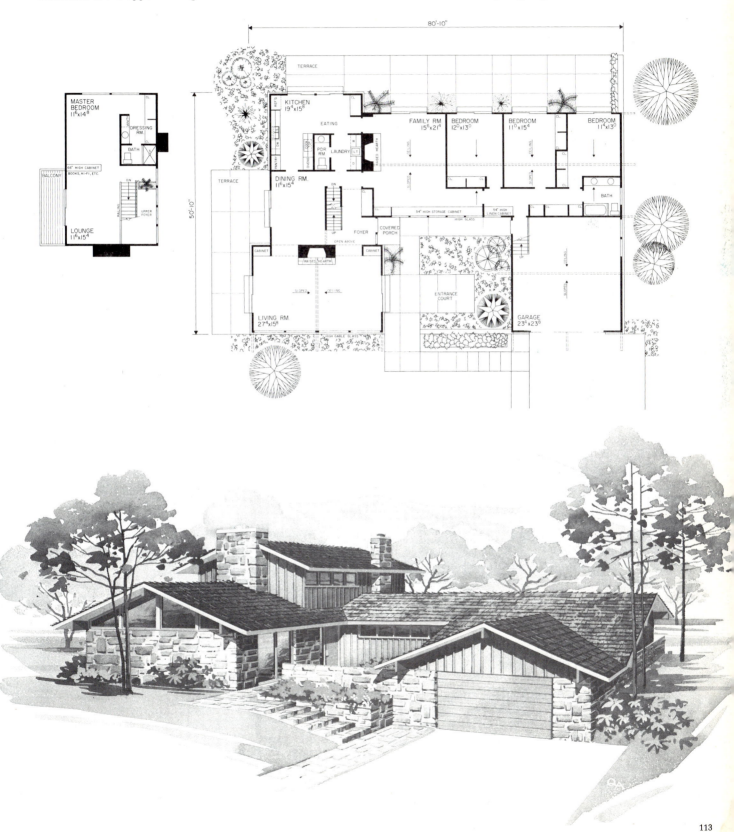

Design 302518

1,630 Sq. Ft. - First Floor
1,260 Sq. Ft. - Second Floor
43,968 Cu. Ft.

● For those who have a predilection for the Spanish influence in their architecture. Outdoor oriented, each of the major living areas on the first floor have direct access to the terraces. Traffic patterns are excellent.

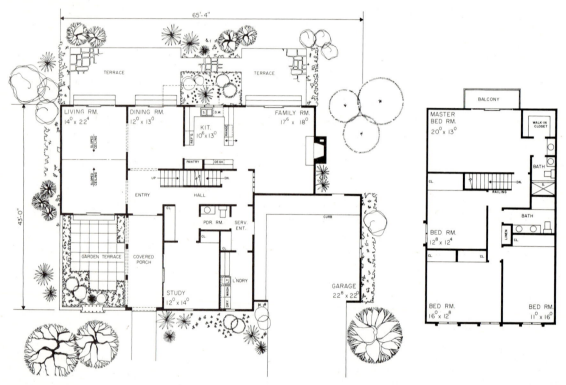

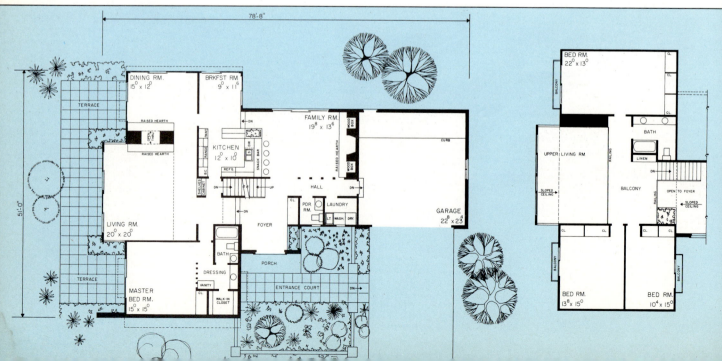

Design 302517

1,767 Sq. Ft. - First Floor
1,094 Sq. Ft. - Second Floor
50,256 Cu. Ft.

● Wherever built - north, east, south, or west - this home will surely command all the attention it deserves. And little wonder with such a well-designed exterior and such an outstanding interior. List your favorite features.

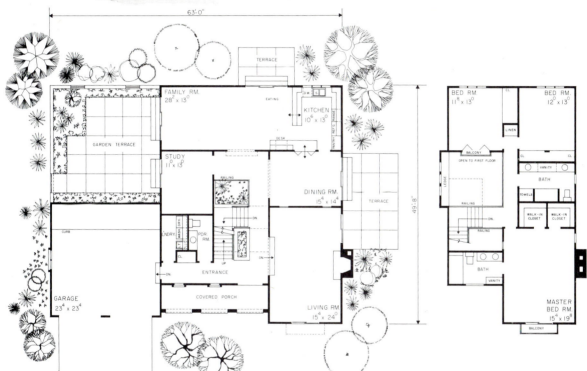

Design 302512

2,074 Sq. Ft. - First Floor
1,116 Sq. Ft. - Second Floor
41,500 Cu. Ft.

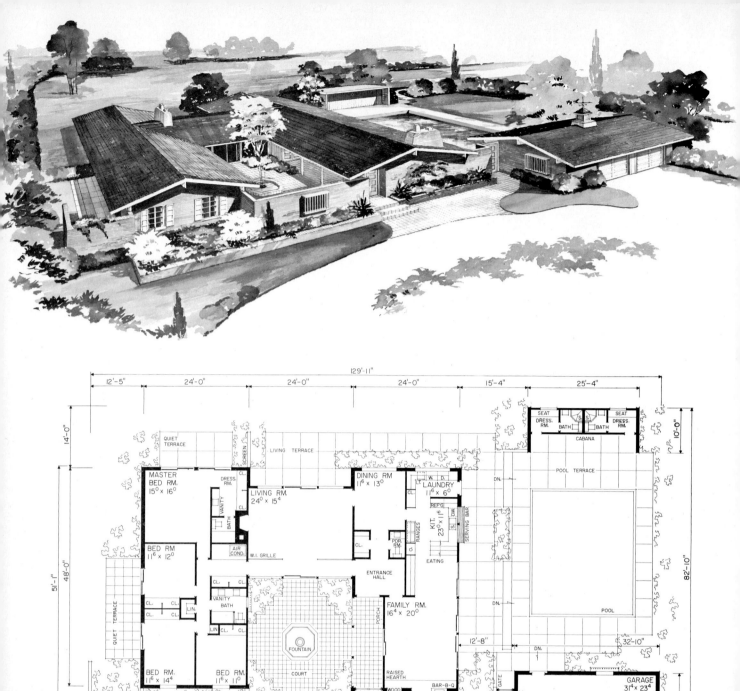

Design 301756 *2,736 Sq. Ft.; 29,139 Cu. Ft.*

● Reminiscent of the West and impressive, indeed. If you are after something that is luxurious in both its appearance and its livability this design should receive your consideration. This rambling ranch house, which encloses a spacious and dramatic flower court, is designed for comfort and privacy indoors and out. Study the outdoor areas. Notice the seclusion each of them provides. Three bedrooms, plus a master suite with dressing room and bath form a private bedroom wing. Formal and informal living areas serve ideally for various types of entertaining. There is excellent circulation of traffic throughout the house. The kitchen is handy to the formal dining room and the informal family room. Don't miss raised hearth fireplace.

116

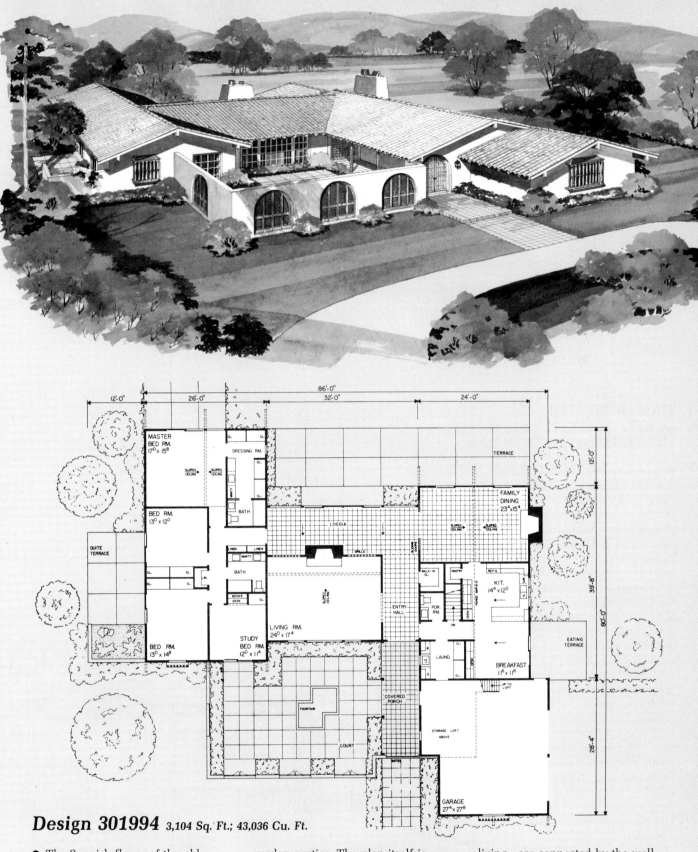

Design 301994 3,104 Sq. Ft.; 43,036 Cu. Ft.

● The Spanish flavor of the old Southwest is delightfully captured by this sprawling ranch house. Its L-shape and high privacy wall go together to form a wide open interior court. This will be a great place to hold those formal and/or informal garden parties. The plan itself is wonderfully zoned. The center portion of the house is comprised of the big, private living room with sloped ceiling. Traffic patterns will noiselessly skirt this formal area. The two wings—the sleeping and informal living—are connected by the well-lighted and spacious loggia. In the sleeping wing, observe the size of the various rooms and the fine storage. In the informal living wing, note the big family room and breakfast room that family members will enjoy.

Design 302628
649 Sq. Ft. - Main Level; 672 Sq. Ft. - Upper Level
624 Sq. Ft. - Lower Level; 25,650 Cu. Ft.

● Impressive! This split-level design is housed in a distinctive Rustic exterior. Its interior has lots of extras, too. Like a wet bar and game storage in the family room. A beamed ceiling, too, and a sliding glass door onto the terrace. In short, a family room designed to make your life easy and enjoyable. There's more. A living room with a traditionally styled fireplace and built-in bookshelves. And a dining room with a sliding glass door that opens to a second terrace. Here's the appropriate setting for those times when you want a touch of elegance. A sunny kitchen, too. It features a built-in oven and range, pantry, broom closet and plenty of space for a breakfast table. A convenient laundry room as well. Four large bedrooms, or three plus a study, if that arrangement suits you better. Also on the upper level is two full back-to-back baths for economical plumbing. This home has style and space to serve any family admirably.

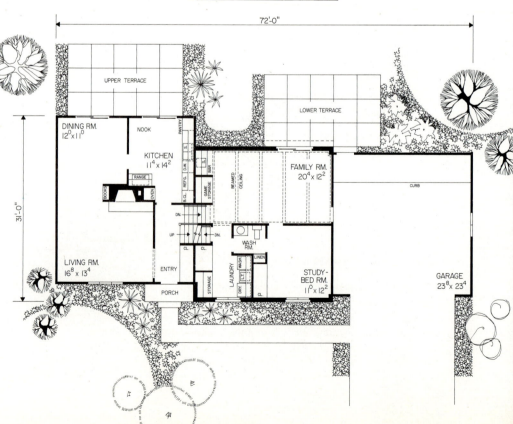

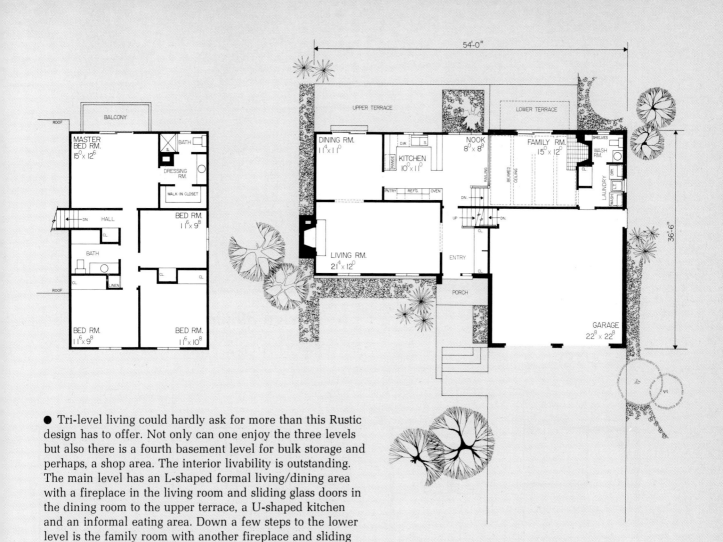

● Tri-level living could hardly ask for more than this Rustic design has to offer. Not only can one enjoy the three levels but also there is a fourth basement level for bulk storage and perhaps, a shop area. The interior livability is outstanding. The main level has an L-shaped formal living/dining area with a fireplace in the living room and sliding glass doors in the dining room to the upper terrace, a U-shaped kitchen and an informal eating area. Down a few steps to the lower level is the family room with another fireplace and sliding doors to the lower terrace, a washroom and laundry. The upper level houses all of the sleeping facilities including three bedrooms, bath and master suite.

Design 302608
728 Sq. Ft. - Main Level; 874 Sq. Ft. - Upper Level
310 Sq. Ft. - Lower Level; 27,705 Cu. Ft.

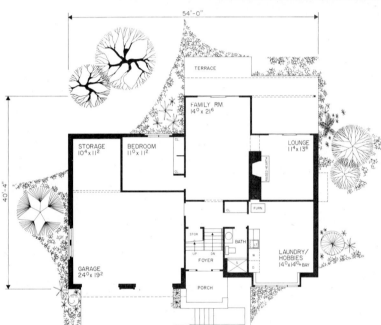

Design 302843

1,861 Sq. Ft. - Upper Level
1,181 Sq. Ft. - Lower Level; 32,485 Cu. Ft.

● Bi-level living will be enjoyed to its fullest in this Spanish styled design. There is a lot of room for the various family activities. Informal living will take place on the lower level in the family room and lounge. The formal living and dining rooms, sharing a thru-fireplace, are located on the upper level.

Design 302846
2,341 Sq. Ft. - Main Level; 1,380 Sq. Ft. - Lower Level; 51,290 Cu. Ft.

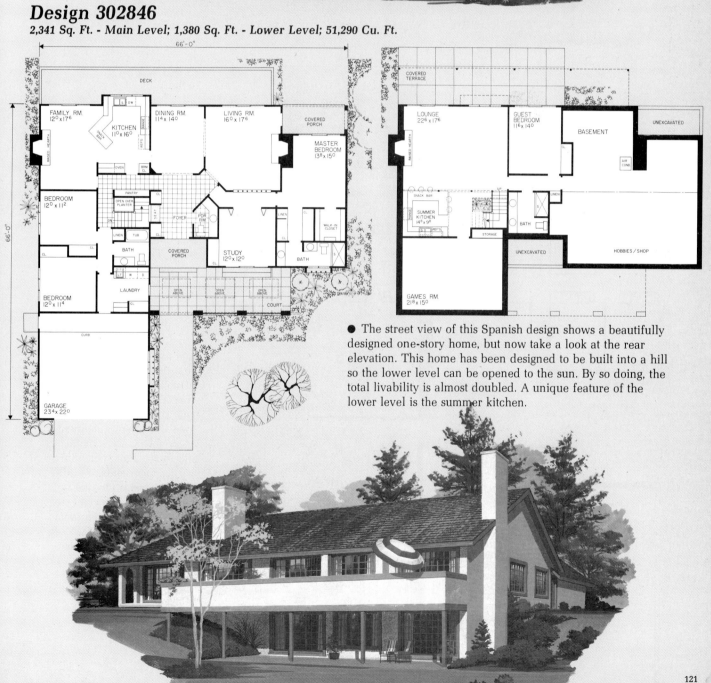

● The street view of this Spanish design shows a beautifully designed one-story home, but now take a look at the rear elevation. This home has been designed to be built into a hill so the lower level can be opened to the sun. By so doing, the total livability is almost doubled. A unique feature of the lower level is the summer kitchen.

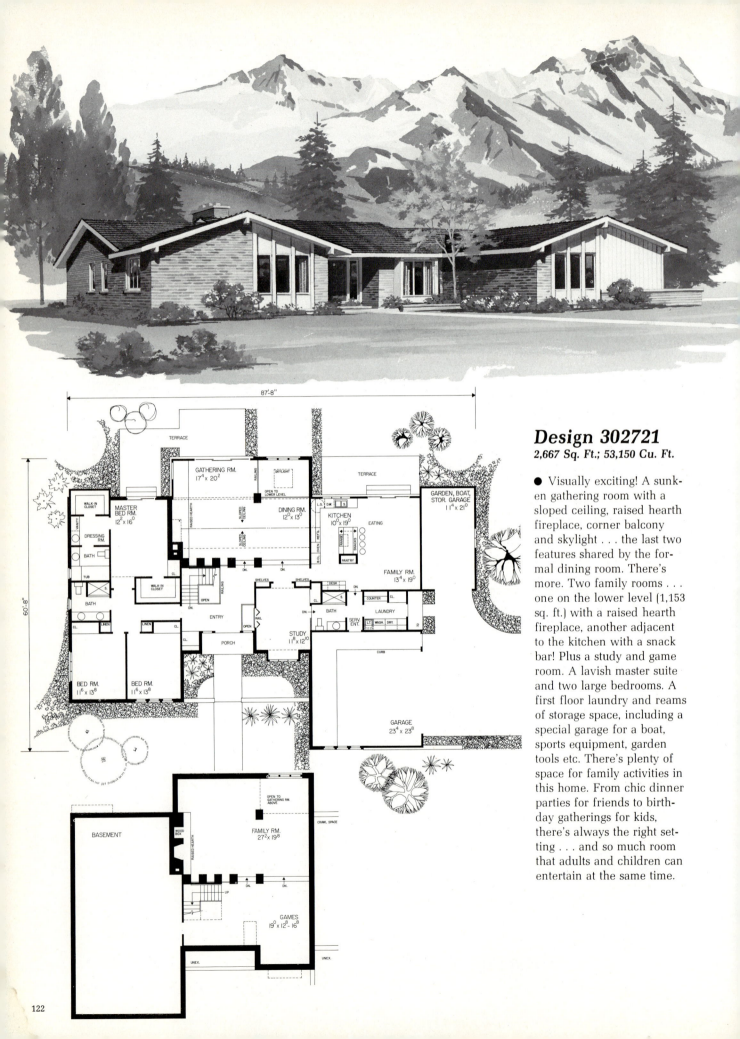

Design 302721
2,667 Sq. Ft.; 53,150 Cu. Ft.

● Visually exciting! A sunken gathering room with a sloped ceiling, raised hearth fireplace, corner balcony and skylight . . . the last two features shared by the formal dining room. There's more. Two family rooms . . . one on the lower level (1,153 sq. ft.) with a raised hearth fireplace, another adjacent to the kitchen with a snack bar! Plus a study and game room. A lavish master suite and two large bedrooms. A first floor laundry and reams of storage space, including a special garage for a boat, sports equipment, garden tools etc. There's plenty of space for family activities in this home. From chic dinner parties for friends to birthday gatherings for kids, there's always the right setting . . . and so much room that adults and children can entertain at the same time.

THE BUDGET SERIES . . . . *represents the publication of a representative*

group of Home Planners' designs in four different size categories. Generally, the smaller the house, the smaller the required building budget. And, conversely, the larger the house, the larger the required building budget. However, as we know, with varying and more expensive specifications the smaller of two houses can cost more to construct. This series of books is edited by square footage sizes. Since construction costs per square foot is an acceptable manner in which to estimate total costs, the low-budget book has the smaller houses; the unrestricted budget book the largest houses. Usually, the local building association can provide square footage costs.

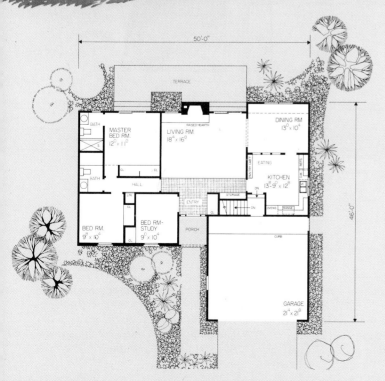

Design 302707 1,267 Sq. Ft.; 27,125 Cu. Ft.

● Here is a charming Early American adaptation that will serve as a picturesque and practical retirement home. Also, it will serve admirably those with a small family in search of an efficient, economically built home. The living area, highlighted by the raised hearth fireplace, is spacious. The kitchen features eating space and easy access to the garage and basement. The dining room is adjacent to the kitchen and views the rear yard. Then, there is the basement for recreation and hobby pursuits. The bedroom wing offers three bedrooms and two full baths. Don't miss the sliding doors to the terrace from the living room and the master bedroom. The storage units are plentiful including a pantry cabinet in the eating area of the kitchen.

THE LOW BUDGET HOME . . .

as featured in this book averages 1,505 sq. ft. This includes an 1,165 sq. ft. average for the one-story designs and an 1,812 average for two-stories. 1½-story and multi-level designs fall within this range. The small home will have appeal for the first time, entry-level buyer, the two-member family, as well as the retired couple. The small home offers efficient living patterns and does not require a large piece of property. In areas where land values are high this can be a significant consideration. As these designs can attest, the low budget home can be as delightful to look at as the larger home.

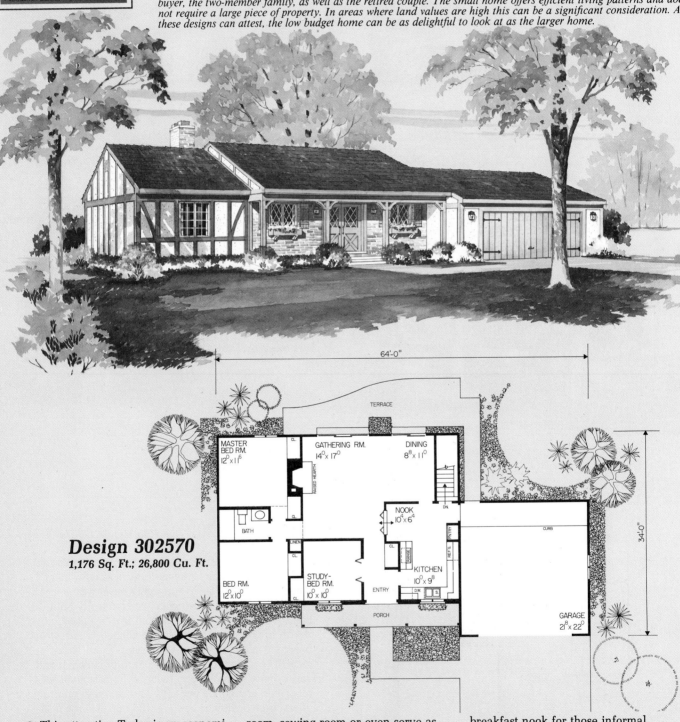

Design 302570

1,176 Sq. Ft.; 26,800 Cu. Ft.

● This attractive Tudor is an economically built design which will cater admirably to the living patterns of the retired couple. In addition to the two bedrooms this plan offers a study which could double ideally as a guest room, sewing room or even serve as the TV room. The living area is a spacious L-shaped zone for formal living and dining. The efficient kitchen is handy to the front door and overlooks the front yard. It features a convenient breakfast nook for those informal meals. Handy to the entry from the garage and the yard are the stairs to the basement. Don't overlook the attractive front porch and the window flower boxes.

124

Design 302505
1,366 Sq. Ft.; 29,329 Cu. Ft.

● This design offers you a choice of three distinctively different exteriors. Which is your favorite? Blueprints show details for all three optional elevations.

A study of the floor plan reveals a fine measure of livability. In less than 1,400 square feet there are features galore. An excellent return on your construction dollar. In addition to the two eating areas and the open planning of the gathering room, the indoor-outdoor relationships are of great interest. The basement may be developed for recreational activities.

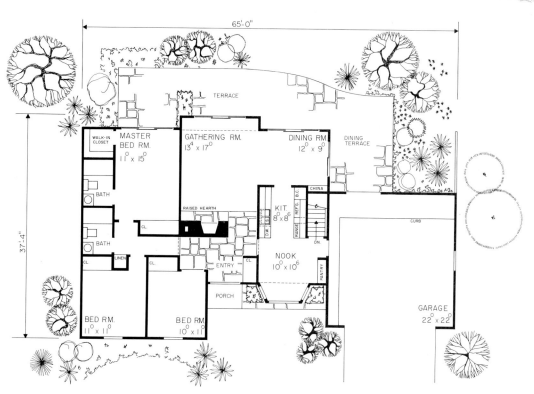

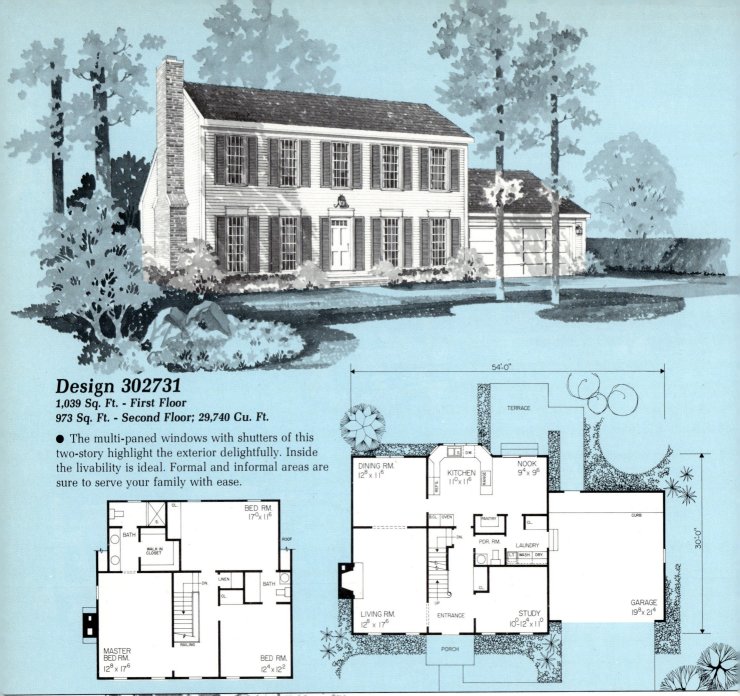

Design 302731

1,039 Sq. Ft. - First Floor
973 Sq. Ft. - Second Floor; 29,740 Cu. Ft.

● The multi-paned windows with shutters of this two-story highlight the exterior delightfully. Inside the livability is ideal. Formal and informal areas are sure to serve your family with ease.

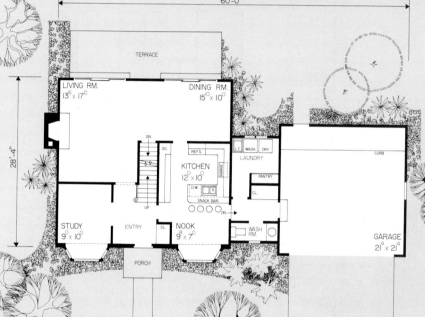

Design 302558

1,030 Sq. Ft. - First Floor
840 Sq. Ft. - Second Floor; 27,120 Cu. Ft.

● This relatively low-budget house is long on exterior appeal and interior livability. It has all the features to assure years of convenient living. Make a list of your favorite features.

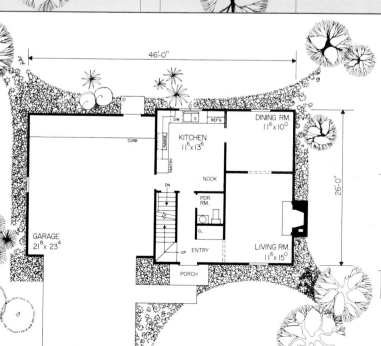

Design 302622

624 Sq. Ft. - First Floor
624 Sq. Ft. - Second Floor; 19,864 Cu. Ft.

● Appealing design can envelope little packages, too. Here is a charming, Early Colonial adaptation with an attached two-car garage to serve the young family with a modest building budget.

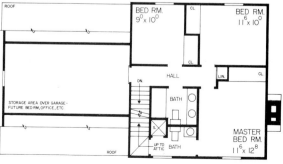

Design 301365
975 Sq. Ft. - First Floor
583 Sq. Ft. - Second Floor
20,922 Cu. Ft.

● This snug little story-and-a-half has three bedrooms, plus a study with built-in desk and bookshelves! It also has two baths, formal and informal dining areas, a good-sized living room and two-car garage.

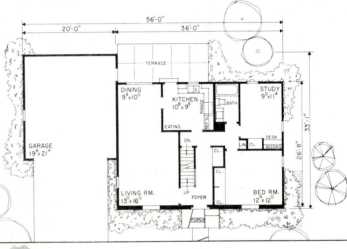

Design 301372
768 Sq. Ft. - First Floor
432 Sq. Ft. - Second Floor
17,280 Cu. Ft.

● Low cost livability could hardly ask for more. Here is an enchanting Colonial exterior and a four bedroom floor plan. Note stairs to basement and carport.

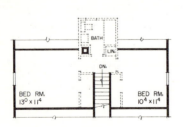

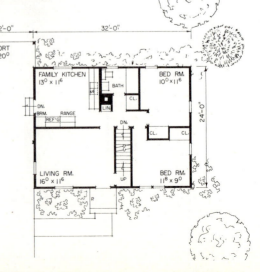

Design 303189
884 Sq. Ft. - First Floor
598 Sq. Ft. - Second Floor
18,746 Cu. Ft.

● Four bedrooms, two baths, a large kitchen/dining area, plenty of closets, a full basement and an attached two-car garage are among the highlights of this design. Note the uniqueness of the second floor.

Design 302162
741 Sq. Ft. - First Floor
504 Sq. Ft. - Second Floor
17,895 Cu. Ft.

● This economical design delivers great exterior appeal and fine livability. In addition to kitchen eating space there is a separate dining room.

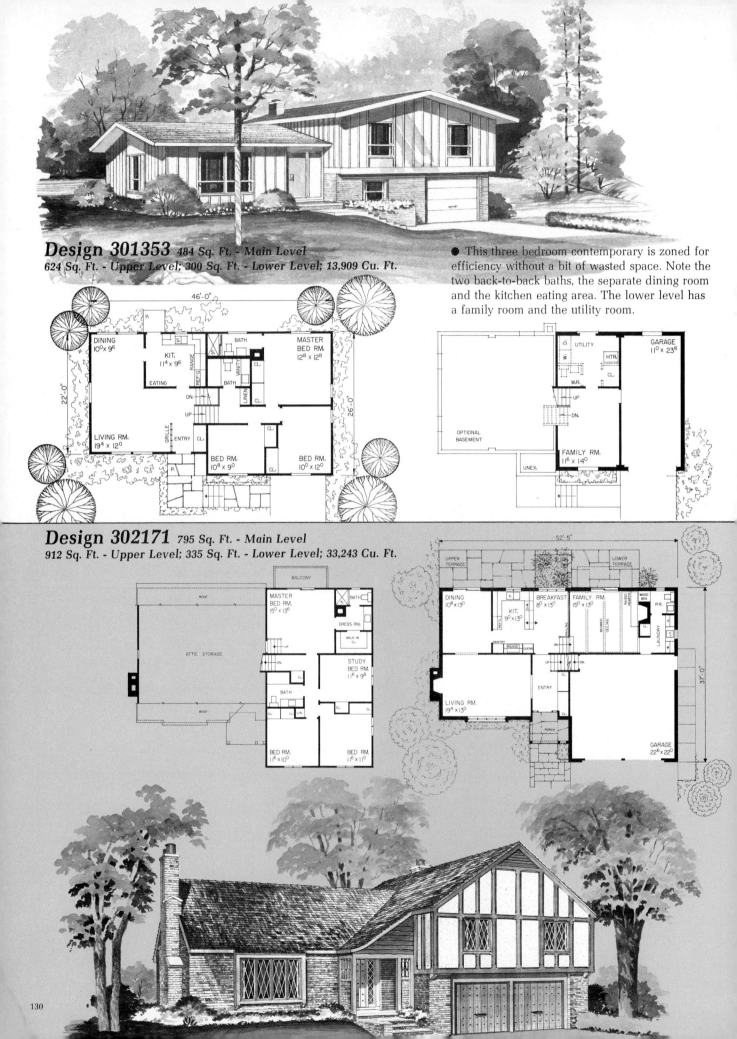

Design 301353
484 Sq. Ft. - Main Level
624 Sq. Ft. - Upper Level; 300 Sq. Ft. - Lower Level; 13,909 Cu. Ft.

● This three bedroom contemporary is zoned for efficiency without a bit of wasted space. Note the two back-to-back baths, the separate dining room and the kitchen eating area. The lower level has a family room and the utility room.

DINING 10⁰ x 9⁶
KIT. 11⁴ x 9⁶
EATING
BATH
MASTER BED RM. 12⁸ x 12⁸
LIVING RM. 19⁴ x 12⁰
ENTRY
BED RM. 10⁸ x 9⁰
BED RM. 10⁰ x 12⁰
46'-0"
22'-0"
26'-0"

UTILITY
GARAGE 11⁰ x 23⁸
HTR
OPTIONAL BASEMENT
FAMILY RM. 11⁶ x 14⁰
UNEX.

Design 302171
795 Sq. Ft. - Main Level
912 Sq. Ft. - Upper Level; 335 Sq. Ft. - Lower Level; 33,243 Cu. Ft.

BALCONY
MASTER BED RM. 15⁰ x 13⁶
BATH
DRESS. RM.
WALK-IN
ATTIC STORAGE
ROOF
STUDY BED RM. 11⁶ x 9⁸
BATH
BED RM. 11⁶ x 10⁰
BED RM. 11⁶ x 11⁰

52'-5"
UPPER TERRACE
LOWER TERRACE
DINING 10⁸ x 13⁰
KIT. 9⁰ x 13⁰
BREAKFAST 8⁰ x 13⁰
FAMILY RM. 15⁰ x 13⁰
WOOD BOX
PANTRY
RANGE
OVENS
LAUNDRY
LIVING RM. 19⁴ x 13⁰
ENTRY
PORCH
GARAGE 22⁶ x 22⁰
37'-0"

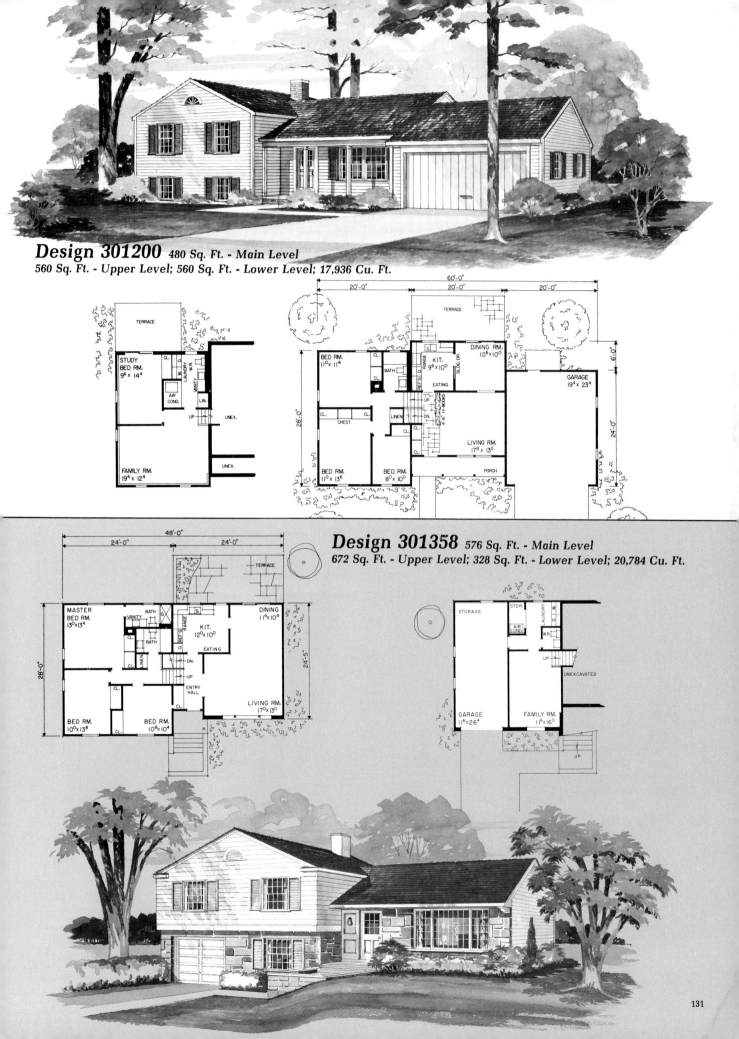

Design 301200 480 Sq. Ft. - Main Level
560 Sq. Ft. - Upper Level; 560 Sq. Ft. - Lower Level; 17,936 Cu. Ft.

Lower Level:
- TERRACE
- STUDY BED RM. 9⁶ x 14⁴
- W.R. / D / W / LAUNDRY / VANITY
- CL.
- AIR COND.
- LIN.
- UP
- UNEX.
- FAMILY RM. 19⁴ x 12⁴
- UNEX.

Main/Upper Level (60'-0" / 20'-0" / 20'-0" / 20'-0"):
- TERRACE
- BED RM. 11⁰ x 11⁴
- CL.
- BATH
- CL.
- DINING RM. 10⁶ x 10⁰
- S.
- REF'S. / RANGE
- KIT. 9⁶ x 10⁰
- SLDG. DR.
- EATING
- GARAGE 19⁴ x 23⁴
- 6'-0"
- 24'-0"
- 28'-0"
- CL. / CL. / CHEST
- LINEN
- CL.
- UP / DN.
- 4-6" HI BOOKS
- LIVING RM. 17⁸ x 13⁰
- BED RM. 11⁰ x 13⁶
- BED RM. 8⁰ x 10⁰
- PORCH

Design 301358 576 Sq. Ft. - Main Level
672 Sq. Ft. - Upper Level; 328 Sq. Ft. - Lower Level; 20,784 Cu. Ft.

Main Level (48'-0" / 24'-0" / 24'-0"):
- TERRACE
- MASTER BED RM. 13⁰ x 13⁴
- VANITY / BATH / S.
- CL.
- BATH
- RANGE / REF'G.
- KIT. 12⁰ x 10⁰
- S.
- DINING 11⁴ x 10⁴
- LINEN
- DN.
- CL. / UP
- ENTRY HALL
- LIVING RM. 17⁰ x 13⁰
- 24'-5"
- 28'-0"
- BED RM. 10⁰ x 13⁸
- CL.
- BED RM. 10⁸ x 10⁴
- CL.
- P.

Lower Level:
- STORAGE
- STOR.
- AIR COND.
- W / D / LAUNDRY
- W.R.
- UP
- UNEXCAVATED
- GARAGE 11⁶ x 26⁴
- FAMILY RM. 11⁶ x 16⁰
- UP

131

Design 301305 1,382 Sq. Ft.; 16,584 Cu. Ft.

● Order blueprints for any one of the three exteriors shown on these two pages and you will receive details for building this outstanding floor plan at the right. You'll find the appeal of these exteriors difficult to beat. As for the plan, in less than 1,400 square feet there are three bedrooms, two full baths, a separate dining room, a formal living room, a fine kitchen overlooking the rear yard and an informal family room. In addition, there is the attached two-car garage. Note the location of the stairs when this plan is built with a basement. Each of the exteriors is predominantly brick - the front of Design 301305 (above) features both stone and vertical boards and battens with brick on the other three sides. Observe the double front doors of Design 301382 (below) and the Contemporary design, 301383 (bottom). Study the window treatment.

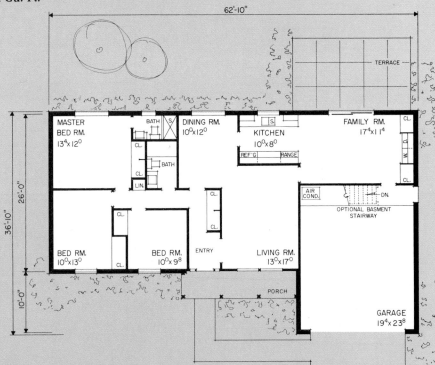

Design 301382
1,382 Sq. Ft.; 17,164 Cu. Ft.

Design 301383
1,382 Sq. Ft.; 15,448 Cu. Ft.

Design 301307 1,357 Sq. Ft.; 14,476 Cu. Ft.

● These three stylish exteriors have the same practical, L-shaped floor plan. Design 301307 (above) features a low-pitched, wide-overhanging roof, a pleasing use of horizontal siding and brick and an enclosed front flower court. Design 301380 (below) has its charm characterized by the pediment gables, the effective window treatment and the masses of brick. Design 301381 (bottom) is captivating because of its hip-roof, its dentils, panelled shutters and lamp post. Each of these three designs has a covered front porch. Inside, there is an abundance of livability. The formal living and dining area is spacious, and the U-shaped kitchen is efficient. There is informal eating space, a separate laundry and a fine family room. Note the sliding glass doors to the terrace. The blueprints include details for building either with or without a basement. Observe the pantry of the non-basement plan.

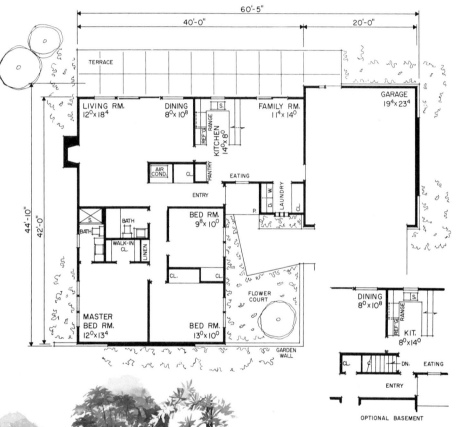

Design 301380
1,399 Sq. Ft.; 17,709 Cu. Ft.

Design 301381
1,399 Sq. Ft.; 17,937 Cu. Ft.

THE AFFORDABLE HOME . . . *is represented here by a selection*

of houses a step larger than those found in the prior section. The designs featured in the plan book average 2,052 square feet. They range from a 1,581 square foot average for the one-story houses to 2,261 for the two-stories and 2,381 for the multi-levels. As the square footage has increased, so has the amount of livability that each house delivers. This can be evidenced by the more frequent presence of the family room, additional bath facilities, the inclusion of breakfast rooms and separate dining rooms, and generally larger sized rooms. And, of course, more storage facilities become possible, too.

Design 302624

904 Sq. Ft. - Main Level; 1,120 Sq. Ft - Upper Level
404 Sq. Ft. - Lower Level; 39,885 Cu. Ft.

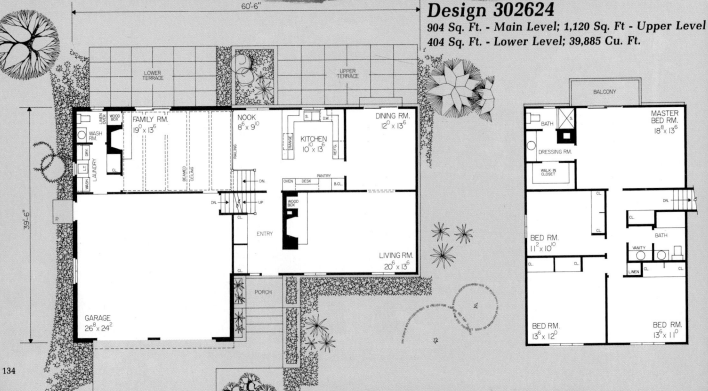

Design 302842
156 Sq. Ft. - Entrance Level; 1,038 Sq. Ft. - Upper Level
1,022 Sq. Ft. - Lower Level; 25,630 Cu. Ft.

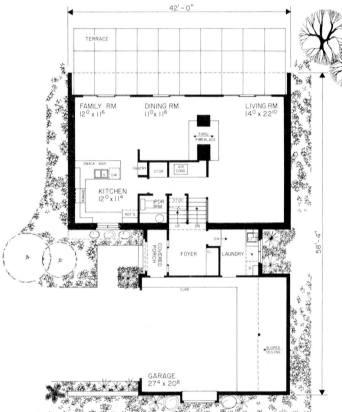

● This narrow, 42 foot width, house can be built on a narrow lot to cut down overall costs. Yet its dramatic appeal surely is worth a million. The projecting front garage creates a pleasing curved drive. One enters this house through the covered porch to the entrance level foyer. At this point the stairs lead down to the living area consisting of formal living room, family room, kitchen and dining area then up the stairs to the four bedroom-two bath sleeping area. The indoor-outdoor living relationship at the rear is outstanding.

Design 302596

1,489 Sq. Ft. - First Floor
982 Sq. Ft. - Second Floor; 38,800 Cu. Ft.

● Captivating as a New England village!
From the weathervane atop the garage
to the roofed side entry and paned windows, this home is perfectly detailed.

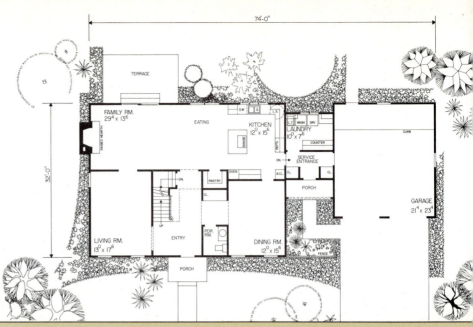

Design 302559

1,388 Sq. Ft. - First Floor
809 Sq. Ft. - Second Floor; 36,400 Cu. Ft.

● Imagine, a 26 foot living room
with fireplace, a quiet study with
built-in bookshelves and excellent
dining facilities. Within such an
appealing exterior, too.

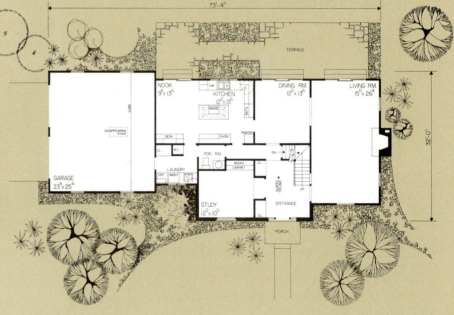

Design 302563

1,500 Sq. Ft. - First Floor
690 Sq. Ft. - Second Floor; 38,243 Cu. Ft.

● You'll have all kinds of fun deciding
just how your family will function in
this dramatically expanded half-house.
There is lots of attic storage, too.
Observe three-car garage.

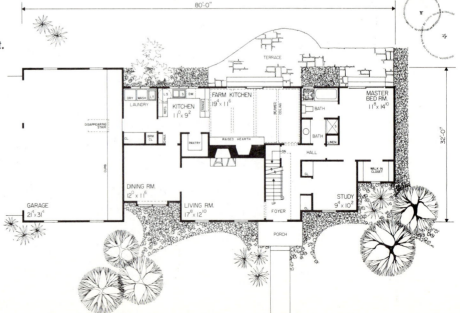

Design 302733 1,177 Sq. Ft. - First Floor; 1,003 Sq. Ft. - Second Floor; 32,040 Cu. Ft.

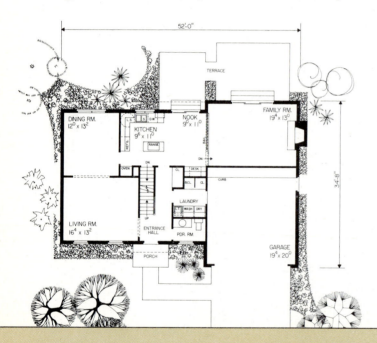

● This is definitely a four bedroom Colonial with charm galore. The kitchen features an island range and other built-ins. All will enjoy the sunken family room with fireplace, which has sliding glass doors leading to the terrace. Also a basement for recreational activities with laundry remaining on first floor for extra convenience.

● The appeal of this Colonial home will be virtually everlasting. It will improve with age and service the growing family well. Imagine your family living here. There are four bedrooms, 2½ baths, plus plenty of first floor living space.

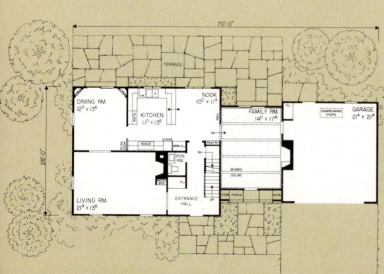

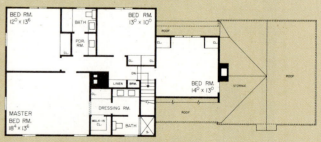

Design 302211
1,214 Sq. Ft. - First Floor
1,146 Sq. Ft. - Second Floor; 32,752 Cu. Ft.

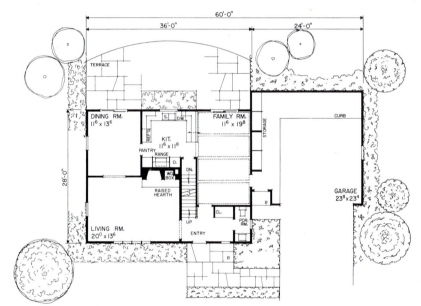

● A Garrison type adaptation that projects all the romance of yesteryear. The narrow horizontal siding, the wide corner boards, the window detailing, the overhanging second floor and the massive, centered chimney help set this home apart.

Design 301849 1,008 Sq. Ft. - First Floor
1,080 Sq. Ft. - Second Floor; 31,153 Cu. Ft.

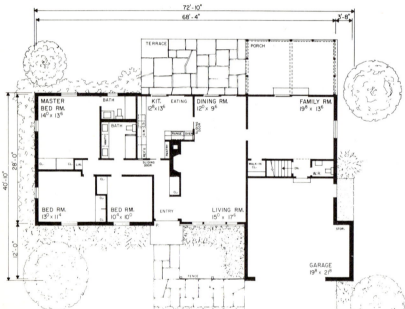

Design 301100
1,752 Sq. Ft.; 34,304 Cu. Ft.

● This modest sized, brick veneer home has a long list of things in its favor—from its appealing exterior to its feature-packed interior. All of the elements of its exterior complement each other to result in a symphony of attractive design features. The floor plan features three bedrooms, two full baths, an extra wash room, a family room, kitchen eating space, a formal dining area, two sets of sliding glass doors to the terrace and one set to the covered porch, built-in cooking equipment, a pantry and vanity with twin lavatories. Further, there is the living room fireplace, attached two-car garage with a bulk storage unit and a basement for extra storage and miscellaneous recreational activities. A fine investment.

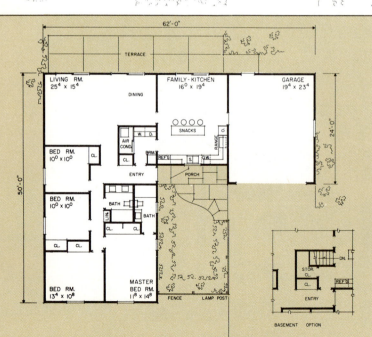

Design 301343
1,620 Sq. Ft.; 18,306 Cu. Ft.

● This is truly a prize-winner! The traditional, L-shaped exterior with its flower court and covered front porch is picturesque, indeed. The formal front entry routes traffic directly to the three distinctly zoned areas—the quiet sleeping area; the spacious; formal living and dining area; the efficient, informal family-kitchen. A closer look at the floor plan reveals four bedrooms, two full baths, good storage facilities, a fine snack bar and sliding glass doors to the rear terrace. The family-kitchen is ideally located. In addition to being but a few steps from both front and rear entrances, one will enjoy the view of both yards. Blueprints include basement and non-basement details.

Design 301896
1,690 Sq. Ft.; 19,435 Cu. Ft.

● Complete family livability is provided by this exceptional floor plan. Further, this design has a truly delightful traditional exterior. The fine layout features a center entrance hall with storage closet in addition to the wardrobe closet. Then, there is the formal, front living room and the adjacent, separate dining room. The U-shaped kitchen has plenty of counter and cupboard space. There is even a pantry. The family room functions with the kitchen and is but a step from the outdoor terrace. The mud room has space for storage and laundry equipment. The extra wash room is nearby. The large family will find those four bedrooms and two full baths just the answer to sleeping and bath accommodations.

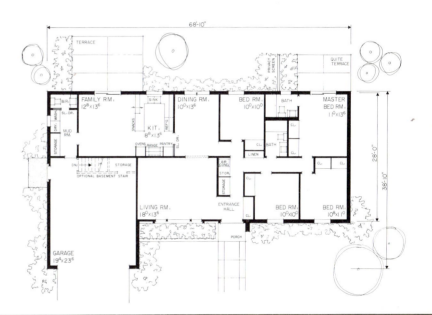

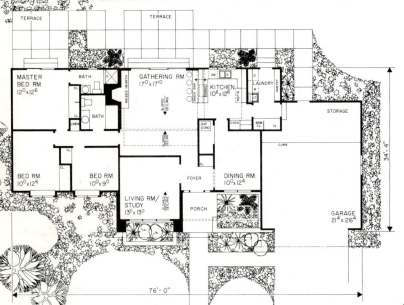

Design 302818
1,566 Sq. Ft.; 20,030 Cu. Ft.

● This is most certainly an outstanding contemporary design. Study the exterior carefully before your journey to inspect the floor plan. The vertical lines are carried from the siding to the paned windows to the garage door. An overhanging hip-roof protects the interior. The front entry is recessed so the overhanging roof creates a covered porch. Note the planter court with privacy wall. The floor plan is just as outstanding. The rear gathering room has a sloped ceiling, raised hearth fireplace, sliding glass doors to the terrace and a snack bar with pass-thru to the kitchen.

OPTIONAL BASEMENT PLAN

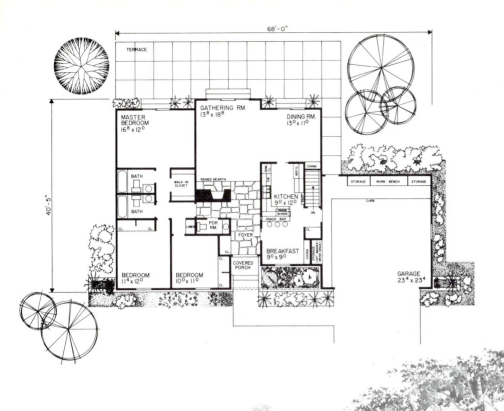

Design 302671
1,589 Sq. Ft.; 36,210 Cu. Ft.

● The rustic exterior of this one-story home features vertical wood siding. The entry foyer is floored with flagstone and leads to the three areas of the plan: sleeping, living and work center. The sleeping area has three bedrooms, the master bedroom has sliding glass doors to the rear terrace. The living area, consisting of gathering and dining rooms, also has access to the terrace. The work center is efficiently planned. It houses the kitchen with snack bar, breakfast room with built-in china cabinet and stairs to the basement. This is a very livable plan.

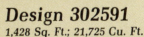

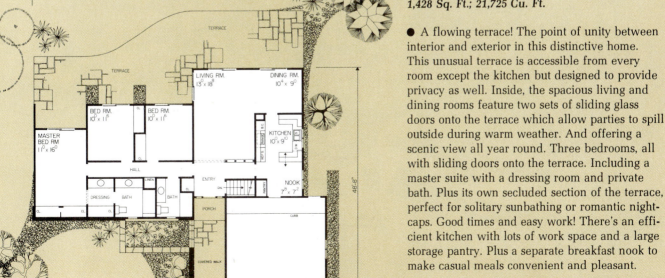

Design 302591
1,428 Sq. Ft.; 21,725 Cu. Ft.

● A flowing terrace! The point of unity between interior and exterior in this distinctive home. This unusual terrace is accessible from every room except the kitchen but designed to provide privacy as well. Inside, the spacious living and dining rooms feature two sets of sliding glass doors onto the terrace which allow parties to spill outside during warm weather. And offering a scenic view all year round. Three bedrooms, all with sliding doors onto the terrace. Including a master suite with a dressing room and private bath. Plus its own secluded section of the terrace, perfect for solitary sunbathing or romantic nightcaps. Good times and easy work! There's an efficient kitchen with lots of work space and a large storage pantry. Plus a separate breakfast nook to make casual meals convenient and pleasant.

143

THE EXPANDED BUDGET HOME . . . *delivers*

*most, if not all, of the amenities the active, growing family generally seeks to assure the joys of up-scale livability. Houses in this category of designs average 2,551 square feet with one-story plans averaging 2,069; two-stories, 2,735; and multi-levels, 2,825. These are sizes of houses where the breakfast room supports the formal dining room; the family room supplements the living room; the study/guest room complements the bedrooms. Further, these houses will have bigger laundries; often a powder room **and** a washroom; more spacious foyers and larger master bedrooms. Surely a house to deliver all the "needs" and most of the "wants".*

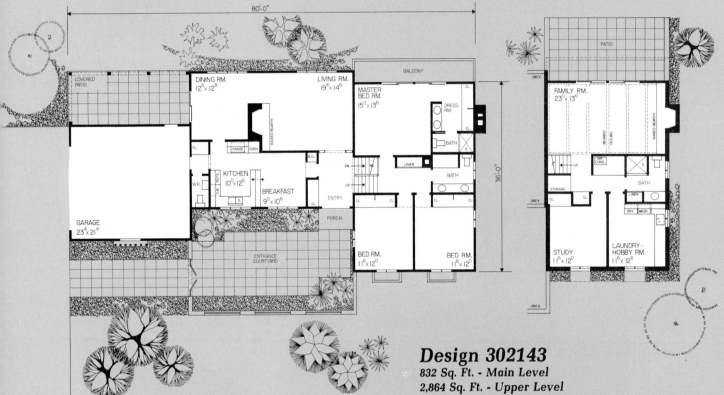

Design 302143

832 Sq. Ft. - Main Level
2,864 Sq. Ft. - Upper Level
864 Sq. Ft. - Lower Level; 27,473 Cu. Ft.

Design 302650
1,451 Sq. Ft. - First Floor
1,091 Sq. Ft. - Second Floor; 43,555 Cu. Ft.

● The rear view of this design is just as appealing as the front. The dormers and the covered porch with pillars is a charming way to introduce this house to the on-lookers. Inside, the appeal is also outstanding. Note the size (18 x 25) of the gathering room which is open to the dining room. Kitchen-nook area is very spacious and features an island range, built-in desk and more. It is a great convenience having the laundry in the service area which is close to the kitchen. Imagine, a fireplace in both the gathering room and the master bedroom! Make special note of the front and rear service entrances.

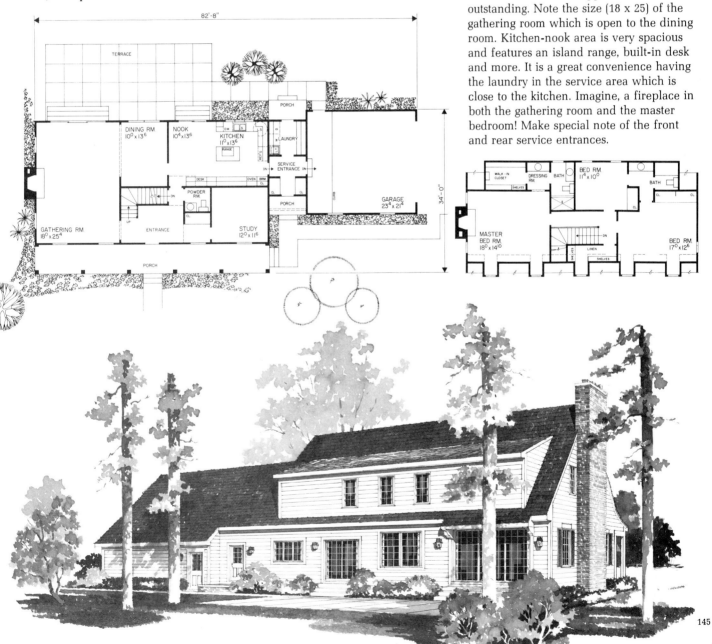

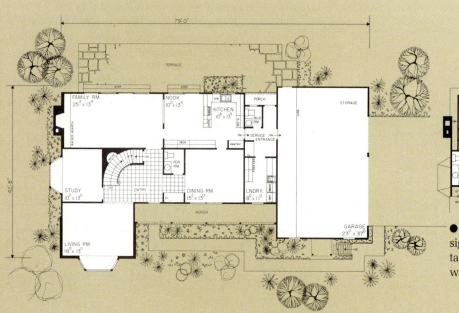

Design 302513
1,799 Sq. Ft. - First Floor
1,160 Sq. Ft. - Second Floor
47,461 Cu. Ft.

● What an appealing story-and-a-half design. Delightful, indeed, is the colonial detailing of the garage. The large entry hall with its open curving staircase is dramatic.

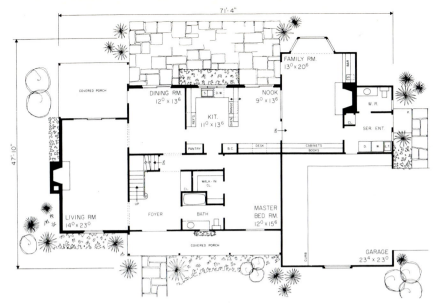

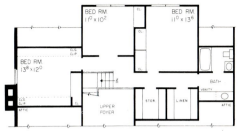

Design 302500
1,851 Sq. Ft. - First Floor
762 Sq. Ft. - Second Floor
43,052 Cu. Ft.

● The large family will enjoy the wonderful living patterns offered by this charming home. Don't miss the covered rear porch and the many features of the family room.

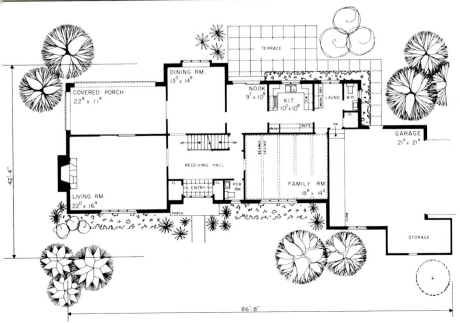

Design 302338
1,505 Sq. Ft. - First Floor
1,219 Sq. Ft. - Second Floor
38,878 Cu. Ft.

● A spacious receiving hall is a fine setting for the welcoming of guests. Here traffic flows effectively to all areas of the plan. Outstanding livability throughout the entire plan.

147

Design 302538

1,503 Sq. Ft. - First Floor
1,095 Sq. Ft. - Second Floor; 44,321 Cu. Ft.

● This Salt Box is charming, indeed. The livability it has to offer to the large and growing family is great. The entry is spacious and is open to the second floor balcony. For living areas, there is the study in addition to the living and family rooms.

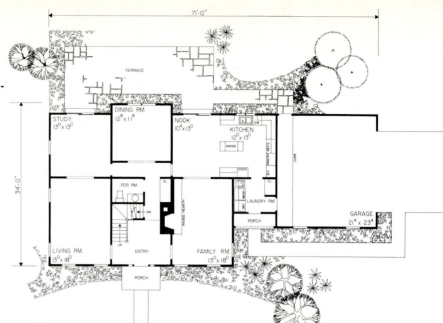

Design 302188

1,440 Sq. Ft. - First Floor
1,280 Sq. Ft. - Second Floor; 40,924 Cu. Ft.

● This design is characteristic of early America and its presence will create an atmosphere of that time in our heritage. However, it will be right at home wherever located. Along with exterior charm, this design has outstanding livability to offer its occupants.

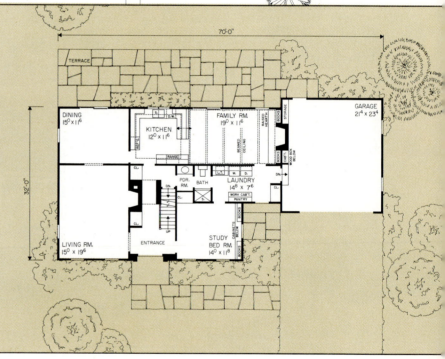

Design 302253

1,503 Sq. Ft. - First Floor
1,291 Sq. Ft. - Second Floor; 44,260 Cu. Ft.

● The overhanging second floor sets the character of this Early American design. Study the features, both inside and out.

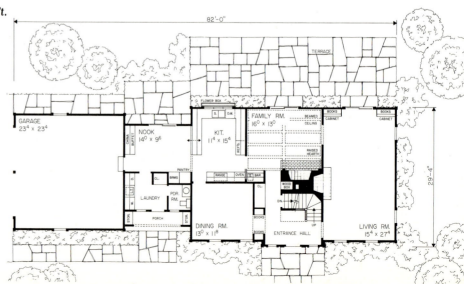

148

Design 302594
2,294 Sq. Ft.; 42,120 Cu. Ft.

● A spectacular foyer! It is fully 21'
long and offers double entry to the
heart of this home. Other highlights include a 21' by 21' gathering room complete with sloped ceiling, raised hearth
fireplace and sliding glass doors.
There's a formal dining room, too. Plus
a well-located study which insures
space for solitude or undisturbed work.
The kitchen features a snack bar and a
breakfast nook with another set of sliding doors. For more convenience, a
pantry and first-floor laundry. In the
master suite, a dressing room with entry
to the bath, four closets and sliding
doors onto the terrace! Two more bedrooms if you wish to convert the study
or one easily large enough for two children with a dressing area and private
entry to the second bath.

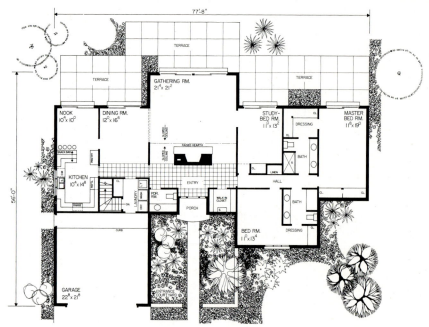

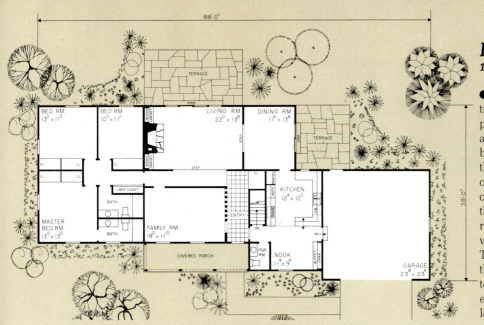

Design 302360
1,936 Sq. Ft.; 37,026 Cu. Ft.

● The charming characteristics of this traditional one-story are many. Fine proportion and pleasing lines assure a long and rewarding study. A list of them may begin with the fine window treatment, the covered front porch with its stolid columns, the raised panelled door, the carriage lamp, the horizontal siding, and the cupola. Inside, the family's everyday routine will enjoy all the facilities which will surely guarantee pleasurable living. The formal rear sunken living room and the dining room function with their own terraces. A 3½ foot high wall with turned wood posts on top separate the excellent family room from the entry hall.

Design 302867
2,388 Sq. Ft.; 49,535 Cu. Ft.

● A live-in relative would be very comfortable in this home. This design features a self-contained suite (473 sq. ft.) consisting of a bedroom, bath, living room and kitchenette with dining area. This suite is nestled behind the garage away from the main areas of the house. The rest of this traditional one-story house faced with fieldstone and vertical wood siding is also very livable. One whole wing houses the four family bedrooms and bath facilities. The center of the plan has a front U-shaped kitchen and breakfast room. Formal dining room and large gathering room will enjoy the view of the backyard. The large rear covered porch will receive much use.

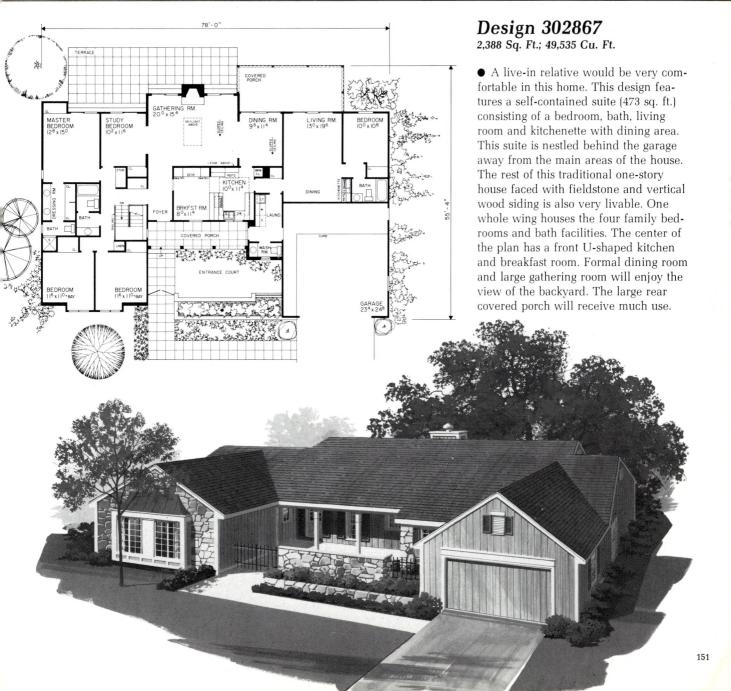

Design 302123
1,624 Sq. Ft. - First Floor
1,335 Sq. Ft. - Second Floor; 42,728 Cu. Ft.

● Inside there is close to 3,000 square feet of uniquely planned floor area. The spacious, well-lighted entry has, of course, a high sloping ceiling. A second floor balcony looks down from above. This area features two walk-in closets. Between the dining and living rooms is a thru fireplace which may be enjoyed from either room. Between the garage and the family room is the laundry and the compartmented powder room. The second floor ceilings slope and, consequently, add to the feeling of spaciousness.

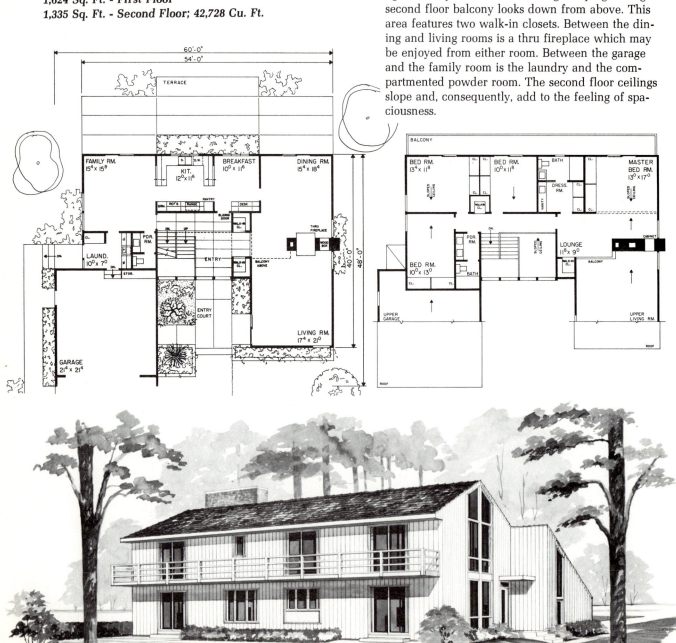

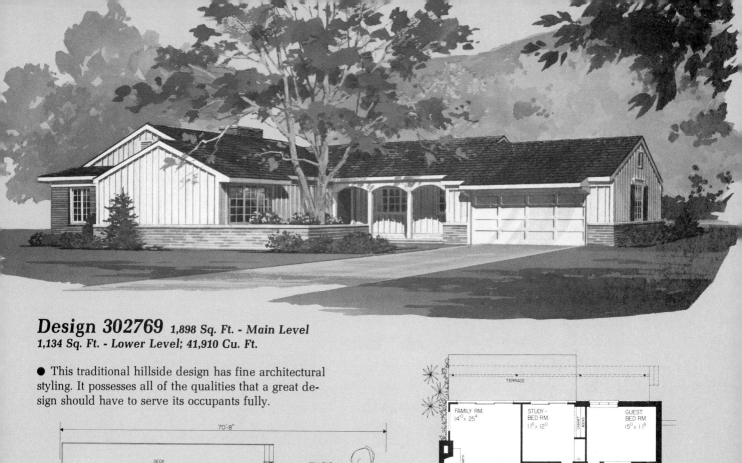

Design 302769 1,898 Sq. Ft. - Main Level
1,134 Sq. Ft. - Lower Level; 41,910 Cu. Ft.

● This traditional hillside design has fine architectural styling. It possesses all of the qualities that a great design should have to serve its occupants fully.

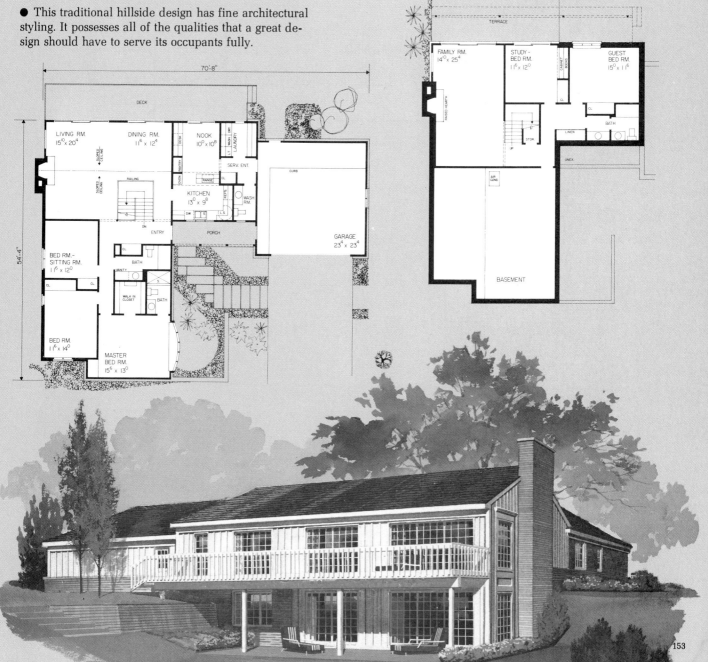

153

THE UNLIMITED BUDGET HOME . . . will ap-

peal to those with large families, maybe live-in relatives; those with large building sites, and the desire and where-withal to satisfy all the family needs, plus all of their wants. Since budgetary restrictions are not a factor, the econo-mies of simple, rectangular construction need not be employed. This results in a variety of floor plan configurations which give birth to unique exteriors and appealing indoor-outdoor living relationships. Functional terraces, court-yards, covered porches, decks and balconies help assure the utmost in outdoor fun. A study of this sampling of houses reveals what luxurious living can be like.

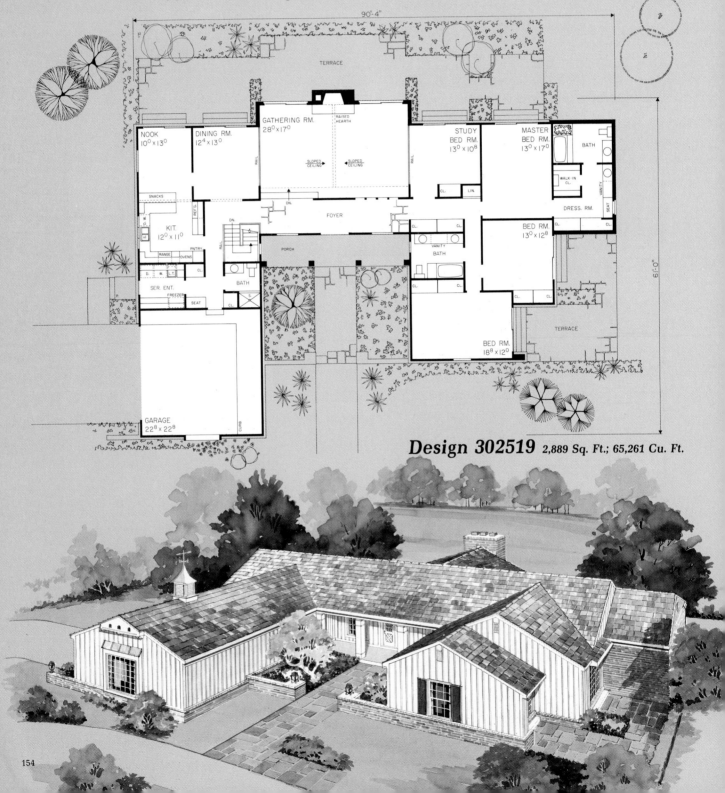

Design 302519 2,889 Sq. Ft.; 65,261 Cu. Ft.

Design 302779 3,225 Sq. Ft.; 70,715 Cu. Ft.

● This French design is surely impressive. The exterior appearance will brighten any area with its French roof, paned-glass windows, masonry brick privacy wall and double front doors. The inside is just as appealing. Note the unique placement of rooms and features. Enter this home into the entry hall. It is large and leads to each of the areas in this plan. To the left, the formal dining room is outstanding. While serving a formal dinner one can enter by way of the butler's pantry (notice it's size and that it has a sink). To the right of the entry is a sizable parlor and beyond that is the three bedroom sleeping area. The gathering room with fireplace, sliding glass doors and adjacent study is in the back of the plan. The work center is also outstanding. There is the U-shaped kitchen, island range, snack bar, breakfast nook, pantry plus washroom and large laundry near service entrance.

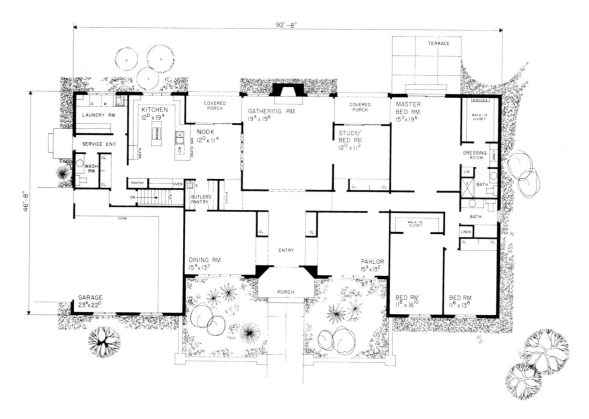

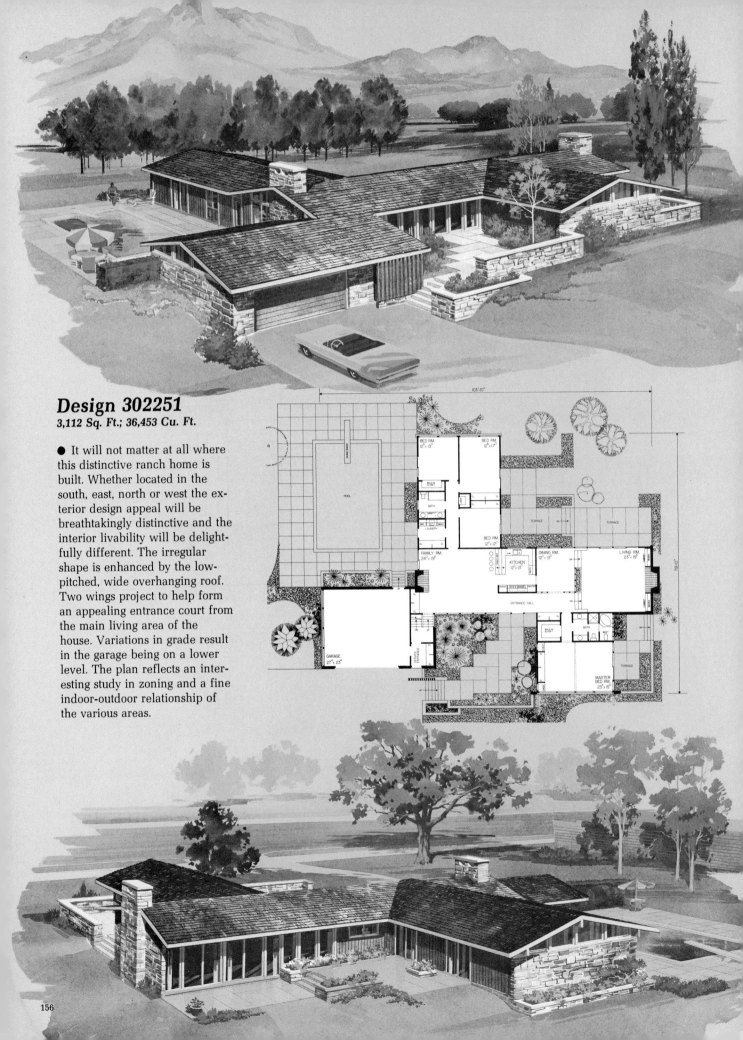

Design 302251
3,112 Sq. Ft.; 36,453 Cu. Ft.

● It will not matter at all where this distinctive ranch home is built. Whether located in the south, east, north or west the exterior design appeal will be breathtakingly distinctive and the interior livability will be delightfully different. The irregular shape is enhanced by the low-pitched, wide overhanging roof. Two wings project to help form an appealing entrance court from the main living area of the house. Variations in grade result in the garage being on a lower level. The plan reflects an interesting study in zoning and a fine indoor-outdoor relationship of the various areas.

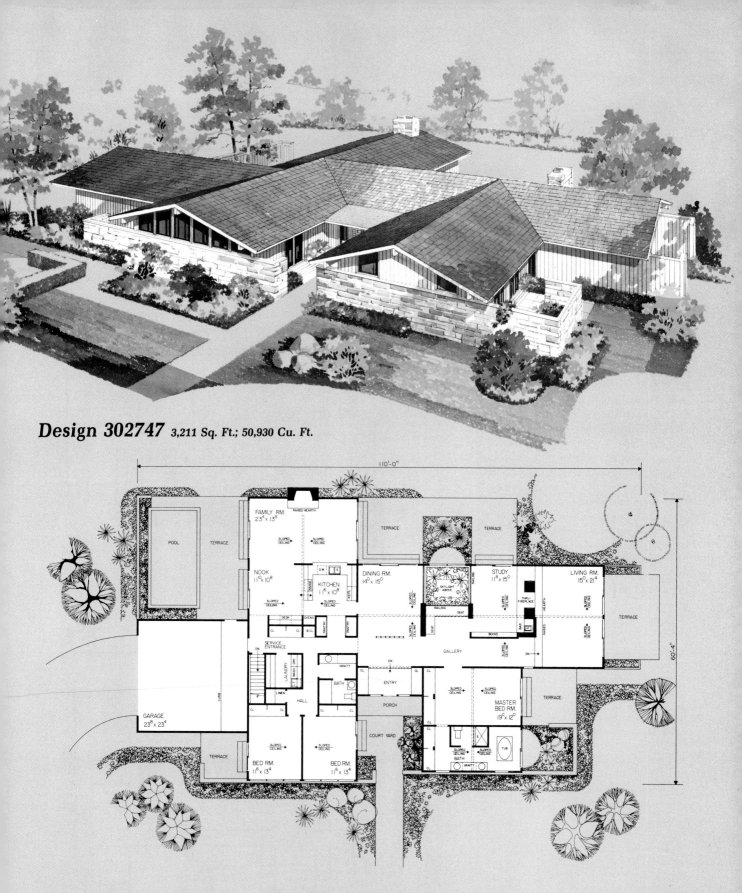

Design 302747 3,211 Sq. Ft.; 50,930 Cu. Ft.

● This home will provide its occupants with a glorious adventure in contemporary living. Its impressive exterior seems to foretell that great things are in store for even the most casual visitor. A study of the plan reveals a careful zoning for both the younger and older family members. The quiet area consists of the exceptional master bedroom suite with private terrace, the study and the isolated living room. For the younger generation, there is a zone with two bedrooms, family room and nearby pool. The kitchen is handy and serves the nook and family rooms with ease. Be sure not to miss the sloping ceilings, the dramatic planter and the functional terrace.

Design 302766
2,711 Sq. Ft.; 59,240 Cu. Ft.

● A sizeable master bedroom with a dressing area featuring two walk-in closets, a twin lavatory and compartmented bath. Two-bedroom children's area with full bath and supporting study. Formal living and dining zone separated by a thru-fireplace. A spacious kitchen-nook with a cheerfully informal sun room just a step away through sliding glass doors. The service area has a laundry, storage, wash room and stairs to basement. An array of sliding glass doors leading to outdoor living on the various functional terraces. These are but some of the highlights of this appealing L-shaped traditional. Be sure to note the large number of sizeable closets for a variety of uses.

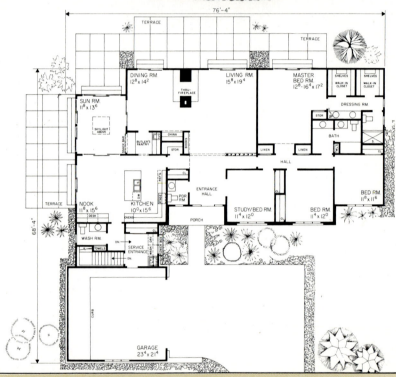

Design 302778
2,761 Sq. Ft.; 41,145 Cu. Ft.

● No matter what the occasion, family and friends alike will enjoy the sizeable gathering room. A spacious 20' x 23', this room has a thru fireplace to the study and two sets of sliding glass doors to the large rear terrace. Indoor-outdoor living can also be enjoyed from the dining room, study and master bedroom. There is also a covered porch accessible through sliding glass doors in the dining room and breakfast nook.

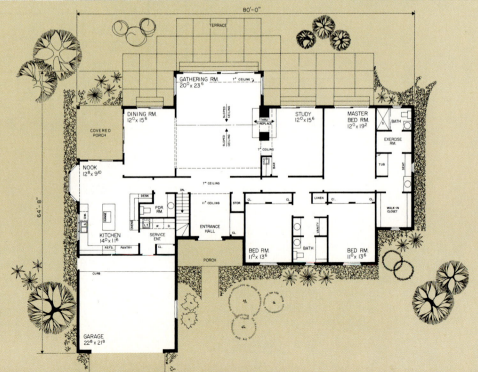

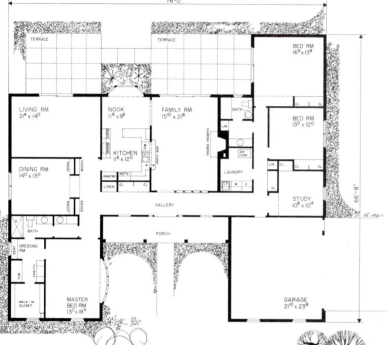

Design 302784
2,980 Sq. Ft.; 41,580 Cu. Ft.

● The projection of the master bedroom and garage create an inviting U-shaped area leading to the covered porch of this delightful traditionally styled design. After entering through the double front doors, the gallery will lead to each of the three living areas: the sleeping wing of two bedrooms, full bath and study; the informal area of the family room with raised hearth fireplace and sliding glass doors to the terrace and the kitchen/nook area (the kitchen has a pass-thru snack bar to the family room); and the formal area consisting of a separate dining room with built-in china cabinets and the living room. Note the privacy of the master bedroom.

Design 301228 2,583 Sq. Ft. - First Floor; 697 Sq. Ft. - Second Floor; 51,429 Cu. Ft.

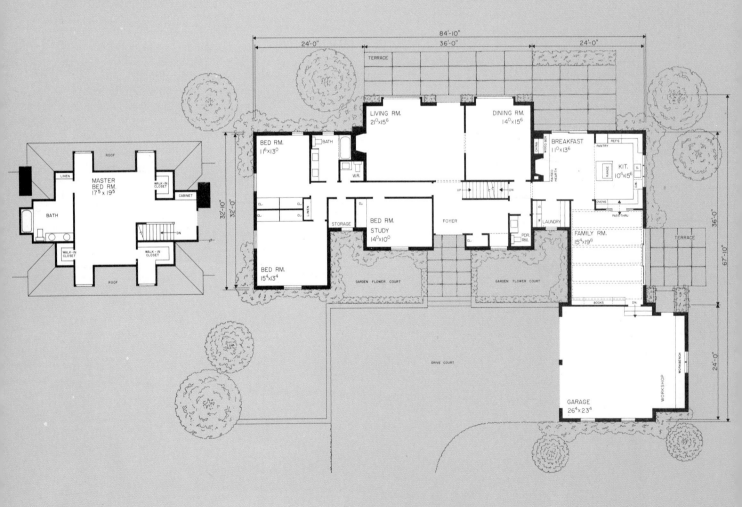

● This beautiful house has a wealth of detail taken from the rich traditions of French Regency design. The roof itself is a study in pleasant dormers and the hips and valleys of a big flowing area. A close examination of the plan shows the careful arrangement of space for privacy as well as good circulation of traffic. The spacious formal entrance hall sets the stage for good zoning. The informal living area is highlighted by the updated version of the old country kitchen. Observe the fireplace, and the barbecue. While there is a half-story devoted to the master bedroom suite, this home functions more as a one-story country estate design than as a 1½ story.

Design 302543

2,345 Sq. Ft. - First Floor
1,687 Sq. Ft. - Second Floor; 76,000 Cu. Ft.

● Certainly a dramatic French adaptation highlighted by effective window treatment, delicate cornice detailing, appealing brick quoins and excellent proportion. Stepping through the double front doors the drama is heightened by the spacious entry hall with its two curving staircases to the second floor. The upper hall is open and looks down to the hall below. There is a study and a big gathering room which look out on the raised terrace. The work center is outstanding. The garage will accommodate three cars.

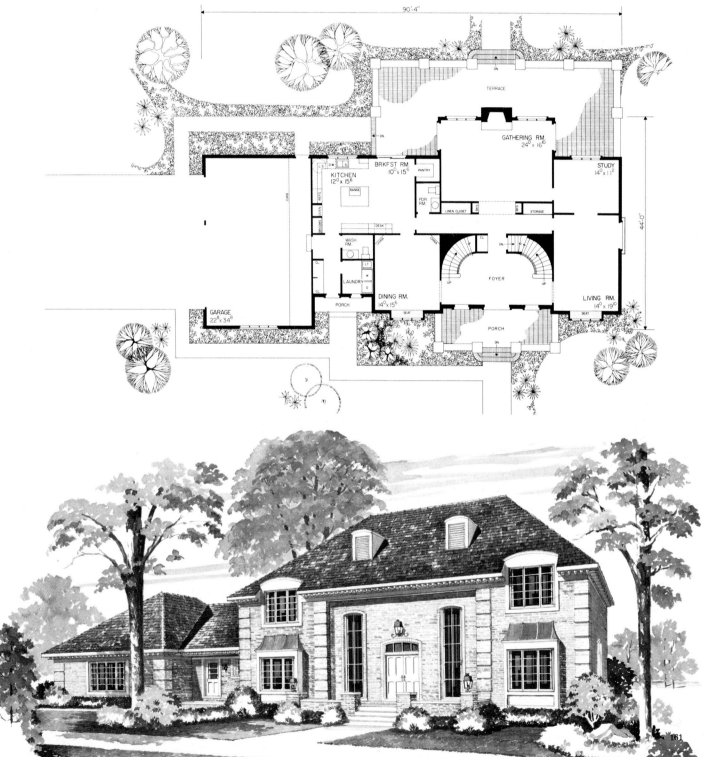

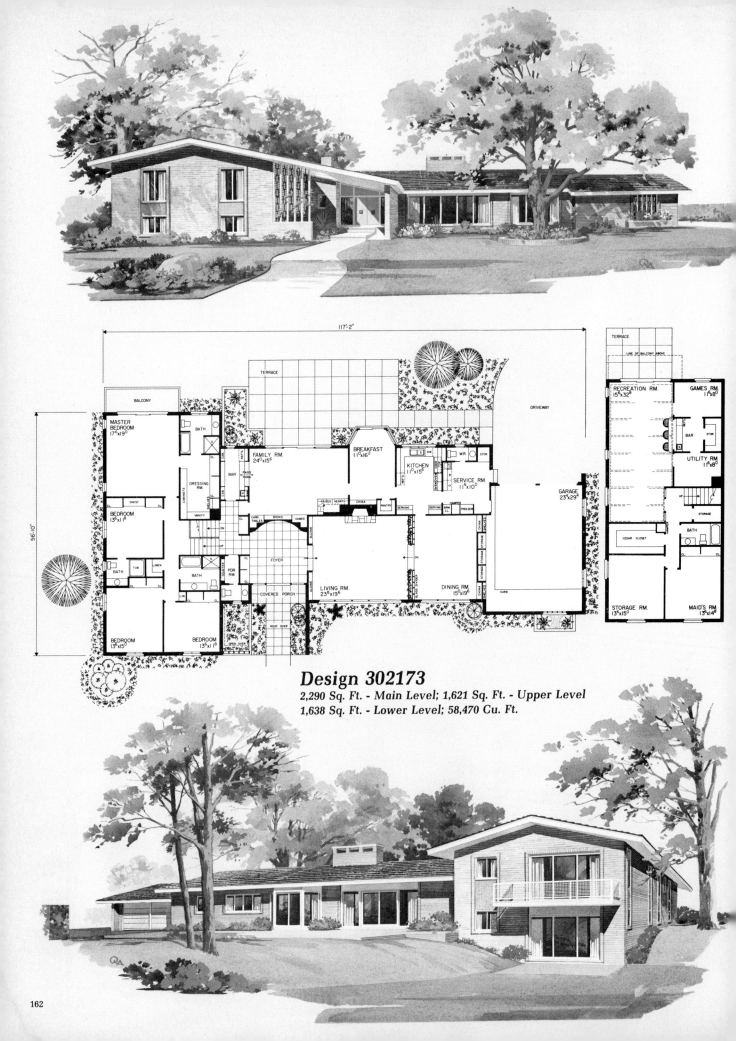

Design 302173

2,290 Sq. Ft. - Main Level; 1,621 Sq. Ft. - Upper Level
1,638 Sq. Ft. - Lower Level; 58,470 Cu. Ft.

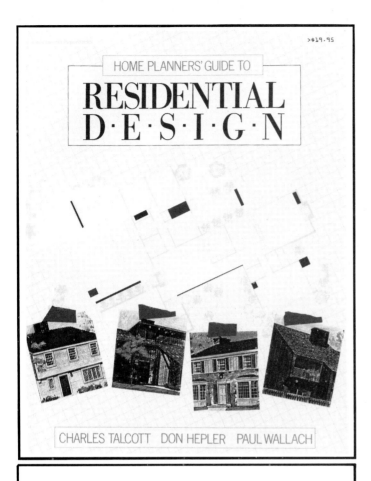

Contents

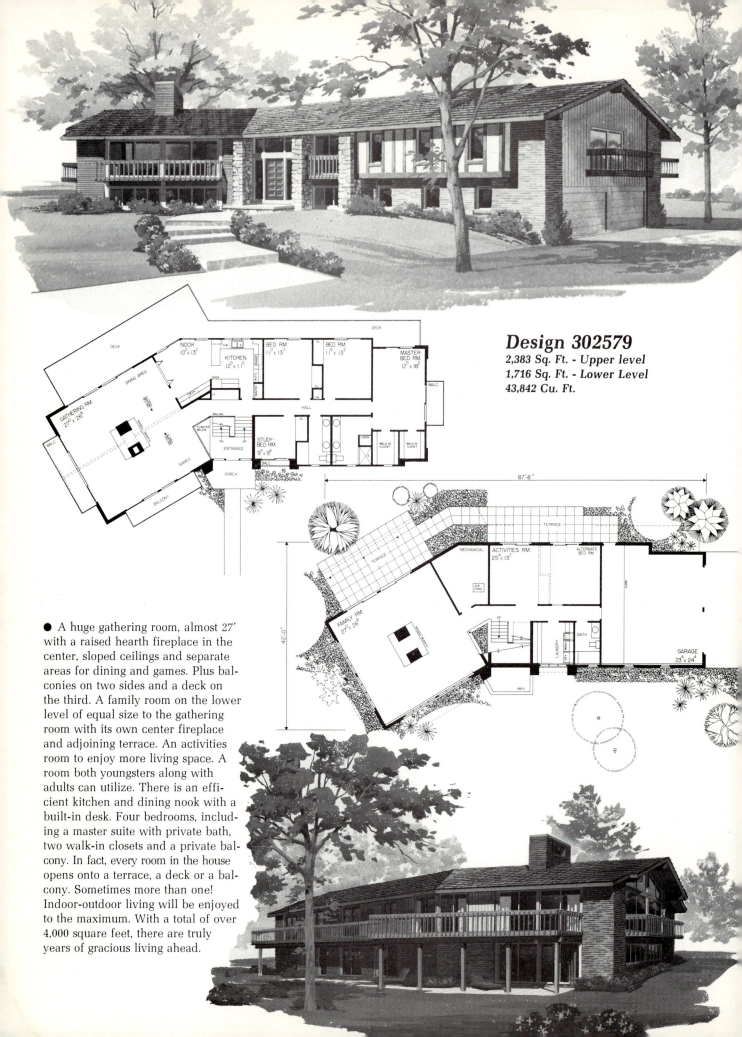

Design 302579
2,383 Sq. Ft. - Upper level
1,716 Sq. Ft. - Lower Level
43,842 Cu. Ft.

● A huge gathering room, almost 27'
with a raised hearth fireplace in the
center, sloped ceilings and separate
areas for dining and games. Plus balconies on two sides and a deck on
the third. A family room on the lower
level of equal size to the gathering
room with its own center fireplace
and adjoining terrace. An activities
room to enjoy more living space. A
room both youngsters along with
adults can utilize. There is an efficient kitchen and dining nook with a
built-in desk. Four bedrooms, including a master suite with private bath,
two walk-in closets and a private balcony. In fact, every room in the house
opens onto a terrace, a deck or a balcony. Sometimes more than one!
Indoor-outdoor living will be enjoyed
to the maximum. With a total of over
4,000 square feet, there are truly
years of gracious living ahead.

All The "TOOLS" You And Your Builder Need

. . . to, first select an exterior and a floor plan for your new house that satisfy your tastes and your family's living patterns . . .

. . . then, to review the blueprints in great detail and obtain a construction cost figure . . . also, to price out the structural materials required to build . . . and, finally, to review and decide upon the specifications to which your home is to be built. Truly, an invaluable set of "tools" to launch your home planning and building programs.

1. THE PLAN BOOKS

Home Planners' unique Design Category Series makes it easy to look at and study only the types of designs for which you and your family have an interest. Each of six plan books features a specific type of home, namely: Two-Story, 1½ Story, One-Story Over 2000 Sq. Ft., One-Story Under 2000 Sq. Ft., Multi-Levels and Vacation Homes. In addition to the convenient Design Category Series, there is an impressive selection of other current titles. While the home plans featured in these books are also to be found in the Design Category Series, they, too, are edited for those with special tastes and requirements. Your family will spend many enjoyable hours reviewing the delightfully designed exteriors and the practical floor plans. Surely your home or office library should include a selection of these popular plan books. Your complete satisfaction is guaranteed.

2. THE CONSTRUCTION BLUEPRINTS

There are blueprints available for each of the designs published in Home Planners' current plan books. Depending upon the size, the style and the type of home, each set of blueprints consists of from five to ten large sheets. Only by studying the blueprints is it possible to give complete and final consideration to the proper selection of a design for your next home. The blueprints provide the opportunity for all family members to familiarize themselves with the features of all exterior elevations, interior elevations and details, all dimensions, special built-in features and effects. They also provide a full understanding of the materials to be used and/or selected. The low-cost of our blueprints makes it possible and indeed, practical, to study in detail a number of different sets of blueprints before deciding upon which design to build.

3. THE MATERIALS LIST

A list of materials is an integral part of the plan package. It comprises the last sheet of each set of blueprints and serves as a handy reference during the period of construction. Of course, at the pricing and the material ordering stages, it is indispensable.

4. THE SPECIFICATION OUTLINE

Each order for blueprints is accompanied by one Specification Outline. You and your builder will find this a time-saving tool when deciding upon your own individual specifications. An important reference document should you wish to write your own specifications.

The Design Category Series

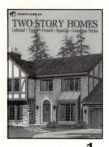

1.

360 TWO STORY HOMES

English Tudors, Early American Salt Boxes, Gambrels, Farmhouses, Southern Colonials, Georgians, French Mansards, Contemporaries. Interesting floor plans for both small and large families. Efficient kitchens, 2 to 6 bedrooms, family rooms, libraries, extra baths, mud rooms. Homes for all budgets.
288 Pages, $6.95

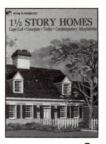

2.

150 1½ STORY HOMES

Cape Cod, Williamsburg, Georgian, Tudor and Contemporary versions. Low budget and country-estate feature sections. Expandable family plans. Formal and informal living and dining areas along with gathering rooms. Spacious, country kitchens. Indoor-outdoor livability with covered porches and functional terraces.
128 Pages, $3.95

3.

210 ONE STORY HOMES OVER 2,000 Sq. Ft.

All popular styles. Including Spanish, Western, Tudor, French, and other traditional versions. Contemporaries Gracious, family living patterns. Sunken living rooms, master bedroom suites, atriums, courtyards, pools. Fine indoor-outdoor living relationships. For modest to country-estate budgets.
192 Pages, $4.95

4.

315 ONE STORY HOMES UNDER 2,000 Sq. Ft.

A great selection of traditional and contemporary exteriors for medium and restricted budgets. Efficient, practical floor plans. Gathering rooms, formal and informal living and dining rooms, mud rooms, indoor-outdoor livability. Economically built homes. Designs with bonus space livability for growing families.
192 Pages, $4.95

5.

215 MULTI-LEVEL HOMES

For new dimensions in family living. A captivating variety of exterior styles, exciting floor plans for flat and sloping sites. Exposed lower levels. Balconies, decks. Plans for the active family. Upper level lounges, excellent bath facilities. Sloping ceilings. Functional outdoor terraces. For all building budgets.
192 Pages, $4.95

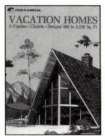

6.

223 VACATION HOMES

Features A-Frames, Chalets, Hexagons, economical rectangles. One and two stories plus multi-levels. Lodges for year 'round livability. From 480 to 3238 sq. ft. Cottages sleeping 2 to 22. For flat or sloping sites. Spacious, open planning. Over 600 illustrations. 120 Pages in full color. Cluster homes selection. For lakeshore or woodland leisure living.
176 Pages, $4.95

The Exterior Style Series

7.

120 EARLY AMERICAN PLANS

and Other Colonial Adaptations is an outstanding and unique plan book for the home and professional library. Devoted exclusively to Early American architectural interpretations adapted for today's living patterns. Exquisitely detailed exteriors retain all the charm of a proud heritage. One-story, 1½ and two-story and multi-level designs for varying budgets.
112 Pages, $2.95

8.

125 CONTEMPORARY HOME PLANS

Here is an exciting book featuring a wide variety of home designs for the 1980's and far beyond. The exteriors of these delightfully illustrated houses are refreshing with their practical and progressive "new look". The floor plans offer new dimensions in living highlighting such features as gathering rooms, cathedral ceilings and interior balconies. House designs of all sizes.
112 Pages, $2.95

9.

135 ENGLISH TUDOR HOMES

and other Popular Family Plans is a favorite of many. The current popularity of the English Tudor home design is phenomenal. Here is a book which is loaded with Tudors for all budgets. There are one-story, 1½ and two-story designs, plus multi-levels and hillsides from 1,176 to 3,849 sq. ft. There is a special 20 page section of Early American Adaptations.
104 Pages, $2.95

The Budget Series

11.

175 LOW BUDGET HOMES

A special selection of home designs for the modest or restricted building budget. An excellent variety of Traditional and Contemporary designs. One-story, 1½ and two-story and split-level homes. Three, four and five bedrooms. Family rooms, extra baths, formal and informal dining rooms. Basement and non-basement designs. Attached garages and covered porches.
96 Pages, $2.95

12.

165 AFFORDABLE HOME PLANS

This outstanding book was specially edited with a wide selection of houses and plans for those with a medium building budget. While none of these designs are considered low-cost; neither do they require an unlimited budget to build. Square footages range from 1,428. Exteriors of Tudor, French, Early American, Spanish and Contemporary are included.
112 Pages, $2.95

13.

142 HOME DESIGNS FOR EXPANDED BUILDING BUDGETS

A family's ability to finance and need for a larger home grows as its size and income increases. This selection highlights designs which house an average square footage of 2,551. One-story plans average 2,069; two-stories, 2,735; multi-levels, 2,825. Spacious homes featuring raised hearth fireplaces, open planning and efficient kitchens.
112 Pages, $2.75

The Full Color Series

116 TRADITIONAL and CONTEMPORARY PLANS

A beautifully illustrated home plan book in complete, full color. One, 1½, two-story and split-level designs featured in all of the most popular exterior styles. Varied building budgets will be satisfied by the numerous plans for all budget sizes. Designs for flat and hillside sites, including exposed lower levels. It will make an ideal gift item.

14.

96 Pages in Full Color, $5.95

122 HOME DESIGNS

This book has full color throughout. More than 120 eye-pleasing, colored illustrations. Tudor, French, Spanish, Early American and Contemporary exteriors featuring all design types. The interiors house efficient, step-saving floor plans. Formal and informal living areas along with convenient work centers. Two to six bedroom sleeping areas. A delightful book for one's permanent library.

15.

96 Pages in Full Color, $5.95

114 TREND HOMES

Heritage Houses, Energy Designs, Family Plans - these, along with Vacation Homes, are in this new plan book in full color. The Trend Homes feature unique living patterns. The revered Heritage Houses highlight the charm and nostalgia of Early America. Solariums, greenhouses, earth-sheltered and super-insulated houses are the Energy Designs. Vacation homes feature A-frames and chalets.

16.

104 Pages in Full Color, $5.95

450 HOUSE PLANS

For those who wish to review and study perhaps the largest selection of designs available in a single volume. This edition will provide countless hours of enjoyable family home planning. Varying exterior styles, plus interesting and practical floor plans for all building budgets. Formal, informal living patterns; indoor-outdoor livability; small, growing and large family facilities.

17.

320 Pages, $8.95

136 SPANISH & WESTERN HOME DESIGNS

Stucco exteriors, arches, tile roofs, wide-overhangs, courtyards and rambling ranches are characteristics which make this design selection distinctive. These sun-country designs highlight indoor-outdoor relationships. Solar oriented livability is featured. Their appeal is not limited to the Southwest region of our country.

10.

120 Pages, $2.95

The Plan Books

... are a most valuable tool for anyone planning to build a new home. A study of the hundreds of delightfully designed exteriors and the practical, efficient floor plans will be a great learning and fun-oriented family experience. You will be able to select your preferred styling from among Early American, Tudor, French, Spanish and Contemporary adaptations. Your ideas about floor planning and interior livability will expand. And, of course, after you have selected an appealing home design that satisfies your long list of living requirements, you can order the blueprints for further study of your favorite design in greater detail. Surely the hours spent studying the portfolio of Home Planners' designs will be both enjoyable and rewarding ones.

1 Frontal Sheet

2 Foundation Plan

3 Detailed Floor Plan

4 House Cross-Sections

5 Interior Elevations

6 Exterior Elevations

7 Material List

Before You Order

1. STUDY THE DESIGNS . . . found in Home Planners current publications. As you review these delightful custom homes, you should keep in mind the total living requirements of your family — both indoors and outdoors. Although we do not make changes in plans, many minor changes can be made prior to the period of construction. If major changes are involved to satisfy your personal requirements, you should consider ordering one set of blueprints and having them redrawn locally. Consultation with your architect is strongly advised when contemplating major changes.

2. HOW TO ORDER BLUEPRINTS . . . After you have chosen the design that satisfies your requirements, or if you wish to select one that you wish to study in more detail, simply clip the accompanying order blank and mail with your remittance. However, if it is not convenient for you to send a check or money order, you can use your credit card, or merely indicate C.O.D. shipment. Postman will collect all charges, including postage and C.O.D. fee. C.O.D. shipments are not permitted to Canada or foreign countries. Should time be of essence, as it sometimes is with many of our customers, your telephone order usually can be processed and shipped in the next day's mail. Simply call toll free 1-800-521-6797, (Michigan residents call collect 0-313-477-1854).

3. OUR SERVICE . . . Home Planners makes every effort to process and ship each order for blueprints and books within 48 hours. Because of this, we have deemed it unnecessary to acknowledge receipt of our customers orders. See order coupon for the postage and handling charges for surface mail, air mail or foreign mail.

4. A NOTE REGARDING REVERSE BLUEPRINTS . . . As a special service to those wishing to build in reverse of the plan as shown, we do include an extra set of reversed blueprints for only $25.00 additional with each order. Even though the lettering and dimensions appear backward on reversed blueprints, they make a handy reference because they show the house just as it's being built in reverse from the standard blueprints — thereby helping you visualize the home better.

5. OUR EXCHANGE POLICY . . . Since blueprints are printed up in specific response to your individual order, we cannot honor requests for refunds. However, the first set of blueprints in any order (or the one set in a single set order) for a given design may be exchanged for a set of another design at a fee of $10.00 plus $3.00 for postage and handling via surface mail; $4.00 via air mail.

TO: **HOME PLANNERS, INC., 23761 RESEARCH DRIVE FARMINGTON HILLS, MICHIGAN 48024**

Please rush me the following:

_____ SET(S) BLUEPRINTS FOR DESIGN NO(S). _____ $_____
Single Set, $95.00; Additional Identical Sets in Same Order $25.00 ea.
4 Set Package of Same Design, $145.00 (Save $25.00)
7 Set Package of Same Design, $180.00 (Save $65.00)
(Material Lists and 1 Specification Outline included)
_____ SPECIFICATION OUTLINES @ $3.00 EACH . . . . $_____

Michigan Residents add 4% sales tax $_____

FOR POSTAGE AND HANDLING PLEASE CHECK ✓ & REMIT
☐ $3.00 Added to Order for Surface Mail (UPS) – Any Mdse.
☐ $4.00 Added for Priority Mail of One-Three Sets of Blueprints.
☐ $6.00 Added for Priority Mail of Four or more Sets of Blueprints. } $_____
☐ For Canadian orders add $2.00 to above applicable rates

☐ C.O.D. PAY POSTMAN
(C.O.D. Within U.S.A. Only)   TOTAL in U.S.A. funds $_____

PLEASE PRINT
Name _____
Street _____
City _____ State _____ Zip _____

CREDIT CARD ORDERS ONLY: Fill in the boxes below   Prices subject to change without notice

Credit Card No. [ ][ ][ ][ ][ ][ ][ ][ ][ ][ ][ ][ ][ ][ ]   Expiration Date Month/Year [ ][ ][ ][ ]

CHECK ONE: ☐ **VISA** ☐ **MasterCard**

Order Form Key BK130   Your Signature _____

How many sets of blueprints should be ordered?

This question is often asked. The answer can range anywhere from 1 to 7 sets, depending upon circumstances. For instance, a single set of blueprints of your favorite design is sufficient to study the house in greater detail. On the other hand, if you are planning to get cost estimates, or if you are planning to build, you may need as many as seven sets of blueprints. Because the first set of blueprints in each order is $95.00, and because additional sets of the same design in each order are only $25.00 each (and with package sets even more economical), you save considerably by ordering your total requirements now. To help you determine the exact number of sets, please refer to the handy check list.

BLUEPRINT ORDERS SHIPPED WITHIN 48 HOURS OF RECEIPT!

TO: **HOME PLANNERS, INC., 23761 RESEARCH DRIVE FARMINGTON HILLS, MICHIGAN 48024**

Please rush me the following:

_____ SET(S) BLUEPRINTS FOR DESIGN NO(S). _____ $_____
Single Set, $95.00; Additional Identical Sets in Same Order $25.00 ea.
4 Set Package of Same Design, $145.00 (Save $25.00)
7 Set Package of Same Design, $180.00 (Save $65.00)
(Material Lists and 1 Specification Outline included)
_____ SPECIFICATION OUTLINES @ $3.00 EACH . . . . $_____

Michigan Residents add 4% sales tax $_____

FOR POSTAGE AND HANDLING PLEASE CHECK ✓ & REMIT
☐ $3.00 Added to Order for Surface Mail (UPS) – Any Mdse.
☐ $4.00 Added for Priority Mail of One-Three Sets of Blueprints.
☐ $6.00 Added for Priority Mail of Four or more Sets of Blueprints. } $_____
☐ For Canadian orders add $2.00 to above applicable rates

☐ C.O.D. PAY POSTMAN
(C.O.D. Within U.S.A. Only)   TOTAL in U.S.A. funds $_____

PLEASE PRINT
Name _____
Street _____
City _____ State _____ Zip _____

CREDIT CARD ORDERS ONLY: Fill in the boxes below   Prices subject to change without notice

Credit Card No. [ ][ ][ ][ ][ ][ ][ ][ ][ ][ ][ ][ ][ ][ ]   Expiration Date Month/Year [ ][ ][ ][ ]

CHECK ONE: ☐ **VISA** ☐ **MasterCard**

Order Form Key BK130   Your Signature _____

How Many Blueprints Do You Need?

___OWNER'S SET

___BUILDER (Usually requires at least 3 sets: 1 as legal document; 1 for inspection; and at least 1 for tradesmen — usually more.)

___BUILDING PERMIT (Sometimes 2 sets are required.)

___MORTGAGE SOURCE (Usually 1 set for a conventional mortgage; 3 sets for F.H.A. or V.A. type mortgages.)

___SUBDIVISION COMMITTEE (If any.)

___TOTAL NO. SETS REQUIRED

Blueprint Ordering Hotline –

Phone toll free: 1-800-521-6797. Orders received by 11 a.m. (Detroit time) will be processed the same day and shipped to you the following day. Use of this line restricted to blueprint ordering only. Michigan residents simply call collect 0-313-477-1854.

Kindly Note: When ordering by phone, please state Order Form Key No. located in box at lower left corner of blueprint order form.

In Canada Mail To:
Home Planners, Inc., 20 Cedar St. North Kitchener, Ontario N2H 2W8
Phone: (519) 743-4169

The Blueprints

1. FRONTAL SHEET.
Artist's landscaped sketch of the exterior and ink-line floor plans are on the frontal sheet of each set of blueprints.

2. FOUNDATION PLAN.
¼" Scale basement and foundation plan. All necessary notations and dimensions. Plot plan diagram for locating house on building site.

3. DETAILED FLOOR PLAN.
¼" Scale first and second floor plans with complete dimensions. Cross-section detail keys. Diagrammatic layout of electrical outlets and switches.

4. HOUSE CROSS-SECTIONS.
Large scale sections of foundation, interior and exterior walls, floors and roof details for design and construction control.

5. INTERIOR ELEVATIONS.
Large scale interior details of the complete kitchen cabinet design, bathrooms, powder room, laundry, fireplaces, paneling, beam ceilings, built-in cabinets, etc.

6. EXTERIOR ELEVATIONS.
¼" Scale exterior elevation drawings of front, rear, and both sides of the house. All exterior materials and details are shown to indicate the complete design and proportions of the house.

7. MATERIAL LIST.
Complete lists of all materials required for the construction of the house as designed are included in each set of blueprints.

THIS BLUEPRINT PACKAGE will help you and your family take a major step forward in the final appraisal and planning of your new home. Only by spending many enjoyable and informative hours studying the numerous details included in the complete package, will you feel sure of, and comfortable with, your commitment to build your new home. To assure successful and productive consultation with your builder and/or architect, reference to the various elements of the blueprint package is a must. The blueprints, material list and specification outline will save much consultation time and expense. Don't be without them.

The Material List

With each set of blueprints you order you will receive a material list. Each list shows you the quantity, type and size of the non-mechanical materials required to build your home. It also tells you where these materials are used. This makes the blueprints easy to understand.

Influencing the mechanical requirements are geographical differences in availability of materials, local codes, methods of installation and individual preferences. Because of these factors, your local heating, plumbing and electrical contractors can supply you with necessary material take-offs for their particular trades.

Material lists simplify your material ordering and enable you to get quicker price quotations from your builder and material dealer. Because the material list is an integral part of each set of blueprints, it is not available separately.

Among the materials listed:

• Masonry, Veneer & Fireplace • Framing Lumber • Roofing & Sheet Metal • Windows & Door Frames • Exterior Trim & Insulation • Tile Work, Finish Floors • Interior Trim, Kitchen Cabinets • Rough & Finish Hardware

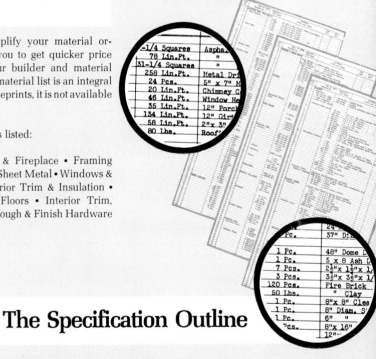

The Specification Outline

This fill-in type specification lists over 150 phases of home construction from excavating to painting and includes wiring, plumbing, heating and air-conditioning. It consists of 16 pages and will prove invaluable for specifying to your builder the exact materials, equipment and methods of construction you want in your new home. One Specification Outline is included free with each order for blueprints. Additional Specification Outlines are available at $3.00 each.

CONTENTS
• General Instructions, Suggestions and Information • Excavating and Grading • Masonry and Concrete Work • Sheet Metal Work • Carpentry, Millwork, Roofing, and Miscellaneous Items • Lath and Plaster or Drywall Wallboard • Schedule for Room Finishes • Painting and Finishing • Tile Work • Electrical Work • Plumbing • Heating and Air-Conditioning

THE FULL COLOR PLAN BOOK SERIES ...

presents a segment of the outstanding artwork of Home Planners' in dramatic and exciting fashion. Here are many of the most popular and unique designs in the portfolio illustrated to their best possible advantage. The design representation runs the gamut of sizes, types and styles. This includes houses from 960 to 5,308 square feet; one, 1½, two-story and multi-level designs along with Vacation Homes; Early American, Tudor, French, Spanish, Western and Contemporary styles. A potpourri of designs cater to a variety of tastes.

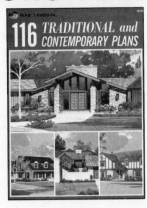

116 TRADITIONAL and CONTEMPORARY PLANS

122 HOME DESIGNS
Tudor • Spanish • French • Early American • Contemporary

114 TREND HOMES
Heritage Houses • Energy Designs • Family Plans

Design 302615
2,563 Sq. Ft. - First Floor
552 Sq. Ft. - Second Floor; 59,513 Cu. Ft.

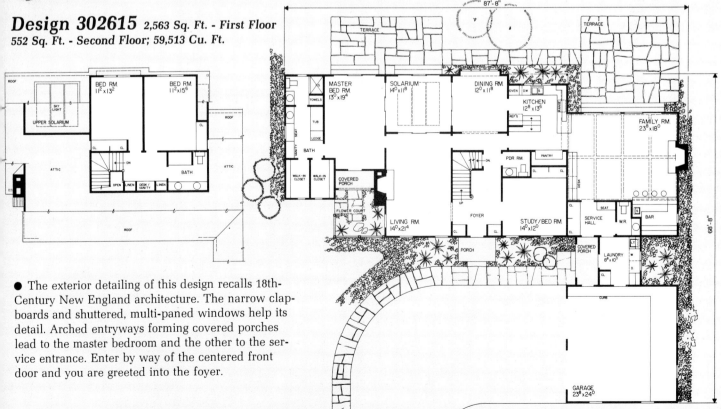

● The exterior detailing of this design recalls 18th-Century New England architecture. The narrow clapboards and shuttered, multi-paned windows help its detail. Arched entryways forming covered porches lead to the master bedroom and the other to the service entrance. Enter by way of the centered front door and you are greeted into the foyer.

● This contemporary, hillside home is very inviting. A large kitchen with an adjacent snack bar makes light meals a breeze. The adjoining breakfast room offers a scenic view through sliding glass doors. Notice the sloped ceiling in the dining and gathering rooms. A fireplace in the gathering room adds a cozy air. An interesting feature is the master bedroom's easy access to the study. Also, take note of the sliding doors in the master bedroom which lead to a private balcony. On the lower level, a large activities room will be a frequently used spot by family members. The fireplace and wet bar add a nice touch for entertaining friends. Take note of the two or optional three bedrooms - the choice is yours. Obviously, this house offers lots of livability and will be a joy to own.

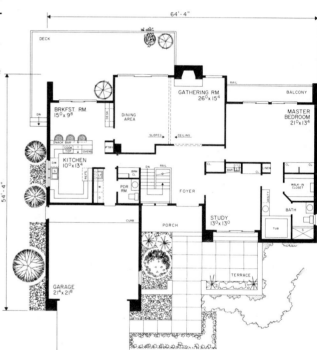

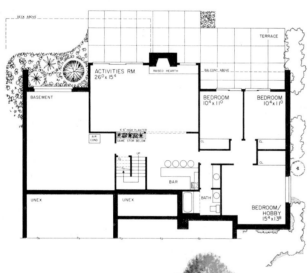

Design 302896 1,856 Sq. Ft. - Main Level
1,454 Sq. Ft. - Lower Level; 43,390 Cu. Ft.

Design 302831

1,758 Sq. Ft. - First Floor
1,247 Sq. Ft. - Second Floor
44,265 Cu. Ft.

● You can incorporate energy-saving features into the elevation of this passive solar design to enable you to receive the most sunlight on your particular site. Multiple plot plans (included with the blueprints) illustrate which elevations should be solarized for different sites and which extra features can be incorporated. The features can include a greenhouse added to the family room, the back porch turned into a solarium or skylights installed over the entry.

Design 302794

1,680 Sq. Ft. - First Floor
1,165 Sq. Ft. - Second Floor
867 Sq. Ft. - Apartment
55,900 Cu. Ft.

● This exceptionally pleasing Tudor design has a great deal of interior livability to offer its occupants. Use the main entrance, enter into the foyer and begin your journey throughout this design. To the left of the foyer is the study, to the right, the formal living room. The living room leads to the rear, formal dining room. This room has access to the outdoors and is conveniently located adjacent to the kitchen. A snack bar divides the kitchen from the family room which also has access to outdoors plus it has a fireplace as does the living room. The second floor houses the family's four bedrooms. Down six steps from the mud room is the laundry and entrance to the garage, up six steps from this area is a complete apartment. This is an excellent room for a live-in relative. It is completely private by gaining access from the outdoor balcony.

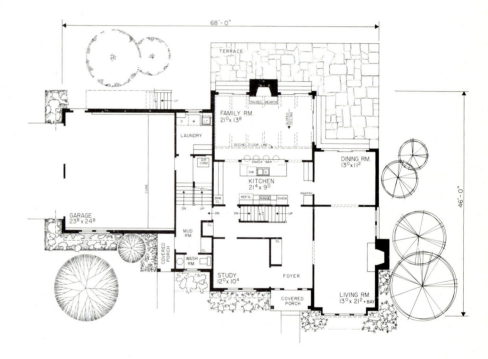

Design 302826
1,112 Sq. Ft. - First Floor
881 Sq. Ft. - Second Floor; 32,770 Cu. Ft.

ALTERNATE KITCHEN / DINING RM./
BREAKFAST RM. FLOOR PLAN

● This is an outstanding example of the type of informal, traditional-style architecture that has captured the modern imagination. The interior plan houses all the features that people want most - a spacious gathering room, formal and informal dining areas, efficient, U-shaped kitchen, master bedroom, two children's bedrooms, second-floor lounge, entrance court and rear terrace and deck. Study all areas of this plan carefully.

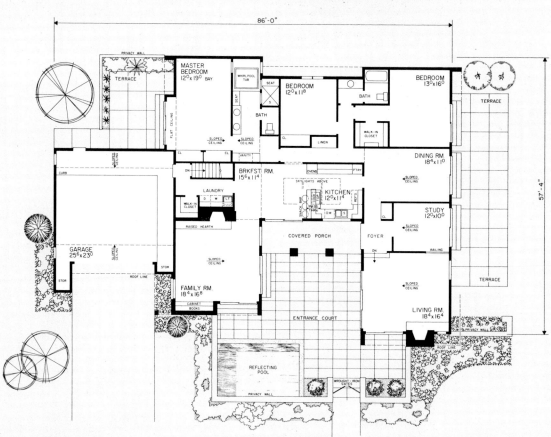

Design 302881 2,346 Sq. Ft.; 60,315 Cu. Ft.

● Energy-efficiency will be obtained in this unique, contemporary design. This plan has been designed for a south facing lot in the temperate zones. There is minimal window exposure on the north side of the house so the interior will be protected. The eastern side of the plan, on the other hand, will allow the morning sunlight to enter. As the sun travels from east to west, the various rooms will have light through windows, sliding glass doors or skylights. The garage acts as a buffer against the hot afternoon sun. The living areas are oriented to the front of the plan. They will benefit from the southern exposure during the cooler months. During the summer months, this area will be shielded from the high, hot summer sun by the overhanging roof. If you plan to build in the south, this house would be ideal for a north facing site. This results in a minimum amount of hot sun for the living areas and a maximum amount of protection from the sun on the rear, southern side of the house.

Design 302181 *2,612 Sq. Ft.; 45,230 Cu. Ft.*

● It is hard to imagine a home with any more eye-appeal than this one. It is the complete picture of charm. The interior is just as outstanding. Sliding glass doors permit the large, master bedroom, quiet, living room and all-purpose family room to function directly with the outdoors. Two fireplaces, built-in china cabinets, bookshelves, complete laundry and kitchen pass-thru to breakfast room are extra features. Although the illustration of this home shows natural quarried stone, you may wish to substitute brick or even siding.

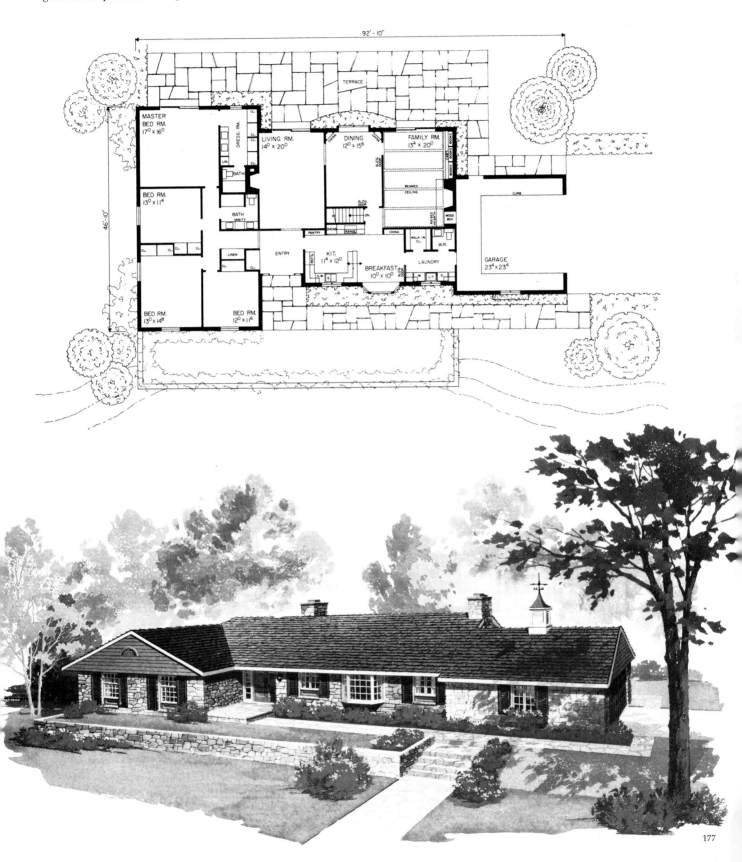

THE MOST POPULAR HOMES BOOKS...

are a fine presentation of the designs and ideas that the readers of Home Planners' books have favored from the current portfolio. Of interest is the wide range of preferencey also like Contemporary houses. Little houses are the favorites of many. But, then too, so are big houses. Simple rectangular designs have captured the fancy of many, as have complicated irregular shapes. A modest, low profile one-story makes the most popular listings; so does a flamboyant, towering three-story. And, of course, Home Planners has some unpopular designs, too. But, in spite of a lack of consensus for such designs, even those have a record that a certain someone, somewhere, loved enough to obtain a blueprint.

Design 302610
1,505 Sq. Ft. - First Floor
1,344 Sq. Ft. - Second Floor; 45,028 Cu. Ft.

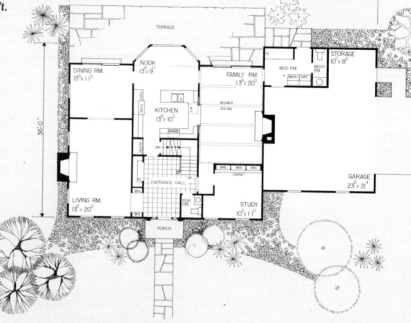

● This full two-story traditional will be worthy of note wherever built. It strongly recalls images of a New England of yesteryear. And well it might; for the window treatment is delightful. The front entrance detail is inviting. The narrow horizontal siding and the corner boards are appealing as are the two massive chimneys. The center entrance hall is large with a handy powder room nearby. The study has built-in bookshelves and offers a full measure of privacy. The interior kitchen has a pass-thru to the family room and enjoys all that natural light from the bay window of the nook. A beamed ceiling, fireplace and sliding glass doors are features of the family room. The mud room highlights a closet, laundry equipment and an extra washroom. Study the upstairs with those four bedrooms, two baths and plenty of closets. An excellent arrangement for all.

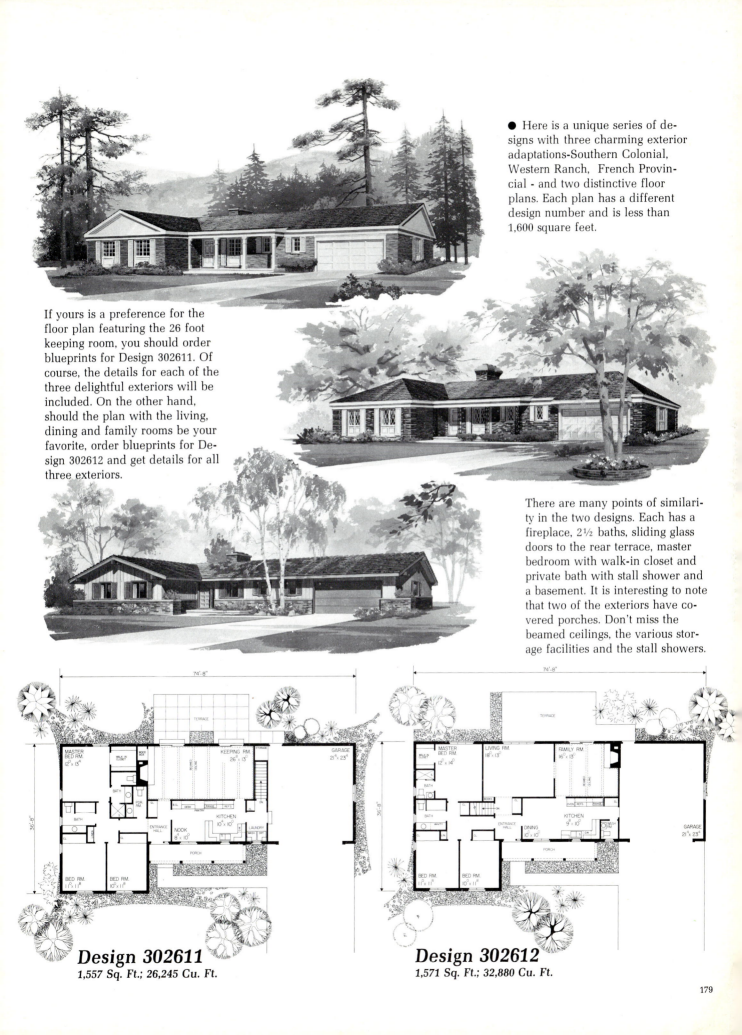

● Here is a unique series of designs with three charming exterior adaptations-Southern Colonial, Western Ranch, French Provincial - and two distinctive floor plans. Each plan has a different design number and is less than 1,600 square feet.

If yours is a preference for the floor plan featuring the 26 foot keeping room, you should order blueprints for Design 302611. Of course, the details for each of the three delightful exteriors will be included. On the other hand, should the plan with the living, dining and family rooms be your favorite, order blueprints for Design 302612 and get details for all three exteriors.

There are many points of similarity in the two designs. Each has a fireplace, 2½ baths, sliding glass doors to the rear terrace, master bedroom with walk-in closet and private bath with stall shower and a basement. It is interesting to note that two of the exteriors have covered porches. Don't miss the beamed ceilings, the various storage facilities and the stall showers.

Design 302611
1,557 Sq. Ft.; 26,245 Cu. Ft.

Design 302612
1,571 Sq. Ft.; 32,880 Cu. Ft.

Design 302534 3,262 Sq. Ft.; 58,640 Cu. Ft.

● The angular wings of this ranch home surely contribute to the unique character of the exterior. These wings effectively balance what is truly a dramatic and inviting front entrance. Massive masonry walls support the wide overhanging roof with its exposed wood beams. The patterned double front doors are surrounded by delight- ful expanses of glass. The raised planters and the masses of quarried stone (make it brick if you prefer) enhance the exterior appeal. Inside, a distinctive and practical floor plan stands ready to shape and serve the living patterns of the active family. The spacious entrance hall highlights sloped ceiling and an attractive open stairway to the lower level recreation area. An impressive fireplace and an abundance of glass are features of the big gathering room. Interestingly shaped dining room and study flank this main living area. The large kitchen offers many of the charming aspects of the family-kitchen of yesteryear. The bedroom wing has a sunken master suite.

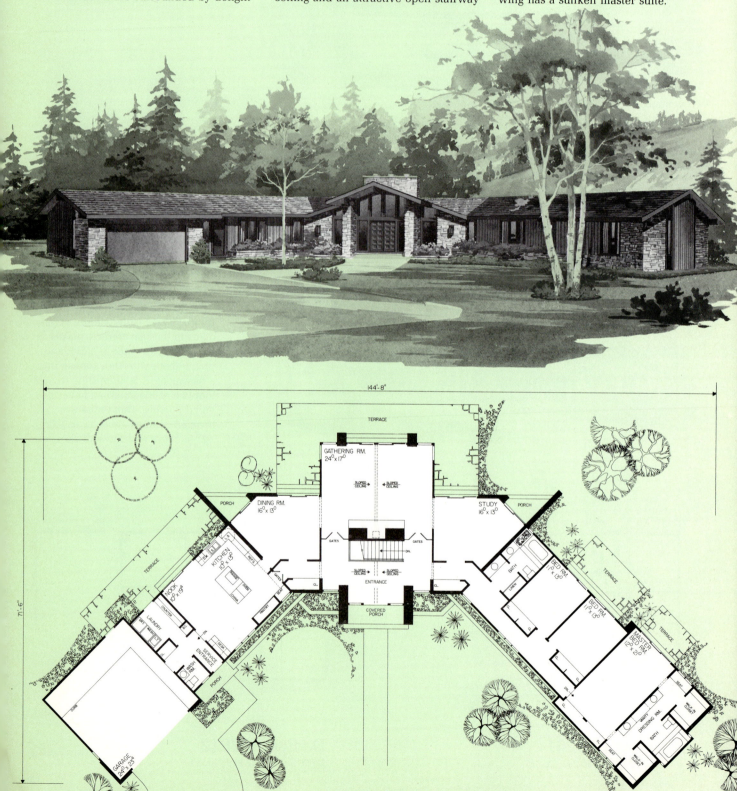

Design 301974 1,680 Sq. Ft. - Main Level; 1,344 Sq. Ft. - Lower Level; 34,186 Cu. Ft.

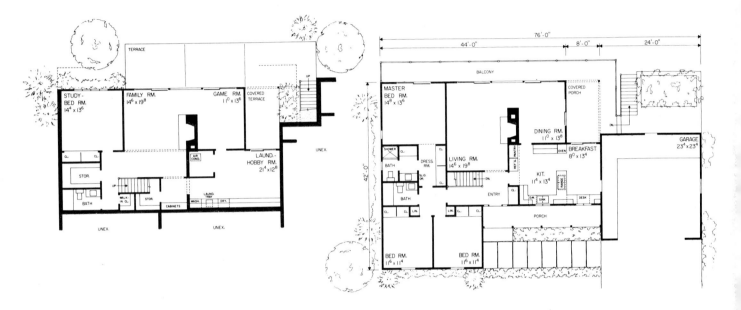

● You would never guess from looking at the front of this traditional design that it possessed such a strikingly different rear. From the front, you would guess that all of its livability is on one floor. Yet, just imagine the tremendous amount of livability that is added to the plan as a result of exposing the lower level - 1,344 square feet of it. Living in this hillside house will mean fun. Obviously, the most popular spot will be the balcony. Then again, maybe it could be the terrace adjacent to the family room. Both the terrace and the balcony have a covered area to provide protection against unfavorable weather. The interior of the plan also will serve the family with ease.

Design 302824
1,550 Sq. Ft.; 34,560 Cu. Ft.

● Low-maintenance and economy in building are the outstanding exterior features of this sharp one-story design. It is sheathed in long-lasting cedar siding and trimmed with stone for an eye-appealing facade. Entrance to this home takes you through a charming garden courtyard then a covered walk to the front porch. The garage extending from the front of the house serves two purposes; to reduce lot size and to buffer the interior of the house from street noise. Sliding glass doors are featured in each of the main rooms for easy access to the outdoors. A sun porch is tucked between the study and gathering rooms. Optional non-basement details are included with the purchase of this design.

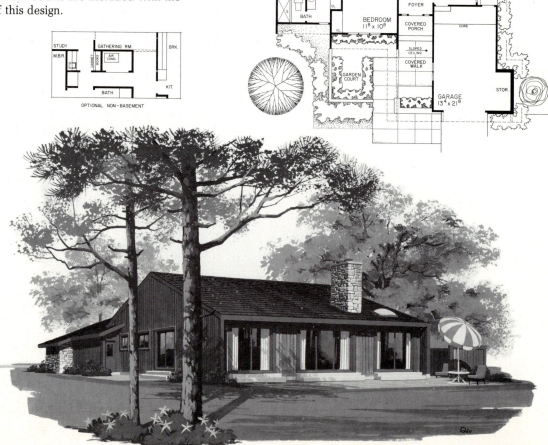

Design 302661
1,020 Sq. Ft. - First Floor
777 Sq. Ft. - Second Floor; 30,745 Cu. Ft.

● Any other starter house or retirement home couldn't have more charm than this design. Its compact frame houses a very livable plan. An outstanding feature of the first floor is the large country kitchen. Its fine attractions include a beamed ceiling, raised hearth fireplace, built-in window seat and a door leading to the outdoors. A living room is in the front of the plan and has another fireplace which shares the single chimney. The rear dormered second floor houses the sleeping and bath facilities.

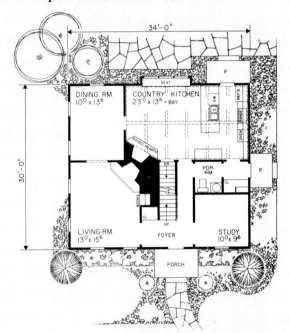

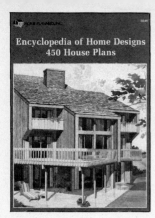

ENCYCLOPEDIA OF HOME DESIGNS . . .

Heritage Houses, Trend Houses, One-Story Homes under 2,000 Square Feet, One-Story Homes over 2,000 Square Feet, 1½-Story Homes, Two-Story Homes, Optional Exteriors & Plans, Multi-Level Homes, Country-Estates Homes, Vacation Homes - these are the ten sections that comprise this 450 design presentation. Within 320 pages there is an outstanding study of just how diverse a group of houses and their plans really can be. Yet, each and every house exterior and interior represents a pleasing, well-proportioned facade and a practical, family oriented floor plan. A selection of designs for housing enthusiasts everywhere.

HERITAGE HOUSES . . . . .

The beauty and charm of early America
is wonderfully captured by the picturesque houses built by our forefathers. For generations, Salt Box, Gambrel, Garrison, Cape Cod, Georgian, Federal and Greek Revival houses and their variations have enhanced our countryside. Today, our architectural history is being reclaimed by families building up-to-date adaptations of these favorite heritage houses of yesteryear. The following pages feature a selection of these famous styles with thoroughly modern floor plans which assure the best in present-day family livability.

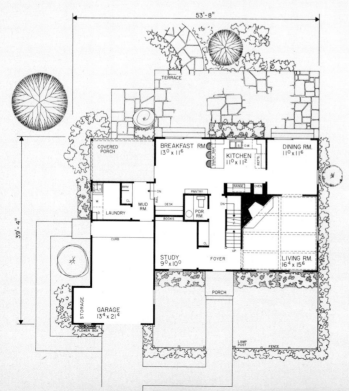

Design 302656 1,122 Sq. Ft. - First Floor
884 Sq. Ft. - Second Floor; 31,845 Cu. Ft.

● This charming Cape cottage possesses a great sense of shelter through its gambrel roof. Dormers at front and rear pierce the gambrel roof to provide generous, well-lit living space on the second floor which houses three bedrooms. This design's first floor layout is not far different from that of the Cape cottages of the 18th century. The large kitchen and adjoining dining room recall cottage keeping rooms both in function and in location at the rear of the house.

ONE-STORY HOMES over 2,000 sq. ft. . . . .

As a home's square footage increases, so does the opportunity to develop a wide variety of features that contribute to more enjoyable living patterns. Of course, as the size of the home escalates so does its cost. The objective should be to make the benefits of increased size cost-effective. This group of one-story homes will cater to the needs of large, active families with expanded building budgets. Square footages range upward to 2889 with four bedrooms predominating. Formal and informal living and dining facilities are represented. Extra baths, laundry rooms, large kitchens and additional storage are among the convenient living highlights of these larger homes.

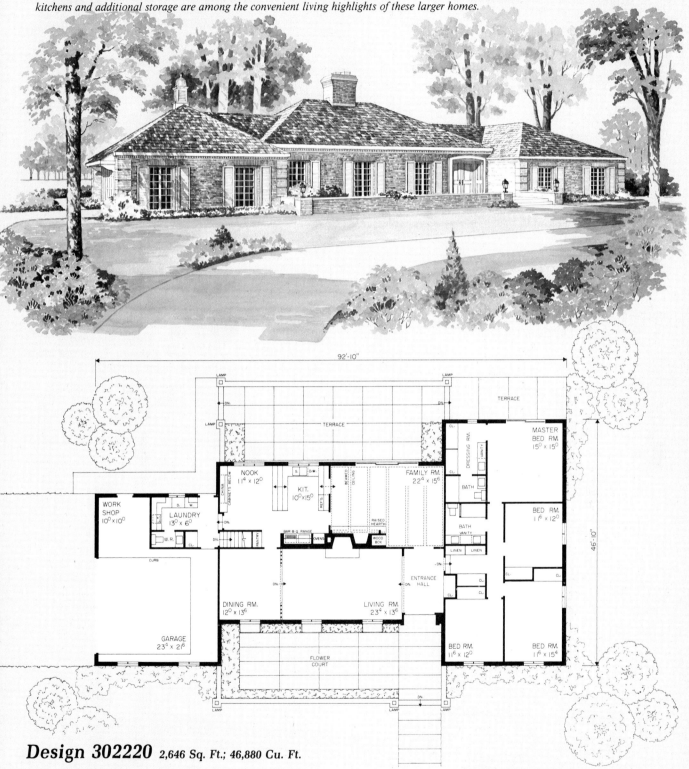

Design 302220 2,646 Sq. Ft.; 46,880 Cu. Ft.

● The gracious formality of this home is reminiscent of a popularly accepted French styling. The hip-roof, the brick quoins, the cornice details, the arched window heads, the distinctive shutters, the recessed double front doors, the massive center chimney, and the de- lightful flower court are all features which set the dramatic appeal of this home. This floor plan is a favorite of many. The four bedroom, two bath sleeping wing is a zone by itself. Fur- ther, the formal living and dining rooms are ideally located. For enter- taining they function well together and look out upon the pleasant flower court. Overlooking the raised living terrace at the rear are the family and breakfast rooms and work center. Don't miss the laundry, extra wash room and work shop in garage.

1½-STORY HOMES

The low profile of the 1½-story home is so often associated with the traditional Cape Cod design. Here is a selection offering variations of the Williamsburg and New England themes. In addition, there is an interesting representation of Tudor and Contemporary styles. Designs for low to expanded budgets range from 1200 to 3477 square feet. Many with first floor bedrooms offer expansible potential. A study of the floor plans will reveal a delightful array of living patterns.

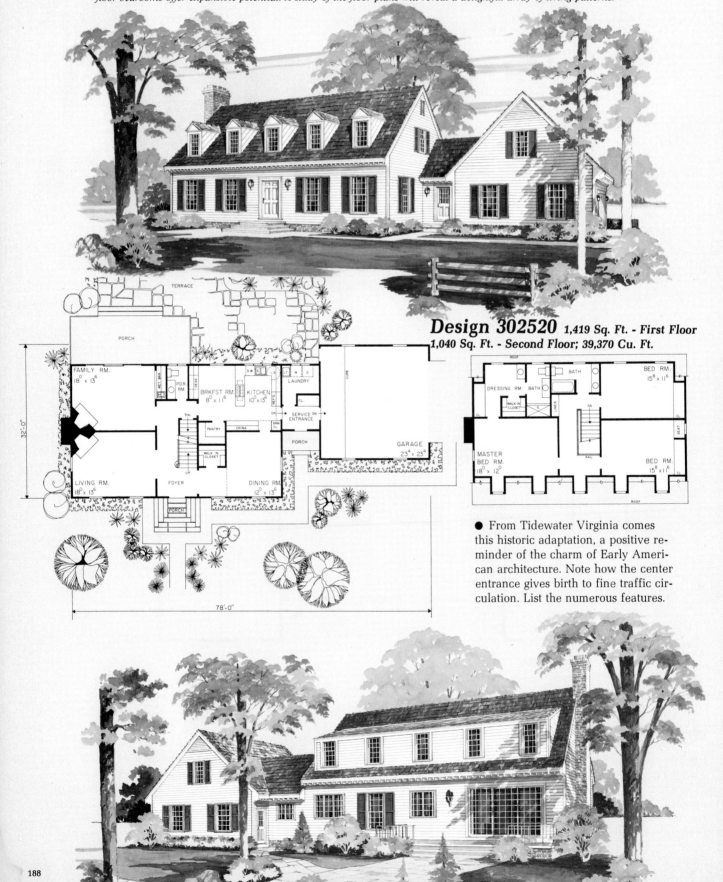

Design 302520
1,419 Sq. Ft. - First Floor
1,040 Sq. Ft. - Second Floor; 39,370 Cu. Ft.

● From Tidewater Virginia comes this historic adaptation, a positive reminder of the charm of Early American architecture. Note how the center entrance gives birth to fine traffic circulation. List the numerous features.

TWO-STORY HOMES . . . .

Your two-story home can contain as many as 3671 square feet (below) or as few as 1216 (page 214). And, of course, it can be anywhere in between. However, regardless of size, if you build a two-story, you can be assured of an economical use of your construction dollar. This is because less roof structure and foundation are required for a two-story than for the same size one-story. Going upstairs to bed provides the two-story with its own stamp of distinction. This selection offers a myraid of examples of how the two-story home can vary in its size, style and variety of living features.

Design 302356

1,969 Sq. Ft. - First Floor
1,702 Sq. Ft. - Second Floor
55,105 Cu. Ft.

● Here is truly an exquisite Tudor adaptation. The exterior with its interesting roof lines, window treatment, stately chimney and its appealing use of brick and stucco, could hardly be more dramatic. Inside, the drama really begins to unfold as one envisions his family's living patterns. The delightfully large receiving hall has a two story ceiling and controls the flexible traffic patterns. The living and dining rooms with the library nearby will cater to the formal living pursuits. The guest room offers another haven for the enjoyment of peace and quiet. Observe the adjacent full bath. Just inside the entrance from the garage is the laundry room. For the family's informal activities there are the interactions of the family room - covered porch - nook - kitchen zone. Notice the raised hearth fireplace, the wood boxes, the sliding glass doors, built-in bar and the kitchen pass-thru.

OPTIONAL EXTERIORS & PLANS . . .

Occasionally, one's enthusiasm for a favorite floor plan may not be matched by a similar feeling about that plan's exterior styling. And, of course, within families, members may differ about their style preferences. The designs in this section offer an excellent opportunity to observe how (with minor modifications) a given floor plan can have different exteriors. This presents an option of which exterior to build. As shown, different types of houses can include variations of Early American, Tudor, Contemporary, French, Spanish and Western as styling options.

Design 301715 1,276 Sq. Ft. - First Floor; 1,064 Sq. Ft. - Second Floor; 31,295 Cu. Ft.

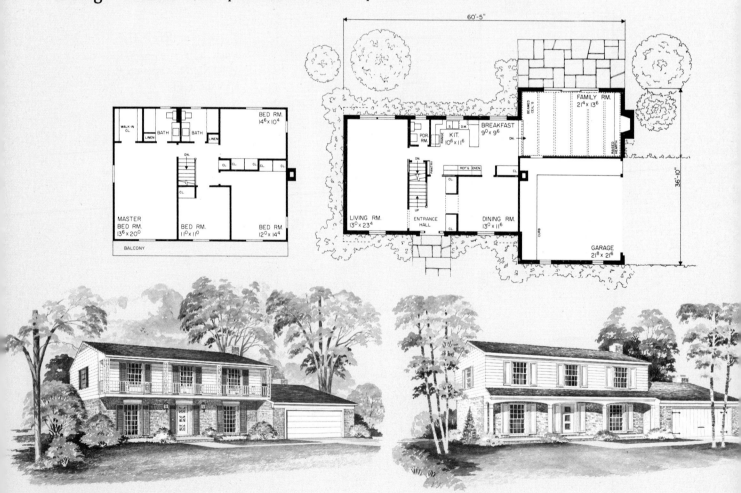

● The blueprints you order for this design show details for building each of these three appealing exteriors. Which do you like best? Whatever your choice, the interior will provide the growing family with all the facilities for fine living.

Multi-Level Homes

For new dimensions in living, the multi-level home can be just what the active family is looking for. Grouped into this section are hillside designs, split-levels and bi-levels. Each type of design offers a distinctive set of living patterns. The hillside home may be two or three levels. However, the bottom level is generally exposed, thus providing an extra full level of cheerful livability. The split-level can have several configurations with each level generally performing a separate function. These levels may be for sleeping, living and recreation. The bi-level, sometimes called a raised one-story, usually has a foyer from which one short flight of stairs leads up to a level, while a second flight leads down to a level. Study the variations of multi-levels on the following pages.

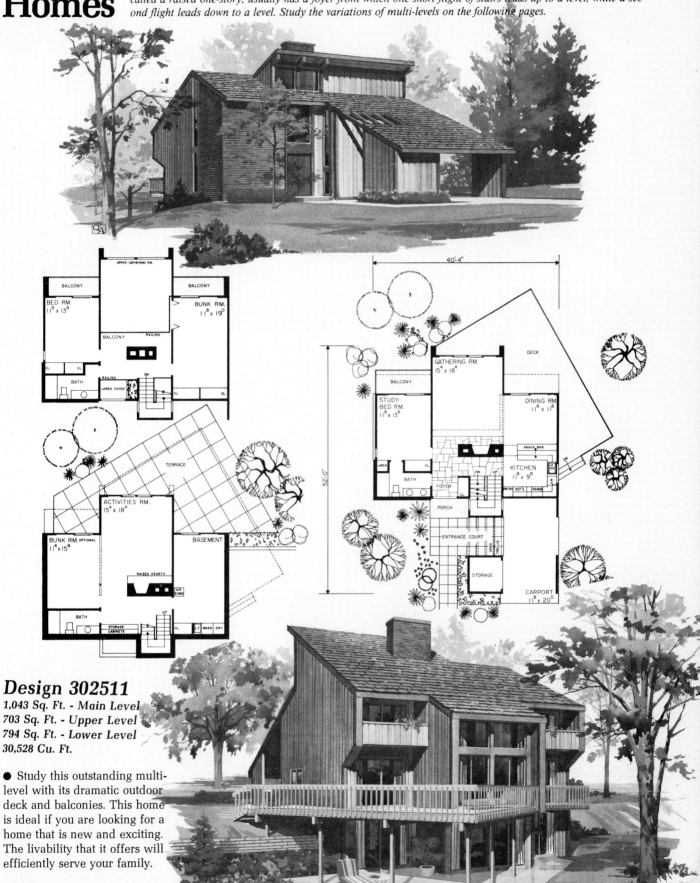

Design 302511

1,043 Sq. Ft. - Main Level
703 Sq. Ft. - Upper Level
794 Sq. Ft. - Lower Level
30,528 Cu. Ft.

● Study this outstanding multi-level with its dramatic outdoor deck and balconies. This home is ideal if you are looking for a home that is new and exciting. The livability that it offers will efficiently serve your family.

COUNTRY-ESTATE HOMES . . . .

Whether situated in the lowlands, in suburbia, or the countryside; in the north, or the south, the estate home is characterized by the gracious formality that seems to foretell of the good life. Space there is in abundance - indoors as well as out. Construction cost factors are but a secondary consideration. There is room for everybody and everybody has a room. The plan affords space for large or small gatherings on any occasion. Yet there will always be a room for privacy, when desired or needed. As shown on the following pages, the country-estate home can be traditional or contemporary in its styling. It can be one, 1½ or two-story, a bi-level or a split-level.

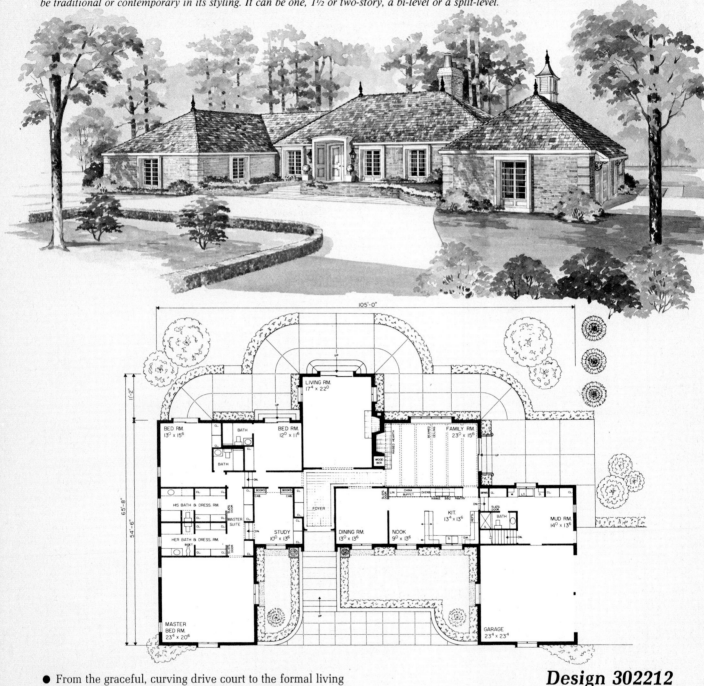

● From the graceful, curving drive court to the formal living room, this expansive, hospitable French country house welcomes the visitor. Truely a house for gracious living.

Design 302212
3,577 Sq. Ft.; 76,208 Cu. Ft.